ATLAS OF MEDIEVAL JEWISH HISTORY

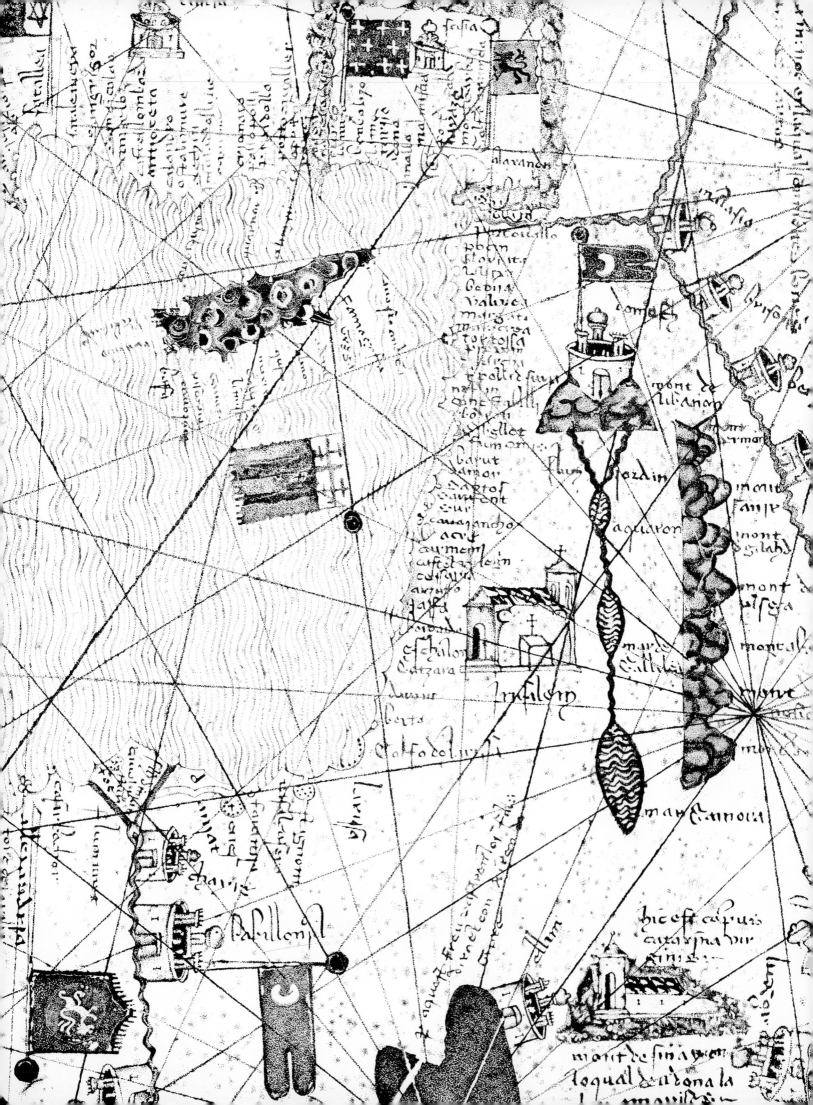

ATLAS OF MEDIEVAL JEWISH HISTORY

HAIM BEINART

SIMON & SCHUSTER

A Paramount Communications Company

New York   London   Toronto   Sydney   Tokyo   Singapore

Cartography, design and production: Carta, Jerusalem

English translation: Moshe Shalvi
Managing editor: Lorraine Kessel

Academic Reference Division
Simon and Schuster
15 Columbus Circle, New York, NY 10023

A Paramount Communications Company

Library of Congress Cataloging-in-Publication Data

Beinart, Haim.
    [Atlas Karta le-toldot 'am Yiśra'el bi-Yeme ha-
benayim. English]
    Atlas of medieval Jewish history / Haim Beinart;
[cartography, design, and production, Carta, Jerusalem;
English translation, Moshe Shalvi].
       p.   cm.
    Translation of: Aṭlas Karṭa le-toldot 'am Yiśra'el
bi-Yeme ha-benayim.
    Includes bibliographical references and indexes.
    ISBN 0-13-050691-5
       1. Jews—History—70-1789—Maps. I. Karṭa
(Firm) II. Title.
    G1034.B413 1992 ⟨G&M⟩
    909'.04924'00223—dc20   92-995
                                          CIP
                                         MAP

Picture Credits: Illustrations on pages 43 and 55 are by courtesy of
The British Museum; those on pages 44 and 56 are by courtesy of The
Hebrew National and University Library; all others are by Carta.

Printed in Israel

INTRODUCTION

Compiling the *Atlas of Medieval Jewish History* entailed a number of problems, the first being the very definition of the term *medieval* in Jewish history. One may even question whether the Jews ever had a medieval age, since the history of the Jewish people is unlike that of other European peoples, who went through Dark Ages before they emerged into the Renaissance. However, since we required a defined period for practical purposes, we adopted an accepted concept and superimposed it on Jewish life. It would be more accurate to say that this atlas encompasses the period of the Jewish people's exile from their land, arranged according to accepted historical periods, beginning with the Barbarian Invasions in the fourth and fifth centuries and continuing to the period after the Chmielnicki Massacres of 1648–1649 and the collapse of the Shabbatean movement.

The advances of scholarly research of our generation on the history of the Jews has necessitated the compilation of this atlas, the first in a series dealing with the history of the Jewish people in the Diaspora.

The maps attempt to present the changes that befell the Jews over a period of more than a thousand years. Despite the many vicissitudes, disasters and trials that befell them during this period, their ties to the Holy Land remained unbroken. This is the common bond that united the Jewish people and it finds its expression in this atlas. The maps illustrate the changes that occurred in the Holy Land and in the Diaspora in chronological order of the events: emigration, expulsion from cities and countries, and forced conversion. While it was impossible to structure the atlas with complete synchronization, the reader can still learn about the movement of Jews from one center to another and how Jewish inspiration and vitality spread from one geographical area to another. We have not always been able to give an exhaustive description of Jewish life in each area, from its inception to its demise. In some regions Jewish life reached full development, both materially and spiritually. In others, the pulse of Jewish community life stopped beating.

A further difficulty was determining political boundaries of states and countries, since these changed from time to time. We have usually followed the accepted practice regarding political boundaries.

The texts that accompany the maps provide a supplementary evaluation and give a geographical-historical expression to the relevant period in the history of the Jews.

The atlas is divided into four sections: the first opens with a description of the Jewish Diaspora in the fourth and fifth centuries and ends with the Crusades; the second opens with the period following the Crusades and ends with the destruction of Jewish communities during the Black Death; the third section ends with the expulsion of the Jews from Spain; and the fourth ends with the devastation resulting from the Chmielnicki Massacres of 1648–1649 and the spiritual upheaval that came after the collapse of the Shabbatean movement. Each of these four major disasters represents the termination of an era.

* * *

This atlas could not have been produced without the aid of students and friends, who gave me invaluable assistance in gathering material and in verification of much of the detail. My thanks are therefore due to Y. Avishur, M. Idel, R. Bonfil, A. Grossman, B. Z. Degani, A. David, M. Nadav, Y. T. Assis, E. Friesel, Y. Y. Kaplan, Y. Kaplan, and M. Riegler.

I also owe thanks to Y. Ben-Zion for the picture of the tombstone at Kabul, and to the photographer Z. Radovan for the pictures of the Ramban Synagogue.

Thanks are also due for the preparation of this atlas to the staff of Carta whose dedication, advice and extensive experience and knowledge have been of infinite assistance throughout.

For the preparation of the English edition my thanks are due to Moshe Shalvi, who translated the Hebrew text into English, and to the staff at Carta, particularly Lorraine Kessel, Anna Gelman, Hanna Tabatchnik and Miriam Dobrusin.

Thanks are also due to Charles E. Smith, President, Paul Bernabeo, Editorial Director, and Stephen Wagley, of Simon and Schuster Academic Reference Division, who coordinated the creation of this English language edition.

Jerusalem,
1992

H. B.

TABLE OF CONTENTS

UNTIL THE BLACK DEATH

UNTIL THE EXPULSION FROM SPAIN

All the nations of the earth,
even the ships that go from
Gaul to Spain are blessed only
for Israel's sake

Babylonian Talmud.

Tombstone of Meliosa, daughter of R.
Judah and Miriam, discovered in Tortosa.
Inscriptions in Hebrew, Latin and Greek.
A Menora and a star similar in shape to a
star of David appear on the tombstone.

FROM THE BARBARIAN INVASIONS OF EUROPE
UNTIL THE CRUSADES

Equestrian statue of Charlemagne.

LEGEND TO SYMBOLS

- •········· Town
- ✿········· Town with Jewish community
- ♈········· Synagogue
- †········· Church
- ⚓········· Port
- ✕········· Battle site
- ➡········· Conquest of city
- ✿⊢········· Massacre of Jews
- ➐········· Expulsion of Jews
- ✦········· Blood libel
- ♨········· Auto-de-fé and burning of Jews at the stake
- ⟵········· Campaign or attack
- ◄◄········· Escape
- ······ ········· Boundary of kingdom or province
- ⌄⌄⌄········· Line of the Reconquest

THE BARBARIAN INVASIONS OF EUROPE   Fifth Century

The invasions of various tribes, collectively called the barbarians, into the boundaries of the Roman Empire caused great changes in Western Europe and only the Eastern Roman Empire — Byzantium — was able to withstand these invasions.

As for the Jews, it was not the barbarian invasions that endangered their survival but rather Byzantium and Christianity. From the time of Constantine the Great (ruled 306–337), who granted imperial favor to Christianity, Christianity sought to populate Palestine with its co-religionists by encouraging both pilgrimages to its holy places and settlement in the country. Bands of Christian monks, "the Christian army," were the standard-bearers of the church militant. Palestine and other Christian centers became arenas for disputations with Jews, and Christianity sought to interpret these disputations as its triumph over Judaism. Christian tradition tells of whole Jewish communities that converted: for example, the entire Jewish community of Menorca was converted by Bishop Severus in 418. It was during this period that Christianity began laying the first foundation for a comprehensive ideology concerning its ascendancy over Judaism. The Jewish people were punished for crucifying Jesus, and the instruments of this punishment were Vespasian and Titus, who, according to this ideology, supported Christianity. An extensive fabric of legends and folktales was woven around the allegation that the Jews crucified Jesus, and the Jewish people were branded as "killers of God." The church declared itself the heir of Judaism, *Verus Israel* ("the true Israel"), and sought proof for this in the Bible. The existence of the Jewish people was necessary to enable the conversion of the pagans to Christianity. Augustine (354–430), bishop of Hippo (north Africa), found a justification for the humiliation of the Jewish people in this interpretation of Psalm 59:11 — "Slay them not, lest my people forget; scatter them by thy power and bring them down…": "Slay them [the Jews] not lest my people (the Christians) forget" the prophecies in the Bible foretelling the realization of Christianity. "And bring them [the Jews] down." These were the tenets that guided Christianity in its war against Judaism over the many generations and upon these foundations it built anti-Jewish public opinion, whose effects were apparent during the entire Middle Ages. Christian propagandists saturated the centers of the ancient world. The most prominent was John Chrysostom (c. 347–407), who determined the character of the struggle against Judaism, a struggle that was necessary for Christianity to emerge victorious in the pagan world. Nonetheless, the church fathers required the assistance of Jewish scholars to interpret and understand the Bible text. One of them, Jerome (Eusebius Sophronius Hieronymus, 342–420, of Bethlehem) required the help of Jewish teachers in Palestine to learn Hebrew for his translation of the Bible into Latin (c. 404).

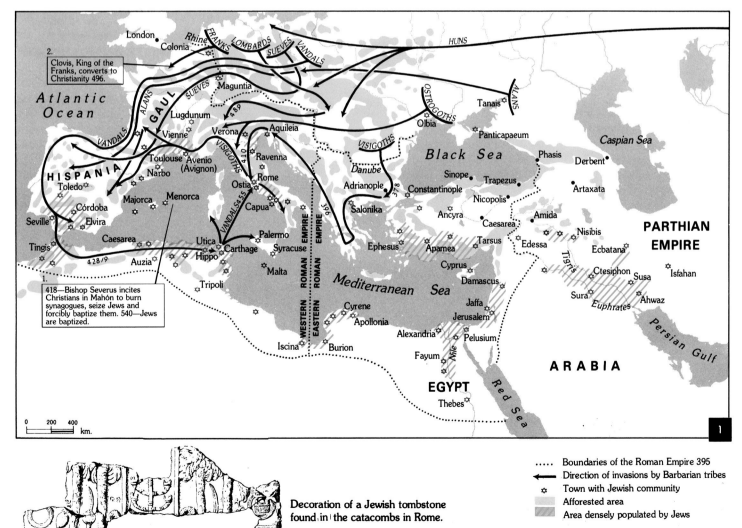

2. Clovis, King of the Franks, converts to Christianity 496.

1. 418—Bishop Severus incites Christians in Mahón to burn synagogues, seize Jews and forcibly baptize them. 540—Jews are baptized.

0   200   400   km.

Decoration of a Jewish tombstone found in the catacombs in Rome.

..... Boundaries of the Roman Empire 395
← Direction of invasions by Barbarian tribes
✡ Town with Jewish community
Afforested area
Area densely populated by Jews

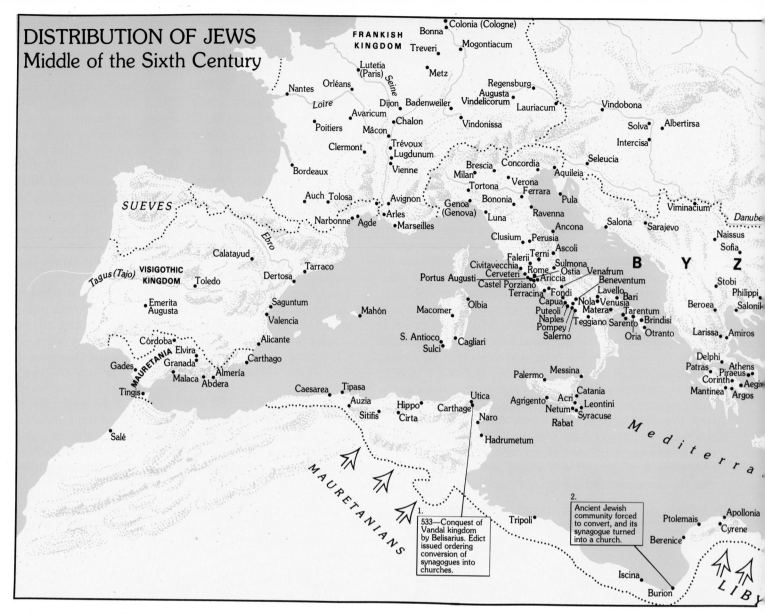

DISTRIBUTION OF JEWS
Middle of the Sixth Century

FRANKISH KINGDOM

Colonia (Cologne) · Bonna · Treveri · Mogontiacum · Lutetia (Paris) · Metz · Nantes · Orléans · Regensburg · Augusta Vindelicorum · Lauriacum · Vindobona · Loire · Dijon · Badenweiler · Avaricum · Chalon · Vindonissa · Solva · Albertirsa · Poitiers · Mâcon · Intercisa · Clermont · Trévoux · Lugdunum · Vienne · Seleucia · Bordeaux · Brescia · Concordia · Milan · Aquileia · Viminacium · Danube · Tortona · Verona · Ferrara · Auch · Tolosa · Genoa (Genova) · Bononia · Pula · Avignon · Luna · Ravenna · Salona · Sarajevo · Naissus · Narbonne · Agde · Arles · Ancona · Sofia

SUEVES

Marseilles · Clusium · Perusia · Calatayud · Terni · Ascoli · Tarraco · Falerii · Sulmona · Civitavecchia · Rome · Ostia · Venafrum · **B Y Z** · Stobi · Philippi · Dertosa · Cerveteri · Ariccia · Beneventum · Castel Porziano · Fondi · Lavello · Bari · Beroea · Saloni · Terracina · Capua · Nola · Venusia · Emerita Augusta · Saguntum · Puteoli · Matera · Tarentum · Larissa · Amiros · Valencia · Naples · Teggiano Sarento · Brindisi · Pompey · Salerno · Oria · Otranto · Delphi · Athens · Patras · Piraeus · Corinth · Aegi · Mantinea · Argos

VISIGOTHIC KINGDOM

Tagus (Tajo) · Toledo · Ebro · Córdoba · Elvira · Alicante · Mahón · Macomer · Olbia · Gades · Granada · Carthago · S. Antioco · Cagliari · Palermo · Messina · Tingis · Malaca · Abdera · Almería · Sulci · Catania · Salé · MAURETANIA · Caesarea · Tipasa · Utica · Agrigento · Acri · Leontini · Auzia · Hippo · Carthage · Naro · Netum · Syracuse · Sitifis · Cirta · Rabat · M e d i t e r r a

MAURETANIANS · Hadrumetum

1. 533—Conquest of Vandal kingdom by Belisarius. Edict issued ordering conversion of synagogues into churches.

2. Ancient Jewish community forced to convert, and its synagogue turned into a church.

Tripoli · Ptolemais · Apollonia · Cyrene · Berenice · Iscina · **LIBY** · Burion

---

Information regarding the Jewish dispersion is sparse. One may learn about the way of life of the Jewish communities from the canons of the church synods that convened in Europe. For example, one of the rulings of the Council of Elvira in southern Spain at the beginning of the fourth century forbade Jews to bless Christian fields and Christians to eat in the company of Jews. These prohibitions were intended to prevent fraternization between Jews and Christians. From this, one may also infer that Jews engaged in agriculture.

In the fifth century church councils increasingly discussed matters involving the Jews. Although Rome was a center of Christianity, the leaders of the church were weak, thus enabling the church councils in various regions to issue canons concerning Jewish affairs.

Anti-Jewish bias was prevalent at the church councils held in France during the Merovingian period and their decisions express the intent to sever social relations between the Jewish and Christian populations. The decisions of these councils determined the relationship of the Merovingian rulers toward the Jews. However, Merovingian France admitted the Jewish refugees who fled from Visigothic persecutions.

Massacre and persecution were the fate of the Jewish communities in the lands conquered by the Byzantine armies. The Emperor Justinian I promulgated a series of Novellae (new laws added to the Corpus Iuris Civilis) intended to harm the Jews and restrict the livelihood of the Jewish population in the Roman Empire. One of the Novellae forbade the public reading of the Torah in Hebrew, permitting the reading only in Greek. The Jews got around this law by composing a corpus of Hebrew liturgical poetry that was incorporated in the prayers and contained references to passages in the Pentateuch.

The victory of Belisarius, commander of Justinian's army, over the Vandals in North Africa (533) put an end to their rule in that territory and from then on the status of the Jews declined in the former Vandal kingdom. The Jews, Donatists and Arians were warned against proselytizing. The status of the Jews further declined with the capture of Burion, the fifth city of the Pentapolis, situated at the southwestern edge of Cyrenaica and the Jews of this ancient community were forced to convert to Christianity and their synagogue was turned into a church. Many Jews fled to the free Berber tribes, who treated them kindly.

The map of Jewish dispersion shows a large Jewish world extending beyond the borders of the Roman Empire, including the Persian Sassanid kingdom. The rulers of this kingdom were generally tolerant toward the Jews, allowing them to establish their own organizations and institutions and thus providing a new political foundation for Jewish self-government through the office of the exilarch, the lay head of the Jewish community.

A distant independent Jewish community in southern Arabia maintained close contact with the Jewish community in the Holy Land and some of its members were priviliged to be buried in Bet She'arim.

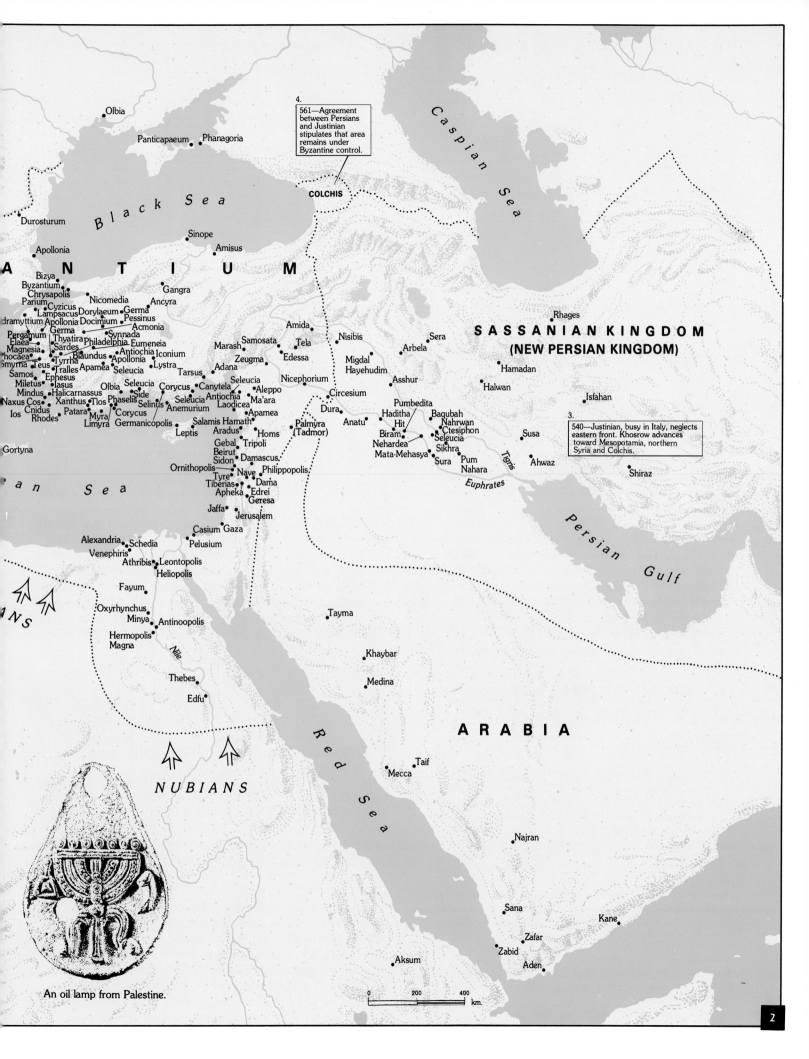

Olbia

Panticapaeum • Phanagoria

Caspian Sea

4.
561—Agreement
between Persians
and Justinian
stipulates that area
remains under
Byzantine control.

COLCHIS

Black Sea

Durosturum

Sinope
Apollonia
Amisus

ANTIUM

Bizya
Byzantium
Chrysopolis   Gangra
Parium   Nicomedia   Ancyra
Cyzicus
Lampsacus Dorylaeum Germa
dramyttium Apollonia Docimium Pessinus
Pergamum Germa   Acmonia
Elaea   Synnada
Magnesia Thyatira Philadelphia Eumeneia
hocaea Sardes Blaundus Antiochia Iconium
Smyrna Tyrrha   Apamea   Lystra
Samos Teus Tralles Seleucia
Miletus Ephesus Iasus
Mindus Halicarnassus Olbia Seleucia Corycus
Naxus Cos Xanthus Tlos Phaselis Side
Ios Cnidus Patara Selinus Seleucia
Rhodes Myra Corycus Anemurium
Limyra Germanicopolis

Amida
Samosata   Tela
Marash   Edessa
Zeugma
Adana
Tarsus   Seleucia
Nicephorium
Canytela
Aleppo
Antiochia Ma'ara
Laodicea
Apamea
Salamis Hamath
Aradus   Homs
Leptis   Tripoli
Gebal
Beirut
Sidon
Ornithopolis   Damascus
Tyre   Nave Philippopolis
Tiberias   Dama
Apheka Edrei
Geresa
Jaffa
Jerusalem

Nisibis

Sera
Arbela

Migdal
Hayehudim
Asshur
Circesium
Dura   Pumbedita
Anatu Haditha Baqubah
Hit Nahrwan
Biram Ctesiphon
Nehardea Seleucia
Mata-Mehasya Sikhra
Sura Pum
Nahara

Palmyra
(Tadmor)

Rhages

SASSANIAN KINGDOM
(NEW PERSIAN KINGDOM)

Hamadan
Halwan

Isfahan

3.
540—Justinian, busy in Italy, neglects
eastern front. Khosrow advances
toward Mesopotamia, northern
Syria and Colchis.

Susa
Ahwaz

Shiraz

Tigris
Euphrates

Persian Gulf

Gortyna

an Sea

Casium Gaza
Alexandria Schedia   Pelusium
Venephiris
Athribis Leontopolis
Heliopolis
ANS
Fayum
Oxyrhynchus
Minya Antinoopolis
Hermopolis
Magna
Nile

Tayma

Khaybar

Medina

Red Sea

ARABIA

Thebes
Edfu

NUBIANS

Taif
Mecca

Najran

Sana
Kane
Zafar
Zabid
Aksum   Aden

An oil lamp from Palestine.

0   200   400
km.

2

15

SYNAGOGUES IN PALESTINE
Second to Sixth Centuries

Byzantine rule sought to deal a blow to the Jewish communities in Palestine and the Diaspora by abolishing the patriarchate. The death of R. Gamaliel the Sixth in 426 brought an end to the harassment of the patriarchate. (The harassment apparently continued until 429.) In spite of the authorities' attempt to badger the Jewish residents of Palestine by dividing the country into three provinces — Prima in the center, Secunda in the north and Tertia in south — the Jewish community remained resolute. A list of

synagogues and their mosaics present a picture of a Jewish community attempting to cope with the edicts of the time. Jews were forbidden to reside in Jerusalem, and Tiberias became the most important Jewish center of the period. The Samaritan community was badly decimated as a result of its first revolt against Byzantine rule in 484, when Emperor Zeno built a church on Mount Gerizim, and the revolt in 529 during the reign of Emperor Justinian I.

THE HIMYAR KINGDOM AND ITS WAR WITH THE ETHIOPIANS
Sixth Century

The kingdom of Himyar and Himyar ben Saba will become strong in Yemen after the departure from there of the tribes of Saba. And the kings of Himyar were called Tuba in the days when the kings of Egypt were called Pharaoh. Their capital was called Zafar and was near the city known today as Sana. And the most famous ruler, Asad abu-Karb, was the first to become a Jew after his return from his war against Persia. He learned of Judaism from Jewish scholars at Medina when he passed through there on his travels. Many people of his land became Jews with him, and the country of Himyar became Jewish until the days of Yosef Du Nuas, whom the king of Ethiopia fought against because of his war against the Christians of Najran who Yosef pursued when he heard what the Christians had done to the Jews of Najran. Because Christianity had spread in Najran in central Arabia when Himyar was Jewish. And the Ethiopians will become strong in Himyar and Yemen and become a colony of Ethiopia for a long time. And the Ethiopian governor of Sana will build a splendid Christian church in the capital in order to capture the hearts of the inhabitants of Arabia for Christianity.

A.M. Habermann, Sefer Gzerot Ashkenaz ve-Tsarfat, *Jerusalem 1946, p. 29*

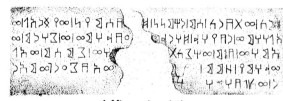

A Himyar inscription.

The Jewish kingdom of Himyar in southern Arabia was a thorn in the flesh of Byzantium, particularly during the Byzantine-Persian wars, because it was located on a major trade route. Byzantium's geopolitical motives for moving against Himyar were founded on the strategic necessity of establishing a southern flanking route to the Persian Gulf. This objective required a base on the Red Sea and an alliance with Ethiopia, the only Christian state in the area. The commercial motive was to maintain an open sea route to India in order to protect the supply of spices and other goods from India and Arabia to the merchants of Rome. However, the Jewish kingdom prevented the passage of Byzantine traders through its territory in retaliation for the persecution of Jews in Byzantium, and Du Nuas, the last king of Himyar, was particularly zealous in this matter. Persia was too weak an ally to render any significant support to the

16

Jewish kingdom of Himyar because it did not share Himyar's political and strategic needs in its relations with Byzantium. Himyar was threatened by the Christian merchant community in Najran and by the Ethiopians. The latter, having formed an alliance with Byzantium, undertook to fight Byzantium's battle with Himyar to settle a score with that kingdom over Ethiopia's loss of control of the straits that led from the Red Sea to the Indian Ocean. Himyar was also weakened by internal strife. King Du Nuas was defeated and died in a battle on the seashore in 525, an event that signified the end of the Himyar kingdom. The Ethiopians destroyed the Jewish communities and the remnants of the independent Jewish kingdom dispersed to the towns and mountains of the Arabian peninsula; many fled to the city of Taif. The Jewish community in Najran was annihilated.

A section of the floor mosaic of Bet Alfa synagogue showing signs of the Zodiac.

1. Wars between Byzantium and Persia sever trade routes from Byzantium to India.

6. Many Jews flee to Ta'if. Jewish community in Najran destroyed.

2. Byzantium avails itself of Christian Ethiopian allies, aiding them with naval and land forces in order to attack Himyar.

4. Himyars avenge themselves on Christian merchant colony of city who collaborated with Ethiopians.

5. 525—Du Nuas fails to repel Ethiopian attack and is killed. Ethiopians kill most of population.

3. 522—Ethiopians invade Himyar, capturing capital city of Zafar, but retreat in face of Du Nuas' army.

Trade routes

WARS BETWEEN PERSIA AND BYZANTIUM 609–629

1. 627—Heraclius defeats Khosrow II.

4. 632—Emperor Heraclius promulgates edict of forced conversion upon Jews of Byzantium.

2. 628—Persians surrender conquered territories to Byzantium. Heraclius embarks on triumphal march.

3. 21 Mar. 629—Heraclius enters Jerusalem in triumphal procession.

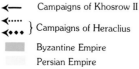

Campaigns of Khosrow II
Campaigns of Heraclius
Byzantine Empire
Persian Empire

THE PERSIAN INVASION OF PALESTINE
614–618

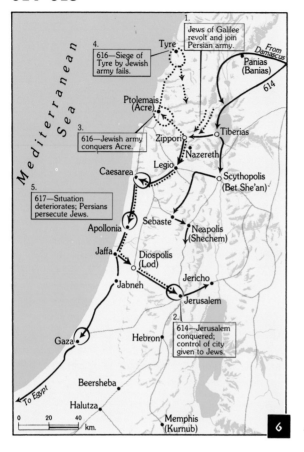

1. Jews of Galilee revolt and join Persian army.

4. 616—Siege of Tyre by Jewish army fails.

3. 616—Jewish army conquers Acre.

5. 617—Situation deteriorates; Persians persecute Jews.

2. 614—Jerusalem conquered; control of city given to Jews.

o   City that opened its gates to Persians
←   Persian army
←···· Jewish army
←┅┅ Persian and Jewish army

In 606 the Persian legions invaded Syria, Palestine and Phoenicia and began to dismember the Byzantine Empire. Palestine was a natural center for Persian-Jewish collaboration since it had a large Jewish community that was a potential counter-force to the Christian population and Byzantine rule. Most of the Jewish population was centered in Galilee, in an area that controlled the route leading from Damascus to Palestine. There was also a concentration of Jews in Jerusalem, so large that the governor of the city tried to force them to convert to Christianty. The fall of Antioch to the Persians severed the land route between Constantinople and Palestine and in 613 the Persians entered Damascus. Jerusalem was captured in 614, and in 619 the Persians conquered Egypt. In all these conquests the Jews and Samaritans received the Persians as liberators, turning many cities over to them. The Persian conquest of Palestine was interpreted by the Jews as the advent of the messianic period of redemption. This ferment was reflected in the eschatological literature of the period and in the increasing number of messianic movements among the Jews.

The Jewish community's euphoria over the Persian conquest was short-lived; the Persians did not fulfill their promises to the Jews and were soon favoring the Christian community and persecuting the Jewish one. In a battle near Nineveh (627), the Byzantines defeated the Persians and proceeded to occupy Ctesiphon (628). With the death of Khosrow (628), the way was open to the conquest of Jerusalem (629), but the days of Byzantine rule too were short-lived. The Islamic conqueror stood at the gate.

THE JEWS IN THE ARABIAN PENINSULA
Beginning of the Seventh Century

- - - Trade routes
✡   City or town with Jewish community
▓   Rainfall area
☐   Oases
░   Sands

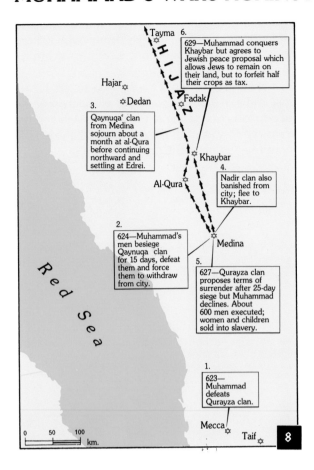

6.
629—Muhammad conquers Khaybar but agrees to Jewish peace proposal which allows Jews to remain on their land, but to forfeit half their crops as tax.

3.
Qaynuqa' clan from Medina sojourn about a month at al-Qura before continuing northward and settling at Edrei.

4.
Nadir clan also banished from city; flee to Khaybar.

2.
624—Muhammad's men besiege Qaynuqa clan for 15 days, defeat them and force them to withdraw from city.

5.
627—Qurayza clan proposes terms of surrender after 25-day siege but Muhammad declines. About 600 men executed; women and children sold into slavery.

1.
623—Muhammad defeats Qurayza clan.

Muhammad had hoped to convert these settlers, but ultimately realizing that he would never succeed, he declared a war of extinction against them.

Relations between Muhammad and the Jews deteriorated, especially after his victory over Abu Jahl of Mecca (in the second year of the Hegira). He now turned against his enemies in Medina, besieging the stronghold of the Jewish clan of Qaynuqa' and forcing them into exile. The Qaynuqa' went by way of Wadi al-Qura to Transjordan and settled at Edrei. Arab sources number the size of the clan as 750 people, excluding women and children. In 627, after an unsuccessful siege by the Meccans against Medina, Muhammad turned against the Jewish clan of Qurayza and forced them to surrender unconditionally. The Qurayza had hoped for mercy and protection from their allies in Muhammad's camp but Muhammad was determined to destroy them.

The fate of the Jews of Khaybar was different from that of the other Jewish clans. They sought allies amongst the Bedouin tribes of the south but Muhammad succeeded in winning the Bedouin over to his side. In 629, after a siege, the Jews of Khaybar turned to Muhammad and sued for peace. Muhammad, apparently weary of war, agreed to a proposal whereby the Jews were allowed to remain on their land on condition that they paid an annual tax of one half of their date harvest. According to the Hadith, this agreement on the distribution of the spoils served as a model for the conquests of Omar. This may explain and justify Omar's methods in conquest.

We know very little about the beginnings of Jewish settlement in the Arabian peninsula. It seems that Jews began to live in oases and urban centers in the first centuries C.E. The settlers engaged in agriculture and commerce and were organized in clans (or, according to some scholars, tribal groups). Their agriculture consisted mainly of date groves, while in commerce they developed the credit system and in the crafts they were blacksmiths, gold- and silversmiths and expert armor makers. Various families were identified by their occupations. The story is told that Muhammad used to buy goods on credit from the Jews.

Medina had a concentration of Jewish tribes; among the large ones were Banu Nadir, Qurayza, Qaynuqa' and some, who claimed to be of priestly descent, called Kahinan. Their strongholds were greater in number than those of the Arabs. The Khaybar Jews resided about a hundred kilometers north of the Medina district and it is possible that this Jewish settlement was larger than Medina. In spite of the vicissitudes in their fortune, the Khaybar community played an important role in the history of the Jewish people. The Jewish settlements in Wadi al-Qura and other oases such as Fadak and Tayma served as asylums for the refugees from southern Arabia after the death of Du Nuas. Jewish residents settled in these areas in proximity to nomadic Bedouin tribes and to the Nadirs, who were sedentary farmers. In spite of the influence of these two groups, the Jews persevered in their own special way of life and did not become nomads like the Bedouin, who changed their abode twice a year.

THE CITY OF MEDINA

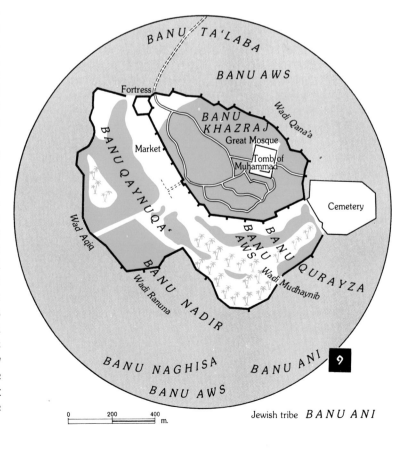

Jewish tribe *BANU ANI*

Now came the turn of the Jewish clans in the southern half of the peninsula and in the oases. This stage of the war is reflected in the text of an agreement containing promises given by Muhammad to the Samuel b. Adaya family in return for an undertaking by the family to pay a poll tax and an annual fixed amount of food products. Muhammad now adopted a policy different from the one used against the Jews of Hijaz and Khaybar. He declared that one must not coerce Jews and Christians to accept the new faith and ordered his officers and tax collectors to limit themselves to taking a poll tax (*jizya*) and a land tax (*karga* or *kharaj*). The majority of Jews were at that time concentrated in the Yemen and those in the north, who joined their brethren in the south, were the ones who renewed contacts with the Babylonian geonim and subsequently with the secular and religious leaders of the Egyptian Jewish community. Others emigrated to Palestine after it was conquered by the armies of Islam.

After Muhammad's death in 632 his successors continued their conquest and expansion. Knowledge of the map of the world at this period is one of the keys to understanding the fate of Judaism, which was from now on poised between the two world powers — Islam and Christianity.

ARABIAN CONQUEST AND THE RISE OF ISLAM   622-721

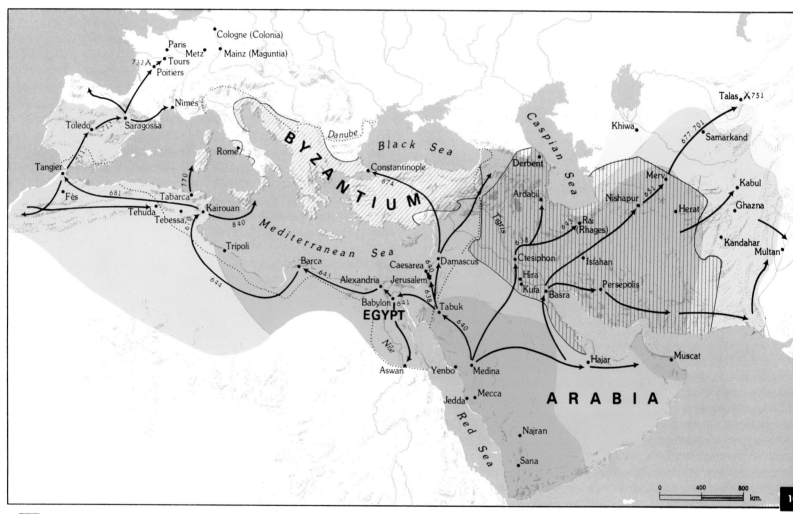

▥	Persian kingdom
⋯⋯	Boundary of Byzantine empire, 565
▨	Byzantine empire, 700
▓	Muhammad's conquests, 622-632
▓	Conquests during reign of first four caliphs, 632-661
░	Conquests during Umayyad caliphate, 661-750
░	Conquests during Abbasid caliphate, 750 onwards
←	Major routes of Arab advances

Islam continued to dominate the Arabian Peninsula, conquering Damascus, Babylonia and Persia. The Arabs invaded Palestine in 634 and by February had already reached the gates of Gaza, defeating the Byzantine army in 636. Jerusalem, still held by the Byzantines, was besieged in 637 and in March–April 638 surrendered to Caliph Omar. In 640 Caesarea, the last Byzantine foothold in Palestine, was taken. The Islamic armies continued their drive through Egypt and North Africa and in 711 crossed the straits separating Europe and Africa, invading and conquering the Iberian Peninsula. They crossed the Pyrenees but were defeated in a battle near Tours (Poitiers) and their advance was halted.

It was clear that the Jews belonged to the *dhimmi* class (the protected people) by virtue of being Jews. Relations with them were therefore determined by the agreements concluded by Muhammad and the practice at that time. However, relations were greatly influenced by the political and social developments in the caliphates.

The Jews tended to live in separate streets, but in this they were not different from members of other faiths. In the Arab city of Fès, Muslims from Kairouan lived in one street and Muslims from Andalusia lived in another street and each community had its own mosque. The Jewish quarter was in the northern part of the city, but there was no fixed Muslim legislation requiring Jews to reside in separate quarters. If such legislation did exist, the Muslims, as a minority, would have segregated themselves in their own quarters. However, in their own quarters Muslims made sure that churches and synagogues were built no higher than mosques and that Muslim houses were no lower than the houses of their neighbors. Segregation existed in the bathhouses, and in many cities separate Jewish baths were built (e.g., Gerona, Granada and elsewhere). Heavy punishment was meted out for sexual intercourse between members of different communities and mixed marriages were strictly forbidden unless the non-Muslim converted to Islam. Muslims were forbidden to bequeath anything to the infidel. In general, *dhimmi* children who converted to Islam lost their right of inheritance and the father of a converted daughter was not entitled to marry her off (and therefore receive her *mohar*).

The superior status of Islam over other religions was further emphasized by distinctions in type and color of clothing. Over the generations, the Muslims added an increasing number of prohibitions and limitations.

VISIGOTHIC SPAIN
Seventh Century

1. 589—Third Church Council of Toledo: King Reccared declares Catholicism sole religion of country. Jews forbidden to marry Christian women or own Christian slaves.

2. 589—Regional council of priests compels all residents to rest on Sunday.

FRANKISH KINGDOM

5. 633—Fourth Church Council of Toledo. Restrictions against Jews and persecution of crypto-Jews.

3. 612—King Sisebut orders release of Christian slaves owned by Jews.

4. 613—King Sisebut expels from Spain Jews who refuse to convert to Christianity. Many Jews convert but secretly continue to observe Judaism.

SUEVES · Duero · León · Burgos · Zamora · BASQUES · Pamplona · Tudela · Saragossa · Calatayud · Escalona · Toledo · Lisbon · Badajoz · Mérida · Guadiana · VISIGOTHS · Seville · Córdoba · Lucena · Elvira · Granada · Gades · Málaga · Adra · Tingis · Ceuta · Toulouse · Agde · Marseilles · Béziers · Narbonne · Perpignan · Gerona · Ebro · Tarragona · Barcelona · Tortosa · Valencia · Elche · Cartagena · Algiers

Byzantine provinces taken by Visigoths, 584-585
Kingdom of Visigoths in 600
o Place with remains of Jewish residence

0 100 200 km.

11

The persecution of the Jews in Visigothic Spain began when the Visigoths converted to Catholicism during the reign of king Reccared (586). From then on the church councils enacted a number of anti-Jewish laws with the intention of eliminating the Jewish community.

King Sisebut, supported by the church councils, inaugurated a series of stringent anti-Jewish laws in 612. The Jewish population was forced to convert and, even then, as converts they were burdened with many restrictions. The church council of 633, during the reign of King Sisenand, was the most severe in its attitude toward the Jewish population and its decisions regarding the Jews were adopted as the law of the land. Nine basic laws (paragraphs 57–65) established a legal network against the Jews and crypto-Jews. Paragraph 65 was the law that forbade Jews and crypto-Jews from holding offices and having any jurisdiction over Christians. This law served in the fifteenth century to forbid Jews and crypto-Jews to hold office and to create anti-Jewish public opinion.

The Visigoths who invaded Spain in 412 ruled for three hundred years as a social upper strata of conquerors that tried to impose the laws of a militant society and church upon the country. They failed to integrate with the indigenous Roman-Spanish community, and also rejected the Jewish minority. Internal intrigues caused their downfall at the beginning of the eighth century.

THE JEWS IN ITALY DURING THE PAPACY OF GREGORY I (THE GREAT) 590–604

1. 591—Bishop of city expels Jews from synagogue on grounds that their prayers disturb those of Christians. Pope Gregory I orders investigation of allegation; if proved valid, Jews must be given alternative site for their synagogue.

3. Pope Gregory orders punishment of Christian fanatics who harrassed Jewish worshipers.

4. Pope Gregory censures an apostate for desecrating a synagogue and orders removal of crosses placed there.

2. 598—Bishop of city confiscates synagogue and houses of learning, converting them into churches. Pope Gregory censures bishop and orders him to pay compensation for buildings and religious artifacts.

5. Although Pope Gregory opposes forced conversion, he orders a group of Jews who wish to convert to be given financial aid and to be baptized immediately, before they change their minds.

0   100   200
km.

12

Area under Langobard control
Area under suzerainty of Byzantine empire

Despite the scant information available on the Jews in Italy in the sixth and seventh centuries, there are sources that indicate Jewish settlement in a number of important Italian cities. Legal autonomy for the Jews of Italy was recognized by an edict of king Theodoric (after 512), in contrast to the policy of the Byzantine emperors, who saw Jewish courts merely as institutions of arbitration. The Jews of Genoa were allowed to repair their synagogue and it was decreed that they were not to be coerced in matters of belief.

The heads of the church in Rome had considerable international influence, but it was only during the papacy of Gregory I (590–604) that the church's attitude to the Jews was given official expression. His papal bull *Sicut Judaeis* determined the church's relationship to the Jews throughout the Middle Ages. The underlying principle of Gregory's bull was the maintenance of the status quo and so, for example, the extent of synagogue activities was restricted to what had been permissible before the publication of the bull. Successive popes in the Middle Ages continued to be guided by *Sicut Judaeis*. However, Gregory's general policy toward the Jews was to refrain from religious compulsion and serious economic persecution. While he permitted Jews to own pagan slaves, he prohibited them from owning pagan slaves who converted to Christianity and totally forbade trading in these slaves. Pagan slaves who worked on Jewish farms and converted and became colons (594), were obliged to pay a fixed rental fee and forbidden to perform any personal service for their Jewish masters. Gregory also supported the persecution of the Jews by the Visigoths in Spain.

The largest concentration of Jews in Italy seems to have been in Sicily, then under Byzantine rule.

Rome had the most ancient Jewish community and communal organization in Italy. The communal leadership had its early origins in the office of the archisynagogus (head of the synagogue) who was assisted by the elders of the community. The Jews of Rome, like the Greeks, Franks, Saxons, Lombards, and Frisians, were called *schola peregrinorum* (a sect of foreigners), and are mentioned as being present at the coronation of emperors in Rome. Rome became the forum for disputations between Jews and Christians on matters of faith.

Pope Gregory I (the Great).

And King Charles sent to the King of Babylonia asking him to send Jews descendants of the House of David. And he agreed and sent him a wise and important person, R. Makhir by name, who was settled in Narbonne . . . and he was given a big landed property in the time the city was conquered from the Israelites . . . And when the city was conquered the King divided it in three parts: one was given to don Eymerich, the city's governor; the second part was given to the local bishop; the third was given to R. Makhir, who became enriched and was granted freedom, and the king gave to the local Jews good laws, signed by the king Charles through privileges, accepted by his descendants. And those who tried persecute them, they would complain to the King who would order reprisals. And immediately order was restored. Narbonne is under the rule of France. And his [R. Makhir's] descendants were in their time leaders at the head of various dispersions.

R. Abraham Ibn Daud, The Book of Tradition I, ed. A. Neubaur, Oxford 1888. Addition to manuscript, p. 82.

CHARLEMAGNE'S EMPIRE

A tombstone in Auch (Elimberris).

Charlemagne (768–814), the central Carolingian figure, had his name linked with many Jewish and Christian legends, one of which is the legend concerning the role he played in the Jewish settlements in Narbonne and Mainz and particularly with the tradition that he was instrumental in having Torah study transferred from Baghdad to Narbonne.

Charlemagne was the first western ruler to send a commercial delegation to the Caliph Harun al-Rashid, and it was this delegation that renewed and revived trade relations between Christian Europe and eastern Islam. A Jew, called Isaac, was a member of the delegation and was the only one to complete the mission and return safely.

The relationship between Charlemagne and the Jews, and the protection he extended to them, is expressed in his edicts. One can assume that the foundations for the charters of privileges for the Jews were laid during his reign.

There are three extant charters of privileges from the Carolingian period, all dating from the reign of Louis the Pious (814–840): one given to R. Domatus; the second to several Jews from Lyons — David, Joseph and their compatriots; the third to Abraham of Saragossa. The three charters provide a wealth of information about the history of the Jews in Europe and particularly in the Carolingian empire. Probably granted in 825, the charters gave protection to the Jews and defined their rights. Each paragraph dealt with a variety of subjects and problems, for example, exemptions from paying certain taxes and excises that were levied on the general population. We also learn from the charters of the considerable Jewish involvement in the slave trade that extended from Bohemia to Muslim Spain. The importance of defining the legal relations between Jews and Christians can be attested to their prominence in the records of judicial proceedings. It is reasonable to assume that the Carolingians instituted the office of *magister Judaeorum,* an imperial official appointed to supervise matters relating to the Jews. The office and its incumbent were destined to rouse the anger of the church in Carolingian France, but also to be emulated in many places.

Relations with the crown were of prime importance since the right of residence for Jews in the Carolingian state, as in every other state, depended upon the crown's approval. A fundamental change in relations with the Jews took place in the Carolingian state, which discarded the Theodosian ordinances and replaced them with the ancient Teutonic laws regarding aliens. The new relations were based upon the ruler's patronage and protection in exchange for the payment of a fixed annual tax.

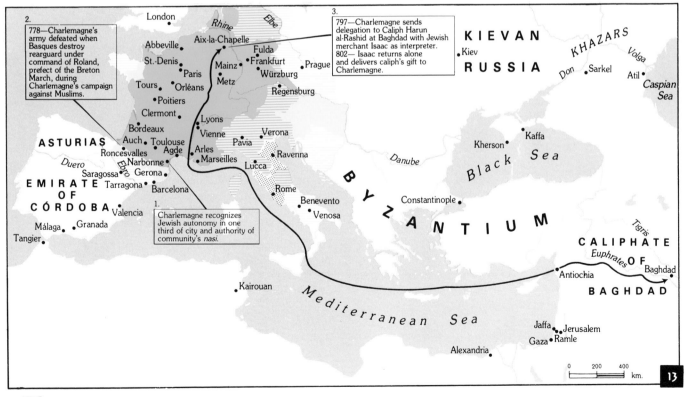

2. 778—Charlemagne's army defeated when Basques destroy rearguard under command of Roland, prefect of the Breton March, during Charlemagne's campaign against Muslims.

3. 797—Charlemagne sends delegation to Caliph Harun al-Rashid at Baghdad with Jewish merchant Isaac as interpreter. 802— Isaac returns alone and delivers caliph's gift to Charlemagne.

1. Charlemagne recognizes Jewish autonomy in one third of city and authority of community's *nasi.*

Frankish kingdom, 768
Charlemagne's conquests
Frontier military districts
Conquered peoples and allies

BOUNDARIES OF THE DIVIDED CAROLINGIAN EMPIRE
843

1. 825—Privileges of Louis the Pious and the reaction of Agobard of Lyon against them.

2. 839—The Priest Bodo converts to Judaism, flees to Saragossa, and becomes active against Christianity.

3. 846—Amulo, successor of Agobard, increases incitement against Jews.

4. 850—Preachers and apostates succeed in baptizing some Jews. In order to protect their children, Jews send them to more secure city of Arles.

..... Boundaries of division of
the Carolingian empire,
according to Treaty of Verdun, 843

The division of the Carolingian Empire after Charlemagne's death did not substantially alter the status of the Jews in the kingdoms. However, the anti-Jewish activities and the writings of Agobard, archbishop of Lyons from 814 to 846, and his pupil, Amulo, archbishop of Lyons from 841, did signify the beginning of a change in attitude. Writings from the second half of the ninth century reveal that there were clergy who preached the forcible conversion of Jews. The Jews strongly objected to these sermons and as a cautionary measure sent their children to take refuge at Arles, where they enjoyed a greater degree of protection.

As a result of the political division in France in the eleventh and twelfth centuries, the Jews found themselves under the jurisdiction either of dioceses that were the owners of cities and towns, or of various feudal barons, to whom the Jewish community paid taxes for rights of residence. There were instances where a Jewish community (such as Narbonne) was obliged to pay an annual tax both to the diocese and to the baron who was the lord of the city.

It is from this period that we have increasing knowledge and information about the Jews in France. In Toulouse it was customary to degrade the Jews by publicly slapping the cheek of the head of the community on Good Friday and only in the twelfth century was this practice replaced by an annual payment to the clergy. Sermons on the death of Jesus incited the Christian masses and often resulted in violence against the Jews. In Béziers, the Christian population was allowed to stone the Jewish quarter on Easter and only in 1160 was this license converted to a one-time payment plus a fixed annual tax to the diocese. It is interesting to note that the basic argument for persecuting the Jews was the accusation of collusion between them and the invading Normans in the south of France and their support for the plundering raids of the Muslims.

THE KHAZARS AND PRESSURE FROM THE CHRISTIAN STATES
Eighth to Tenth Centuries

The conversion of the Khazars to Judaism is described in a number of historical sources of the period. Mas'udi, the Arab historian and traveler, in his book *The Meadows of Gold and Mines of Gems* (943–947), tells of the Khazar king who converted during the reign of Harun al-Rashid (786–809); of Muslims, Christians and Jews who settled in the Khazar city of Atil; of Jewish settlers, refugees from Muslim countries and Greeks who settled in the Khazar kingdom as a result of persecution by the Byzantine emperor, Romanus I Lecapenus (919–944). Other Arab sources relate the conversion story, some telling of the king's disappointment with his Christian faith, and of the talented Jewish polemicist who succeeded in convincing the king (after the former had purportedly poisoned his traveling companion, the Muslim emissary). Other sources report that members of the king's court were Jews; that his judicial court was composed of seven wise men — Jews, Christians, Muslims and pagans; that the basis of the Khazar livelihood was hunting and trading in animal skins, wax and honey. These sources also mention that Jews introduced work methods into the kingdom; that they taught the Khazars to read and write and that only because of their religious separatism were the

Jews able to maintain their independence and avoid being crushed between the Byzantine hammer and the caliphite anvil. However, political considerations were certainly not the only factors that prompted the Khazar king to convert.

The Khazars were constantly at war with their neighbors and Byzantium did everything in its power to destroy the kingdom — even inciting the Alan and Russian tribes to attack the Khazars from the north. This constant state of war prevented the Khazars from attending to the internal matter of Jewish consolidation. There is a general consensus that the Khazar kingdom of the ninth and tenth centuries was a Jewish state with Muslim and Christian minorities, in which the presence of Christians acted as a restraint on Byzantium's treatment of its Jewish population. The persecution of the Jews in Byzantium during the reign of Romanus I Lecapenus could be reciprocated by King Joseph's persecution of the Christians in his kingdom.

Not only international political factors undermined the existence of the Khazar kingdom but also economic ones, such as the lack of a centralized national economy (even by standards of that period). It is true that the capital city of Atil benefited from its strategic location on the crossroads

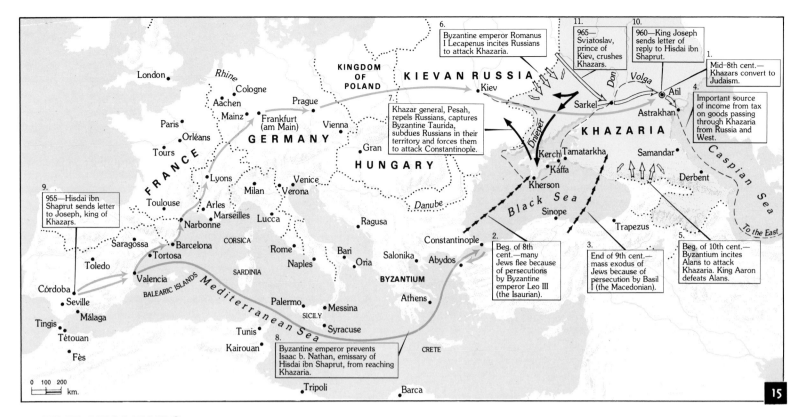

THE KHAZARS

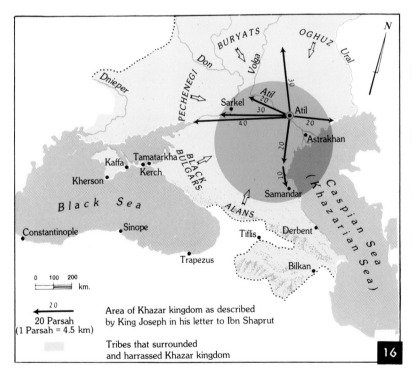

"Let not my lord take it ill, I pray, that I enquire about the number of his forces. May the Lord add to them, how many soever they be, an hundredfold. ...My lord sees that I enquire about this with no other object than that I may rejoice when I hear of the increase of the holy people. I wish too that he would tell me of the number of provinces over which he rules, the amount of tribute paid to him, if they give him tithes, whether he swells continually in the royal city or goes about through the whole extent of his dominions, if there are islands in the neighborhood, and if any of their inhabitants conform to Judaism? If he judges over them? How he goes up to the house of God? With what peoples he wages war? Whether he allows war to set aside the observance of the Sabbath? What kingdoms or nations are on his borders? What are the cities near to his kingdom called Khorasan, Berdaa, and Bab al Abwab? In what way their caravans proceed to his territory? How many kings ruled before him? What were their names, how many years each of them ruled, and what is the current language of the land?"

From letter by Hisdai ibn Shaprut to King of Khazars. Letters of Jews Through the Ages, ed. F. Kobler, Ararat Publishing Society Ltd., London, 1952.

of an important trade route and was, therefore, the major source of national revenue for the kingdom. However, the duties on goods and taxes collected within the state — the extent of which we know practically nothing — still fell short of what the kingdom required.

The apogee of the Khazar kingdom was in the middle of the tenth century, the period of contact between King Joseph and R. Hisdai ibn Shaprut and the emergence of Russian power. According to Russian sources, Sviatoslav, ruler of Kiev (945–972), crushed the Khazars in 965, but they are still mentioned in the Russian Chronicles of 1016 and 1023. Khazars from the city of Tamatarkha (Taman of today)

assisted Mstislav the Brave in his campaign against his brother Yaroslav the Wise (ruled 1019–1054). It is known that in 1078 Oleg, grandson of Yaroslav the Wise, resided in Tamatarkha and the Chronicles relate that in 1079 he was siezed by the Khazars and taken captive to Constantinople. However, in 1083 he was able to avenge himself on the Khazars on behalf of his brother. The Khazars are still mentioned at the beginning of the twelfth century and so it seems that they were active for a considerable period after their defeat by the Russians in 965 and before they finally dispersed among the many Jewish communities.

THE RADHANITE MERCHANTS

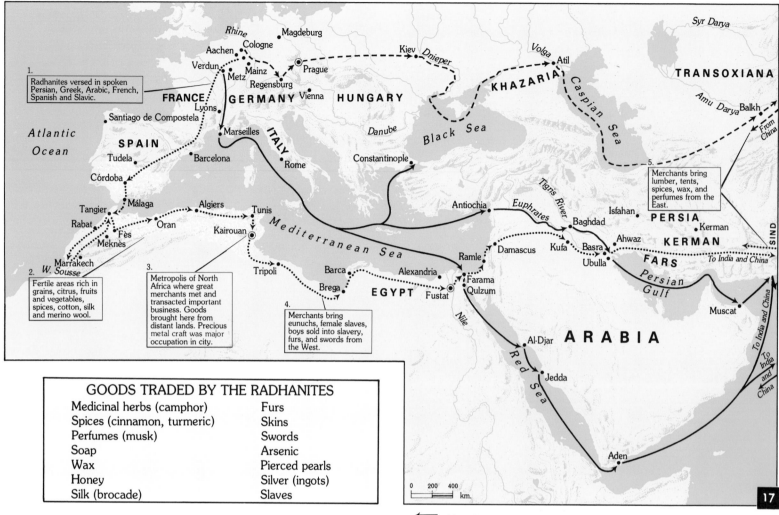

1. Radhanites versed in spoken Persian, Greek, Arabic, French, Spanish and Slavic.

2. W. Sousse
Fertile areas rich in grains, citrus, fruits and vegetables, spices, cotton, silk and merino wool.

3. Metropolis of North Africa where great merchants met and transacted important business. Goods brought here from distant lands. Precious metal craft was major occupation in city.

4. Merchants bring eunuchs, female slaves, boys sold into slavery, furs, and swords from the West.

5. Merchants bring lumber, tents, spices, wax, and perfumes from the East.

GOODS TRADED BY THE RADHANITES

Medicinal herbs (camphor)	Furs
Spices (cinnamon, turmeric)	Skins
Perfumes (musk)	Swords
Soap	Arsenic
Wax	Pierced pearls
Honey	Silver (ingots)
Silk (brocade)	Slaves

⟵⟵ ⟵ ⟵ Major Radhanite trade routes

◉ Trade center

The beginning of the ninth century saw a change in the function of the Mediterranean ports of the Muslim countries. The Muslim fleets grew stronger and were now able to attack Byzantine garrisons on Cyprus, Crete, Sicily and southern Italy. In fact, the Arabs controlled the Mediterranean and the Byzantine navy ceased to play any practical role in the area. North Africa became the link between Muslim ports in the western, southern and eastern Mediterranean. In Egypt, Fustat developed as a trading center, situated between Alexandria and the Red Sea ports on the trade route to India. Due to the political stability of the tenth century, the Muslim countries developed and prospered.

Among the towns that played an important role in developing trade were the new ones — Fès, Marrakech, Meknès, and Rabat — all of them Muslim. Kairouan exceeded them all as the metropolis of North Africa; located on the trade route midway between Alexandria and the ports of western Morocco and Spain and adjacent to the fortified port of Mahdia, it engaged in precious metal crafts, received slaves from Sudan and Byzantium, and goods — oils, dried fruits, turmeric, spices, and leather — from distant places. It was a meeting place for great merchants and their agents and many business transactions were effected there. From the beginning of the ninth until the middle of the eleventh century, considerable wealth was accumulated in Kairouan,

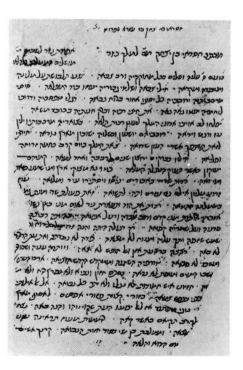

A letter from R. Hisdai ibn Shaprut to Joseph, king of the Khazars.

and palatial private and public buildings were constructed in the town. Merchants, particularly the Jewish ones known as Radhanites, played a major role in international trade. Their caravans traversed many countries, from Europe through North Africa to the Muslim east and on to India. Another land route took them through Europe to the Far East and China.

The origin of the Radhanites is unknown but some think they came from the east. As Radhanite trade declined in the tenth century, it was taken up by the merchants of Kairouan and Fustat. Documents found in the Cairo Genizah contain a wealth of material relating to the international wholesale trade of North Africa as well as a considerable amount of responsa about commercial matters referring to the sages and geonim of Babylon. They reveal the lively trade engaged in by Jewish merchants from different western communities, using

Fustat and Kairouan as their centers. Various documents deal with the resolution of credit problems and litigation between various merchants.

Rabbi Naharay b. Nissim, head of the Babylonian Jewish community in Fustat, engaged in a particularly extensive trade that was of international scope. His commercial establishment operated for more than fifty years in the eleventh century, reaching near and distant lands and dealing with a large variety of goods.

The volume and scope of international Jewish trade demanded the use of new methods of credit. It was these Jewish merchants who introduced the use of the *shufatajiyya* (the equivalent of our check), which inter alia was used to protect the merchants from robbery (as well as from merchant association partnerships of a family nature).

ITALY IN THE FRAMEWORK OF BYZANTIUM AND THE HOLY ROMAN EMPIRE
Ninth to Tenth Centuries

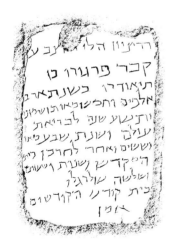

A tombstone in Venosa, southern Italy, from 829.

2. 855—Louis II orders expulsion of Jews from northern Italy. (Decree apparently never implemented.)

3. Bishop Ratherius of Verona complains of excessively tolerant attitude towards Jews.

11. Hananel II gets permission from Byzantine emperor to search empire for family property lost during wars. After peregrinations, settles in Benevento.

1. 850—Church council forbids Jews to serve as tax collectors or arbitrators between Jews and Christians.

4. Shephatiah, head of Jewish community in Oria, cures daughter of Emperor Basil I and consequently obtains cancellation of edict of conversion issued by emperor.

10. 953—*Josippon*, important Jewish historiographic book, written here.

5. Shephatiah acts as intermediary between Byzantine governor and conquering Arab general.

6. 895—Peace treaty signed, bringing Sicily under Muslim control, but battle for southern Italy continues.

7. 925—Hasadiah and 9 rabbis killed by Arabs because of their loyalty to Byzantium.

9. 950—Paltiel b. Hasadiah backs Imam al-Mu'izz and prophesies that he will conquer southern Italy. The Imam takes him to his court at Kairouan. 969—Al-Mu'izz appoints Paltiel minister at Caliphate in Cairo.

8. Physician and philosopher, Shabbetai Donnolo (born in Oria 913) exiled in his youth (925) to Palermo and Africa (ransomed by relatives in Taranto). Eventually became court physician to Byzantine governor of Calabria.

0   100   200   km.

18

The most important political factors for an understanding of this period are the political status of Byzantium in southern Italy, Rome as the papal seat, and the rise of city states in the central and northern parts of the peninsula. This situation did not change very much even after the incorporation of northern Italy into the Holy Roman Empire, nor after the Muslim conquests in southern Italy. In other words, a number of forces, religious or political, combined to rule Italy and within this framework lived the Jewish community, often in very difficult circumstances. In the struggle of power in southern Italy the Muslims tried to oust Byzantium and gain a foothold in Europe.

From 652 until the 820s, Italian cities were at the mercy of Muslim bands based mainly in Tunisia and the adjacent islands, whence they engaged in pillaging raids with no intent to conquer territory. It was only in 827 that actual steps were taken to conquer Sicily and in 831 Palermo became the Muslim capital city on the island. Messina was captured in 843 and Syracuse in 878. In their military campaigns the Muslim invaders took control of the straits of Messina and for a while held Bari and Taranto, presenting a serious threat to Rome. In 846 Rome was invaded and a number of churches were looted. It was only toward the end of the century (895–896) that a peace treaty was signed between Byzantium and the Muslims. Sicily was ceded to the Muslims. At first the island was dependent upon Tunisia, but when Tunisia was conquered by the Fatimids it became part of the Fatimid caliphate. After Cairo became the capital of the Fatimid dynasty their influence on Sicily slackened and the island was ruled by a local family.

The largest Jewish community on the island was at Palermo where the Jewish quarter was located outside the city walls. It was first mentioned in 967 and was probably the residence of the judge Mazliah b. Elijah al-Bazak, believed to be the teacher of the celebrated Talmudist, Nathan b. Jehiel of Rome. In 1030 two Spanish Jews, Hayyim and his son Nissim, assisted the Jews of Sicily by obtaining tax reductions and protection for Jewish merchants who traded with Sicilians. The Jews of Palermo wrote to the rabbis of Kairouan about the activities of Hayyim and Nissim. A Spanish Jew named Moses served at the court of the ruler of Sicily, Tsamtsam a-Dullah, and accompanied the latter on his journey to Egypt.

The Jews of southern Italy engaged in cloth dyeing and silk weaving; many were also farmers. Otranto and Bari were Torah centers and renowned for their scholarship. Evidence of knowledge of Jewish tradition by the Jews of southern Italy can be found in contemporary tombstones engraved in Hebrew.

Historical evidence from northern Italy indicates the existence of small Jewish communities, located chiefly in small and medium-sized towns (Ferrara, Bologna, Modena, Padua, Mantua, Treviso and Milan). There is further evidence that the famous Kalonymos family settled in Lucca in the state of Tuscany (c. ninth century) and there founded a Talmudic academy. Around the year 1000 some members of the family emigrated to Mainz, where they established themselves and founded a yeshiva. The Jews of Tuscany were known to have owned vineyards and their presence in Modena is mentioned in a document dated 1025. Venice was under the influence of Byzantium and in 945 forbade her ship captains to haul Jewish cargo or carry Jewish passengers to the east.

Louis II, grandson of Charlemagne, in 855 ordered the expulsion of Italian Jews from the territories he ruled, but it is doubtful whether this decree was ever implemented.

In 850 the church council at Ticino forbade the employment of Jews as tax collectors or as arbitrators between Jews and Christians, and in Verona Bishop Ratherius repeated the allegations of Agobard of Lyons against the Jews.

Italy was a repository of Jewish traditions and customs and served as a bridge for Jews who passed from the Holy Land mainly into the Holy Roman Empire through Sicily and from there to Egypt and to Byzantium.

THE NORMAN INVASION OF SOUTHERN ITALY

Byzantine Empire, 1025
Areas under Muslim rule

THE AHIMAAZ SCROLL OF GENEALOGIES

The Jewish community of the small town of Oria, located between Taranto and Brindisi, was a center of Jewry in southern Italy under Byzantine rule. The Amittai family was active in Oria for many generations and their descendants included: Shephatiah b. Shabbetai, the poet (d. 886); the doctor, Shabbetai Donnolo (913–after 983) who composed a number of medical texts in Hebrew; Paltiel I (d. 975), astrologer and physician, who was appointed aide to the caliph at the Fatimid court in Egypt and head of the Egyptian Jewish community; and Ahimaaz, the author of one of the first historical descriptions of the period (1054).

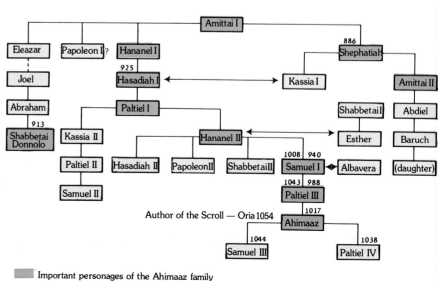

Important personages of the Ahimaaz family

RELIGIOUS FERMENT AND SECTS IN JUDAISM
Until the Twelfth Century

A decorated page in a Karaite Bible.

From the end of the seventh century the Jewish Middle East was the arena for religious sects that claimed that they had the power to redeem the People of Israel. Between the years 685–705 a Jewish sect known as the Isanians was founded in Persia by Abu Isa (Isaac b. Jacob al-Isfahani) also called Obadiah, who claimed to be the Messiah destined to redeem the people of Israel from their dispersion. He led a revolt against the Muslims but was defeated and killed. The basic principles of the sect were asceticism, including the prohibition of eating meat and drinking wine; a ban on divorce; and prayer seven times a day (based on the verse in Psalm 119:164 "seven times daily do I praise Thee"). Some of its tenets anticipate doctrines adopted by Anan, the founder of the Karaite sect. The Isanian sect continued to exist after the death of Abu Isa. Yudghan, Abu Isa's disciple and heir,

declared himself to be a prophet and Messiah, founding a sect that was named after him as Yudghanites. Mushka was the founder of another sect, called the Mushkanites. Somewhat more is known about Moses Haparsi, probably Abu Imran; born in Baghdad, he too founded a religious sect, settling in Zafran near Kermanshah before moving to Tiflis (Tbilisi). His sect, which became known as the Tiflisites, rejected the doctrine of resurrection and other basic tenets of Mosaic law.

The most important sect were the Ananites, named for their founder Anan b. David who, rejecting the Talmudic *halakhah*, saw Jewish life as based solely on the Bible as interpreted by him and his disciples. The sect was subsequently called Karaite and much of its doctrine was based on Muslim influence. The doctrine was developed by Benjamin b. Moses Nahawendi (between 830 and 860) and other scholars who extended the exegesis and added new tenets. Benjamin's legal works, *Sefer Mitzvot* ("Book of Precepts") and *Sefer Dinim* ("Book of Laws"), represent an attempt at a comprehensive code of Karaite law. Hiwi al-Balkhi, probably born in Balkh in Afghanistan, was a contemporary of Benjamin. A free thinker, he rejected both the written and oral law, being influenced by various Persian religious trends. His doctrines did not survive him by many years.

Three outstanding Karaite personalities were: Salmon b. Jeruhim (tenth century), Daniel b. Moses al-Qumisi (ninth to tenth centuries) considered the founder of Karaism in Palestine, and Jacob al-Kirkisani (first half of tenth century), the greatest Karaite philosopher. Most of the Karaites who settled in Jerusalem in the first half of the ninth century joined the *Avelei Zion* ("Mourners of Zion"), a group of Jews devoted to mourning the destruction of the Temple and Jerusalem. (The group also included Rabbanite Jews.)

The existence of the Karaite movement was one of the factors that led to the rabbanite examination of Biblical texts and the subsequent codification of the spelling and reading of the Hebrew Bible (Masorah).

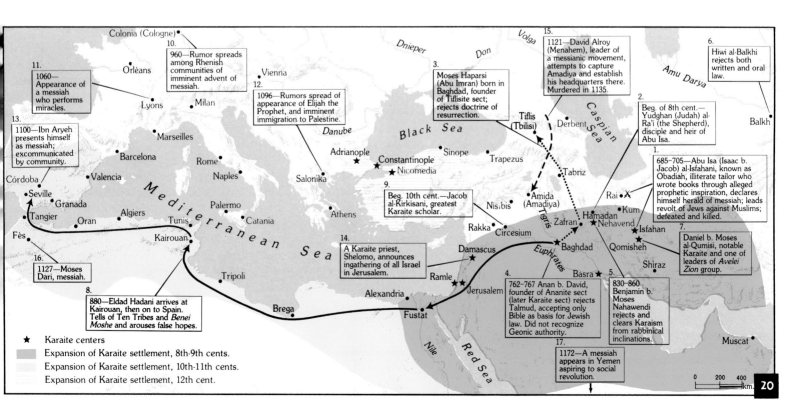

11. 1060—Appearance of a messiah who performs miracles.

10. 960—Rumor spreads among Rhenish communities of imminent advent of messiah.

12. 1096—Rumors spread of appearance of Elijah the Prophet, and imminent immigration to Palestine.

3. Moses Haparsi (Abu Imran) born in Baghdad, founder of Tiflisite sect; rejects doctrine of resurrection.

15. 1121—David Alroy (Menahem), leader of a messianic movement, attempts to capture Amadiya and establish his headquarters there. Murdered in 1135.

6. Hiwi al-Balkhi rejects both written and oral law.

13. 1100—Ibn Aryeh presents himself as messiah; excommunicated by community.

2. Beg. of 8th cent.—Yudghan (Judah) al-Ra'i (the Shepherd), disciple and heir of Abu Isa.

1. 685–705—Abu Isa (Isaac b. Jacob) al-Isfahani, known as Obadiah, illiterate tailor who wrote books through alleged prophetic inspiration, declares himself herald of messiah; leads revolt of Jews against Muslims; defeated and killed.

9. Beg. 10th cent.—Jacob al-Kirkisani, greatest Karaite scholar.

7. Daniel b. Moses al-Qumisi, notable Karaite and one of leaders of *Avelei Zion* group.

14. A Karaite priest, Shelomo, announces ingathering of all Israel in Jerusalem.

4. 762–767 Anan b. David, founder of Ananite sect (later Karaite sect) rejects Talmud, accepting only Bible as basis for Jewish law. Did not recognize Geonic authority.

5. 830–860 Benjamin b. Moses Nahawendi rejects and clears Karaism from rabbinical inclinations.

16. 1127—Moses Dari, messiah.

8. 880—Eldad Hadani arrives at Kairouan, then on to Spain. Tells of Ten Tribes and *Benei Moshe* and arouses false hopes.

17. 1172—A messiah appears in Yemen aspiring to social revolution.

★ Karaite centers
Expansion of Karaite settlement, 8th-9th cents.
Expansion of Karaite settlement, 10th-11th cents.
Expansion of Karaite settlement, 12th cent.

0 200 400
km.

20

THE GAONATE IN BABYLONIA

SURA		PUMBEDITA
	589	Mar Hanan of Iskiya
Rav Mar bar Huna	591	(?) Mar Rav Mari b. R. Dimi (formerly of Firuz-Shapur and Nehardea)
Rav Hanina	614	Mar Rav Hanina of Bei-Gihara (Firuz-Shapur)
		Rav Hana (or Huna)
Rav Huna	650	
Rav Sheshna		
(also called Mesharsheya b. Tahlifa)		
	651	Rav Rabbah
		Rav Bosai
Rav Hanina of Nehar-Pekod	689	Rav Huna Mari b. Rav Joseph
		Rav Hiyya of Mershan
		Mar Rav Ravya (or Mar Yanka)
Rav Hilai ha-Levi of Naresh	694	
Rav Jacob ha-Kohen of Nehar-Pekod	712	
	719	Rav Natronai b. R. Nehemiah
		Rav Judah
Mar Samuel	730	
	739	Rav Joseph
Rav Mari Kohen of Nehar-Pekod	748	Rav Samuel b. Rav Mar
	752(?)	Rav Natroi Kahana b. Rav Mar Amunah
		Rav Abraham Kahana
Rav Aha	756	
Rav Yehudai b. R. Nahman	757	
Rav Ahunai Kahana b. Mar R. Papa	761	Rav Dodai b. Rav Nahman (brother of R. Yehudai, the gaon of Sura)
	764	Rav Hananiah b. R. of Sharsheya
Rav Haninai Kahana b. Mar. R. Huna	769	
	771	Rav Malkha b. R. Aha
	773	Rav Rabbah (Abba) b. R. Dodai
Rav Mari ha-Levi b. R. Mesharsheya	774	
Rav Bebai ha-Levi b. Abba of Nehar-Pekod	777	
	781	Rav Shinoi
	782	Rav Haninai Kahana b. R. Abraham
	785	Rav Huna ha-Levi b. R. Issai
Rav Hilai b. R. Mari	788	Rav Manasseh b. Mar Joseph
	796	Rav Isaiah ha-Levi b. Mar R. Abba
Rav Jacob ha-Kohen b. R. Mordecai	797	
	798	Rav Joseph b. R. Shila
	804	Rav Kahana b. R. Haninai
Rav Ivomai	810	Rav Ivomai
Rav Ivomai, uncle of his predecessor	811	
	814	Rav Joseph b. R. Abba
Rav Zadok b. Mar R. Jesse (or Ashi)	816	Rav Abraham b. R. Sherira

SURA		PUMBEDITA
Rav Hilai b. R. Hanina	818	
Rav Kimoi b. R. Ashi	822	
Rav Moses (Mesharsheya) Kahana b. R. Jacob	825	
	828	Rav Joseph b. R. Hiyya
	833	Rav Isaac b. R. Hananiah
Rav Kohen Zedek b. Ivomai	838	
	839	Rav Joseph b. R. Ravi
	842	Rav Paltoi b. R. Abbaye
Rav Sar Shalom b. R. Boaz	848	
served jointly { Rav Natronai b. R. Hilai	853	
Rav Amram b. Sheshna	857	Mar Rav Aha Kahana b. Rav
	858	Rav Menahem b. R. Joseph b. Hiyya
	860	Rav Mattathias b. Mar Ravi
Rav Nahshon b. R. Zadok	869	Rav Abba (Rabbah) b. R. Ammi
	871	Rav Zemah b. R. Paltoi
Rav Zemah b. Mar R. Hayyim	872	
Rav Malkha	879	
Rav Hai b. R. Nahshon	885	
	890	Rav Hai b. David
Rav Hilai b. R. Natronai	896	
	898	Rav Kimoi b. R. Ahai
Rav Shalom b. R. Mishael	904	
	906	Rav Judah b. R. Samuel (grandfather of R. Sherira)
Rav Jacob b. R. Natronai	911	
	917–26	Rav Mevasser Kahana b. R. Kimoi
Rav Yom Tov Kahana b. R. Jacob	924	
	926–36	Rav Kohen Zedek b. R. Joseph (appointed while predecessor was still living)
Rav Saadiah b. R. Joseph (Rav Saadiah Gaon)	928	
	936	Rav Zemah b. R. Kafnai
	938	Rav Hananiah b. R. Judah
Rav Joseph b. R. Jacob	942–44	
	943	Rav Aaron b. R. Joseph ha-Kohen Sargado
	960	Rav Nehemiah b. R. Kohen Zedek
	968	Rav Sherira b. R. Hananiah
Rav Zemah b. R. Isaac (descendant of Paltoi)	988(?)	
Rav Samuel b. Hophni ha-Kohen	997(?)	
	998	Rav Hai b. R. Sherira
Rav Dosa b. R. Saadiah	1013	
Rav Israel b. R. Samuel b. Hophni	1017	
Rav Azariah ha-Kohen (son of R. Israel?)	1034	
Isaac (?)	1037	
	1038–58	Rav Hezekiah b. David (exilarch and *gaon*)

Baghdad, founded by Caliph al-Mansur (762), attracted many Jewish settlers.

Although the beginnings of the Jewish Diaspora in Babylon preceded the Muslim conquest, the gaonate period coincided with the period of Muslim rule. The decline of the gaonate began with the death of Rav Hai Gaon in 1038. The gaonate period is of special significance in the history of the Jewish people because the Jewish center in Babylon played a decisive role in the life of the nation and had the vigor to withstand the competition with Eretz Israel for the hegemony over Jewish life, and to prevail.

Jewish means of livelihood in Babylon had changed even before the Arab Conquest, when Jews began to assume patterns of life similar to those that would later typify the Jews of Europe during the Middle Ages.

Heavy taxation, revolutions, riots and insecurity forced the agriculturist off his land and obliged him to seek refuge in the cities. This process continued during the entire period of Arab rule. In the first half of the ninth century, Rav Moshe Gaon writes: "In Babylon most people are without land" (*Hemda Genuzah*, 60:65). The small communities and rural settlements diminished, while cities grew and swelled. Jewish population centers disappeared and were replaced by that of Baghdad.

In Baghdad Jewish financial institutions developed to such an extent that their economic influence within the caliphate was considerable. Two Jewish bankers, Joseph b. Phineas and Aaron b. Amram, and their heirs, the sons of Aaron

THE STRUCTURE OF A YESHIVA

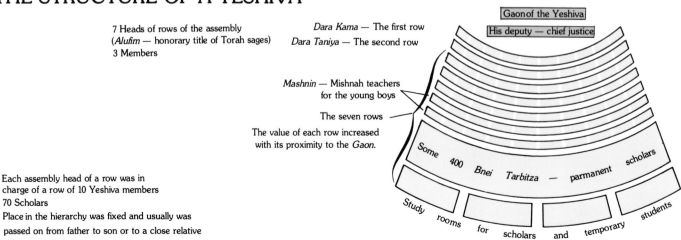

7 Heads of rows of the assembly
(*Alufim* — honorary title of Torah sages)
3 Members

Dara Kama — The first row
Dara Taniya — The second row

Gaon of the Yeshiva

His deputy — chief justice

Mashnin — Mishnah teachers for the young boys

The seven rows

The value of each row increased with its proximity to the *Gaon*.

Some 400 *Bnei Tarbitza* — parmanent scholars

Study rooms for scholars and temporary students

Each assembly head of a row was in charge of a row of 10 Yeshiva members
70 Scholars
Place in the hierarchy was fixed and usually was passed on from father to son or to a close relative

and of Netira, started business operations in the district of Ahwaz (in Persia), later expanding them to trade on an international scale. Documents referring to the two families reveal the extent of their partnership and cooperation in business enterprises. Among their many activities was the lending of money to the vizier of Caliph al Muqtadir, Muhammad ibn Abdullah ibn Yahya (912–913), but there is every indication that they engaged in moneylending prior to this date. They also financed the caliphate, using money deposited with them by Jews and non-Jews and taking as security the tax farming rights in the district of Ahwaz. They engaged in international transfer of funds and were thus able to help in financially supporting the exilarchate and gaonate. Apparently they were the innovators of the *shufatajiyya*, a kind of check-promissory note that could be redeemed by a surrogate.

Even the academies of Sura and Pumbedita could not resist the magnetic pull of Baghdad, and at the end of the ninth century, about 150 years before the waning of the gaonate, they both moved to the city as independent institutions. Each of the academies retained its independence, and preserved its own character, methods of teaching, and public activities. The famous geonim were Rav Saadiah, Rav Samuel b. Hofni and Rav Hai — all residents of Baghdad. However, Babylon could not financially support all its scholars who were taken prisoner in the West, and who, according to legend, brought with them the traditions of the Babylonian Talmud. Poets and grammarians also emigrated to Spain. There was no intrinsic difference between the situation of the Jews in Babylon and their condition in other Islamic countries during the period of Arab rule.

The divisions within the empire of the caliphate and the subsequent founding of emirates in the second half of the eighth century caused basic changes in Jewish life and existence. The following events constituted turning points for the Jews and opened up new opportunities: the separation of Spain from the caliphate in 756 and the subsequent establishing of emirates; Moroccan independence in 788; Tunisian independence in 800; that of Egypt (by Ahmad ibn Tulun) in 868 and of Persia in 935. There was no basic change in relations within the Jewish community nor was there any change in the affinitive relations between the communities of the Jewish diaspora. They all recognized the authority of the central Jewish organizations, the exilarchate and the gaonate, as powerful elements of unity and instruction for the Jewish people. The Palestinian gaonate was acknowledged as an equal partner with its Babylonian counterpart.

Rav Saadiah (882–942) was among the great geonim. He was born in the Fayum district of Egypt, moved to Palestine and, in 922, to Babylon, where he was appointed gaon of the Sura academy in 928. Saadiah waged an unremitting battle against the Karaites and is credited with having stopped their expansion, although his struggle did help them to consolidate as a sect. He was famous for his polemic with the Palestinian gaon, Aaron ben Meir, over the establishing of the Jewish calendar and its festivals, and for his controversy with the exilarch, David ben Zakkai, on matters of authority. His profound spiritual and scholarly activities included works of *halakhah*, exegesis, philosophy, grammar, liturgy, *piyyut* and the translation of the Bible into Arabic.

The Babylonian gaonate came to an end with two great and outstanding figures: Rav Sherira b. Hanina Gaon (c. 906–1006), gaon of Pumbedita from 968 to 1006, and his

son, Rav Hai Gaon (939–1038). Sherira was among the prolific writers of responsa. One of his famous epistles was written in response to an inquiry from Rabbi Jacob b. Nissim b. Shahin of the Kairouan community, who asked for information regarding the Mishnah and Talmud. Sherira's reply was a classic work of Jewish historiography in which he listed the generations of Jewish scholars from the men of the Great Sanhedrin until the period of the gaonate. His son and successor, Rav Hai Gaon, gaon of Pumbedita, was one of the great *halakhists*, a *paytan*, liturgist, judge and writer. With his death, the gaonate in Babylon officially ended.

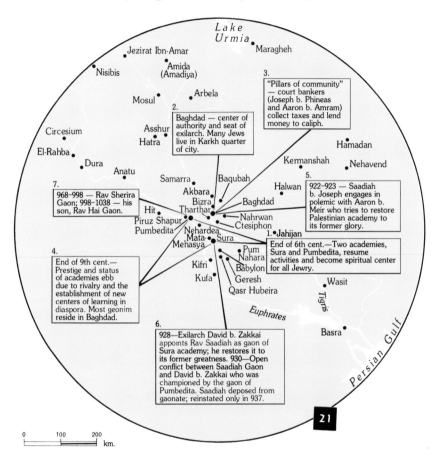

A letter sent from Fustat to R. Hai Gaon.

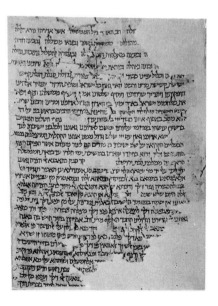

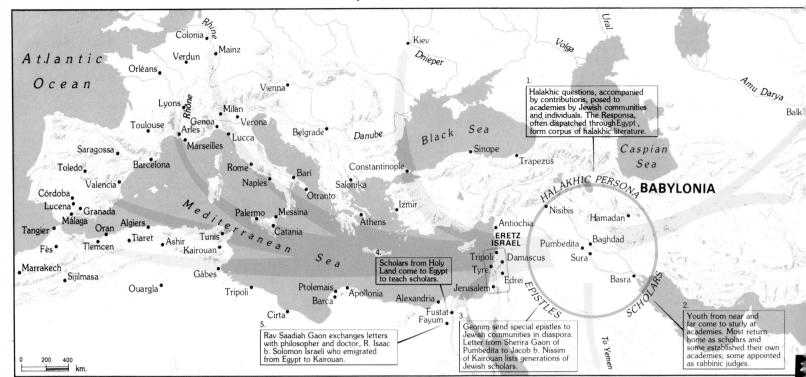

The following labels appear within the map:

1. Halakhic questions, accompanied by contributions, posed to academies by Jewish communities and individuals. The Responsa, often dispatched through Egypt, form corpus of halakhic literature.

2. Youth from near and far come to study at academies. Most return home as scholars and some established their own academies; some appointed as rabbinic judges.

3. Geonim send special epistles to Jewish communities in diaspora. Letter from Sherira Gaon of Pumbedita to Jacob b. Nissim of Kairouan lists generations of Jewish scholars.

4. Scholars from Holy Land come to Egypt to teach scholars.

5. Rav Saadiah Gaon exchanges letters with philosopher and doctor, R. Isaac b. Solomon Israeli who emigrated from Egypt to Kairouan.

The contacts between the Babylonian geonim and the Diaspora were numerous and widespread. The gaonate became the spirtual and halakhic center for Jewry, issuing instructions and guidance both to the eastern and western Jewish communities. The Diaspora connection was important for establishing a consensus regarding halakhic doctrine. Instrumental in achieving this goal were the emissaries sent by the geonim to the Diaspora — students from the Babylonian academies and Rabbinical judges ordained by the geonim. They were the vanguard of the movement that helped create and maintain the Jewish halakhic consensus during the life span of the Babylonian centers of learning. Ties with the Diaspora also found expression in the financial support extended by the Jewish communities to the academies, considerable correspondence about which was found in the Cairo Genizah. These relations also helped to foster international commercial ties in which Jews played a very important role.

Other communities, chiefly in Italy and Germany, had very close ties with the academies in Palestine and they adopted the Palestinian (Eretz Israel) tradition primarily in matters of liturgical poetry.

THE GEONIM OF ERETZ ISRAEL; AND ALIYAH TO ERETZ ISRAEL

General Jawhar conquered Palestine on behalf of the Fatimid Caliph al-Mu'izz after subjugating Egypt in 969. The Fatimids were a branch of the Shi'ite sect who ruled over a Muslim population that was predominately Sunni, and were, therefore, considered foreigners in Palestine, Egypt and Syria. Paltiel (d. 975), a Jew of Oria, served as physician to al-Mu'izz during the conquest of Egypt and was responsible for provisioning the Fatimid army. From his position of influence he was able to assist the Jewish community and when he died he was buried in Eretz Israel. During most of the Fatimid period the rulers employed many Jews, among them the Jewish convert to Islam Yaqub ibn Killis (vizier to Caliph al-Aziz from 978–990), who also aided the Jewish community. The Jewish community in Eretz Israel prospered under Fatimid rule, particularly the large communities of Tyre and Sidon. Jerusalem, Tiberias and Ramle were large and important Jewish centers; small Jewish settlements existed in Transjordan. However, prosperity did not last and in 996 the Fatimid throne was occupied by Caliph al-Hakim (996–1021) who persecuted non-Muslims. To make matters worse, there were calamitous earthquakes in 1034 and 1067 in which

Ramle was particularly badly hit. Eretz Israel as a whole had its share of al-Hakim's harassment but Jerusalem had a double portion with the caliph's Nubian troops wreaking their violence upon Jews and destroying their synagogues. Many Jews were openly killed and survivors were subjected to hard labor.

It was during this period that the Great Yeshiva of Jerusalem moved to Ramle. From 1024 to 1029 an enormous sum of money was cruelly extorted for the state coffers from the Jews of Jerusalem and from the Karaites who had resided in the city for over a hundred years. Pilgrimage to Jerusalem ceased. Only about fifty Jews resided in the city.

The situation improved somewhat during the reign of al-Hakim's successor, al-Zahir (1021–1034), and the Jewish population slowly recovered. However, the disaster of the crusades would follow in 1099.

Despite the dangers on land and sea, Jews continued to make pilgrimages to Eretz Israel, especially during the Feast of Tabernacles. Their destinations were chiefly Jerusalem, the Mount of Olives and Hebron. With them came Jews who wished to settle in Jerusalem. Among the settlers were

Avelei Zion ("Mourners of Zion"), people who "abandoned their families, repudiated their lands of birth, left cities and dwelt in the mountains." "People from the east and the west," who "set their sights on settling in Jerusalem, forsook their possessions and renounced the temporal world." The Karaite scholar, Sahl ben Mazliah, relates that "Jerusalem at this time was a haven for all who fled, a comfort for all mourners and a repose for the poor and humble; wherein resided servants of the Lord who were gathered unto her, one from a town, another from a family; wherein resided dirge singer and eulogizers in Hebrew, Persian and Arabic."

Ramle was an important center for Jews from Babylon, known as *Knesset al-Iraquiin*, just as Jews from Eretz Israel who lived in Egypt were known as *Knesset al-Shamiin*. The Karaites had their own synagogue in Ramle. Eretz Israel also served as a transit point for Jews emigrating from east to west.

Bedouin invasions and disturbances in 1029 and 1030 did not hinder Jewish emigration even from Spain, as is attested in a letter sent from Jersalem to Toledo in 1053 describing the "Sephardim" who resided in Ramle and Jerusalem with their wives and children. Even the Sephardic scholar Joseph ibn Abitur intended to leave Spain and emigrate to Eretz Israel, but one of his friends advised him to go first to Egypt. The story of Rabbi Judah Halevi's *aliyah* typifies a trend among many Jews in those days. Immigrants also came to Eretz Israel from North Africa and Syria. Close ties existed between the Jews of Tripoli and Eretz Israel. Wills from Italy, Egypt and North Africa bear witness to the custom of reinterring the bones of Jewish dead in the Holy Land. There were, however, still many Jews who left Eretz Israel. Those who emigrated to Egypt established communities, such as in Alexandria. Many of the émigrés were learned men and graduates of *yeshivot* and it is reasonable to assume that the educational needs of the Diaspora communities were what motivated them to emigrate in order to teach the Torah.

In contrast to the lack of livelihood in Jerusalem, Ramle was a commercial center, and one of the resident Jews held the title of "The Merchants Clerk." He apparently served as a third-party trustee for disputed property or perhaps he was the "Head of the Merchants," as indicated by the Arabic form of this title. In Tyre Jews were engaged in glass blowing and some were shop owners. Here too the Jews had a functionary called "The Merchants Clerk." Tyre was no less an important Jewish center than Ramle, and when the Seljuks conquered Jerusalem in 1071, the Palestinian academy transferred to Tyre. Jews living in the coastal towns seem to have been better off than those residing in the center of the country (excluding Ramle). Jews were engaged in many trades and particularly dyeing, in which they had a monopoly.

Their financial hardships were further aggravated by the burden of taxes; Jerusalem bore the heaviest tax load.

During this period Eretz Israel was renowned for its geonim

THE GAONATE OF PALESTINE

and its centers of learning. Because of the difficult local conditions, its gaonate was overshadowed by the prosperous Jewish Diaspora of Babylon. A number of geonim in Eretz Israel were members of the ben Meir family, the most important being Aaron b. Meir. The gaon Solomon b. Judah was the head of the community from 1027 to 1051. The gaon Daniel b. Azariah was related to the Babylonian exilarch, David b. Zakkai. The last of the geonim in Eretz Israel were Elijah b. Solomon and his son Abiathar. The latter, who lived during the period of the Crusades, moved to Tripoli where he died in 1109. The Palestinian academy moved to Damascus where it continued to function for about a hundred years under the name "Hatsevi Academy" or "Eretz Hatsevi Academy".

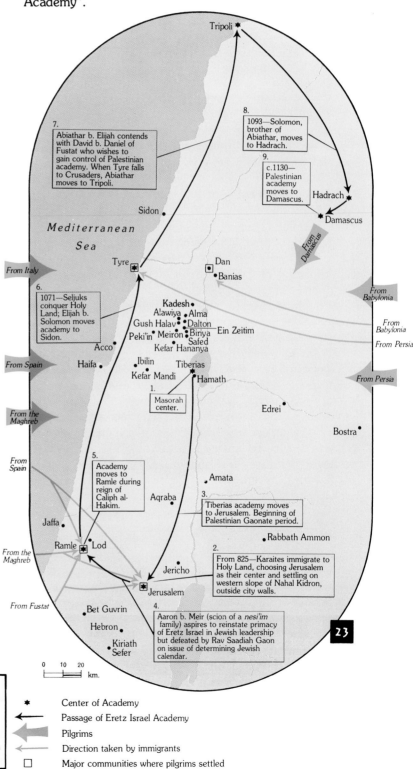

7. Abiathar b. Elijah contends with David b. Daniel of Fustat who wishes to gain control of Palestinian academy. When Tyre falls to Crusaders, Abiathar moves to Tripoli.

8. 1093—Solomon, brother of Abiathar, moves to Hadrach.

9. c.1130—Palestinian academy moves to Damascus.

6. 1071—Seljuks conquer Holy Land; Elijah b. Solomon moves academy to Sidon.

1. Masorah center.

5. Academy moves to Ramle during reign of Caliph al-Hakim.

3. Tiberias academy moves to Jerusalem. Beginning of Palestinian Gaonate period.

2. From 825—Karaites immigrate to Holy Land, choosing Jerusalem as their center and settling on western slope of Nahal Kidron, outside city walls.

4. Aaron b. Meir (scion of a *nesi'im* family) aspires to reinstate primacy of Eretz Israel in Jewish leadership but defeated by Rav Saadiah Gaon on issue of determining Jewish calendar.

0 10 20
km.

★   Center of Academy

←   Passage of Eretz Israel Academy

⬅   Pilgrims

←   Direction taken by immigrants

▢   Major communities where pilgrims settled

c. 844–915	Zemah	988–	Samuel b. Joseph ha-Kohen
c. 915–932	Aaron b. Moses ben Meir	...	Yose b. Samuel
c. 932–934	Isaac (son of Aaron?)	...	Shemaiah
c. 934–948	Ben Meir (brother of Aaron)	1015	Josiah b. Aaron b. Abraham
c. 948–955	Abraham b. Aaron	1020–1027	Solomon b. Joseph ha-Kohen
c. 933–926	Aaron	1027–1051	Solomon b. Judah
933–	Joseph ha-Kohen b. Ezron	1051–1062	Daniel b. Azariah
(2 years)	?	1062–1083	Elijah b. Solomon b. Joseph ha-Kohen
(30 years)	?	1084–1109	Abiathar b. Elijah

THE JEWS OF NORTH AFRICA
Twelfth to Fifteenth Centuries

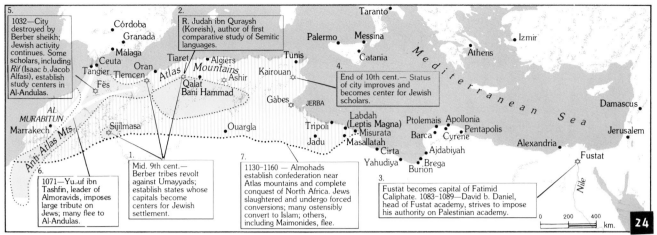

5. 1032—City destroyed by Berber sheikh; Jewish activity continues. Some scholars, including *Rif* (Isaac b. Jacob Alfasi), establish study centers in Al-Andulas.

2. R. Judah ibn Quraysh (Koreish), author of first comparative study of Semitic languages.

4. End of 10th cent.— Status of city improves and becomes center for Jewish scholars.

6. 1071—Yusuf ibn Tashfin, leader of Almoravids, imposes large tribute on Jews; many flee to Al-Andulas.

1. Mid. 9th cent.— Berber tribes revolt against Umayyads; establish states whose capitals become centers for Jewish settlement.

7. 1130–1160 — Almohads establish confederation near Atlas mountains and complete conquest of North Africa. Jews slaughtered and undergo forced conversions; many ostensibly convert to Islam; others, including Maimonides, flee.

3. Fustat becomes capital of Fatimid Caliphate. 1083–1089—David b. Daniel, head of Fustat academy, strives to impose his authority on Palestinian academy.

0   200   400 km.   **24**

✡ Center of Torah and Jewish life
   Berber tribal areas in 9th cent.
   Furthest extent of Almohads (al-Muwahhidun)

The status of the Jews in North Africa as in all other Islamic states was that of a "protected people" (*dhimmi*). The first hundred years of Muslim conquest were rather turbulent; there was no *Pax Islamica*. Naturally this affected Jewish life. During the waning of the Umayyad dynasty and the dawning of the Abbasid rule, a confederation of Berber tribes revolted against the Arab rulers in Kairouan and western Tripolitania. Ibn Rustam, one of the leaders of the revolt, fled and established a new state in central Algeria with its capital at Tiaret. At the same time, another group established a kingdom in the city of Tlemcen. Another Berber tribe established a state in the Tafilalt Oasis, with its capital at Sijilmasa. Despite religious differences, these states became important Jewish centers. Tiaret was the residence of R. Judah ibn Quraysh (Koreish), a well-known ninth-century philologist and renowned author. Jews lived on the island of Jerba, in the region of Jerid to Gabès, and in the area of M'zab, and Ouargla.

When Egypt was conquered and the caliphate established there, Kairouan became "the grand trading center in Africa," as it was designated in a legal document of 978, and a center for Jewish scholars. With the weakening of Fatimid rule in North Africa, government was transferred to the Zirids in Kairouan.

Yusuf ibn Ziri, a Berber and founder of the dynasty, was a loyal servant of the Fatimids in the days when they ruled the Maghreb. He appointed his sons as governors in various places. Eventually they grew strong and severed their relations with the Fatimids in Cairo, recognizing the sovereignty of the Abbasids in distant Baghdad. Soon they established their city of Ashir and Jews from various places were brought there. Rabbi Sherira Gaon and Rabbi Samuel b. Hofni corresponded with Jews of Ashir. Kairouan was not exclusive in its special status as a center for Torah learning and Jewish life. In southern Tunisia the city of Gabès was famous as a "mother city in Israel" and a Torah center. Fès's status as a Torah center was determined by the residence there in the eleventh century of R. Isaac b. Jacob, known as Alfasi author of the *Rif* (born c. 1013 in Qalat Bani Hammad in Algeria, and died 1103 at Lucena in southern Spain). Alfasi was one of the architects of Torah study in Spain and among Jewry in general.

MOROCCO

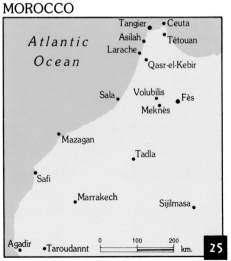

TUNISIA

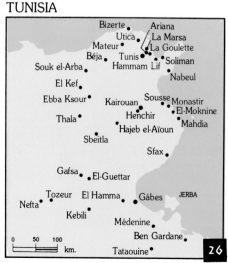

EGYPT

In 1032 Fès was captured by one of the Berber sheikhs who destroyed the town and its Jewish quarter and massacred many of its Jews. However, neither this disaster nor those that preceded or succeeded it arrested Jewish activity. The scholars of Fès continued to correspond with the geonim of Babylon on matters of *halakhah* and the Babylonian geonim, Rabbi Sherira, Rabbi Hai and Rabbi Samuel b. Hofni would send their responsa to "Abraham" or "Tanhum." It is possible that these two were heads of the community and its judges. Several important scholars from Fès moved to Spain where they were among the founders of Torah study centers. The Muslims of that period saw Fès as a Jewish town. Even the Jews of Tiaret and Sijilmasa maintained contact with Babylon and the geonim of Palestine. Berber troops, Umayyad armies from Spain, and Fatimid soldiers caused great destruction in these towns. Despite this, however, there was a resurgence of Jews in these towns. Many engaged in international trade with distant lands. Perhaps the geographical importance of these towns contributed to continuing Jewish settlement. Kairouan played a central role in Jewish relations and contact with Babylon.

In northwestern Africa a number of Berber tribes joined forces to form a religious, social, and military confederation called al-Murabitun, known as the Almoravids, whose doctrines favored a more radical religious orthodoxy. Their leader, Yusuf ibn Tashfin (who founded Marrakech in 1062), set out on campaigns of conquest in Africa and Spain. In 1071 he forced the Jews in his North African domain to pay a huge tribute of 100,000 dinars. Such taxation may explain why so many Jews left North Africa for Spain. However, the rule of the Almoravids cannot be compared to the reign of the Muwahhidun (Almohads), who emerged in the twelfth century and destroyed many Jewish communities.

MUSLIM SPAIN: ECONOMY AND CENTERS OF JEWISH SETTLEMENT
Tenth to Twelfth Centuries

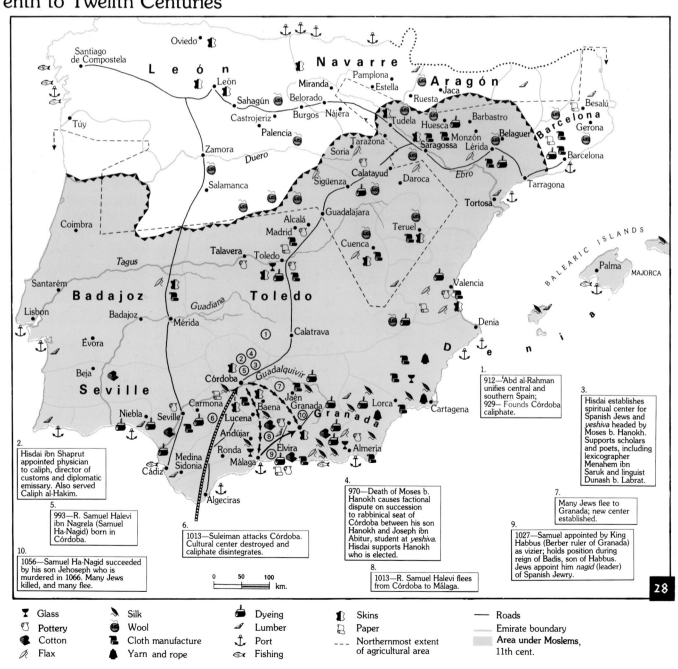

1.
912—'Abd al-Rahman unifies central and southern Spain; 929— Founds Córdoba caliphate.

2.
Hisdai ibn Shaprut appointed physician to caliph, director of customs and diplomatic emissary. Also served Caliph al-Hakim.

3.
Hisdai establishes spiritual center for Spanish Jews and *yeshiva* headed by Moses b. Hanokh. Supports scholars and poets, including lexicographer Menahem ibn Saruk and linguist Dunash b. Labrat.

4.
970—Death of Moses b. Hanokh causes factional dispute on succession to rabbinical seat of Córdoba between his son Hanokh and Joseph ibn Abitur, student at *yeshiva*. Hisdai supports Hanokh who is elected.

5.
993—R. Samuel Halevi ibn Nagrela (Samuel Ha-Nagid) born in Córdoba.

6.
1013—Suleiman attacks Córdoba. Cultural center destroyed and caliphate disintegrates.

7.
Many Jews flee to Granada; new center established.

8.
1013—R. Samuel Halevi flees from Córdoba to Málaga.

9.
1027—Samuel appointed by King Habbus (Berber ruler of Granada) as vizier; holds position during reign of Badis, son of Habbus. Jews appoint him *nagid* (leader) of Spanish Jewry.

10.
1056—Samuel Ha-Nagid succeeded by his son Jehoseph who is murdered in 1066. Many Jews killed, and many flee.

0   50   100
|————————————| km.

28

Icon	Legend	Icon	Legend	Icon	Legend
Glass		Silk		Dyeing	
Pottery		Wool		Lumber	
Cotton		Cloth manufacture		Port	
Flax		Yarn and rope		Fishing	

Skins
Paper
— Roads
— Emirate boundary
--- Northernmost extent of agricultural area
Area under Moslems, 11th cent.

Al Andalus, as the Iberian Peninsula was known, began to prosper during the reign of 'Abd al-Rahman II (822–852). Despite many revolts he built a network of fortifications to defend his kingdom against the Christian incursions and concluded treaties with various Muslim princes. Thus he was able to withstand the Norman invasions of the coastal cities. He also found time to devote to cultural matters and began constructing public building in Córdoba and other places. These buildings are the pride of Spain to this very day. Córdoba also became a center for Jewish spiritual and cultural activity.

At the end of the tenth century, Jacob and Joseph ibn Jau were appointed heads of the Jewish community. Jacob was appointed *nasi* (leader) of all the Jews living in Muslim Spain and in those areas of Morocco and Algeria that were under Muslim Spanish suzerainty. The brothers were wealthy silk merchants and manufacturers. Jacob was appointed tax collector and was allowed to appoint rabbinical judges. Hisdai ibn Shaprut was another major figure in Spanish Jewish life.

Muslim Granada was consolidated in the eleventh century and included the whole of the southeastern part of the peninsula. Rabbi Samuel b. Joseph Halevi ibn Nagrela (Samuel Ha-Nagid) was an outstanding leader of the Jewish community in Granada. Born in Córdoba in 993 he fled to Málaga in 1013 in the wake of the Berber conquest. He had a fine Jewish and general education, including training in Arabic, and soon made a name for himself as a teacher and Arabic stylist to whom people turned for letterwriting skills. Samuel was appointed to the staff of the vizier of Granada. One of his first tasks in Granada was to collect taxes in some of the districts. He soon succeeded in obtaining an important position in king Habbus's administration as minister of finance and later as vizier. His position at court was strengthened during the reign of Badis, son and successor of Habbus. Samuel successfully commanded the king's army from 1038 to 1056. Samuel viewed all his military victories as signs of divine intervention and all of his activities as part of a divine mission in which he was an emissary sent by the Lord to defend his people. Consequently he fulfilled his tasks with a fervor and loyalty uncommon among officials at court. Samuel corresponded with Rabbi Nissim of Kairouan (whose daughter married his eldest son Jehoseph), with R. Hai Gaon, with the heads of the *yeshivot* in Palestine and with the heads of the Jewish community in Egypt. In Spain he maintained a close relationship with, and was patron of, the *paytan* Isaac ibn Khalfun and the poet and philosopher Solomon ibn Gabirol. He exchanged poetry with both of them. In addition to being a poet he was a halakhist and composed a major work in *halakhah*. He was also known as a philologist and writer of theological tracts. During his lifetime there was economic prosperity in Granada, which had many Jewish merchants and craftsmen. The Jewish population of Granada was estimated at five thousand and it was no wonder that the Muslims called the city *Gharnatat al-Yahud* ("Granada of the Jews"). The yeshiva at Granada had many well-known scholars.

In the Muslim area of northern Spain there was a large concentration of Jews in Saragossa. The rulers were the Banu Tujib dynasty, who maintained proper relations with their Christian neighbors in the city. In the second half of the eleventh century a new family, Banu Hud, came to power, originating from Yemen. The city became one of the richest in all of Spain. Most of the Jewish inhabitants were either furriers or were engaged in the flax, clothing and leather industries. In the environs of Saragossa Jews were engaged in farming and viticulture; they traded with the merchants of Barcelona and southern France. The community had a great number of Torah scholars, doctors and intellectuals. At the ruling court there was an atmosphere of tolerance and Jews found ways of serving these rulers. In the 1030s Abu Ishaq Jekuthiel b. Isaac ibn Hasan served as adviser to King Mundhir II. Jekuthiel had a broad Torah and secular education. He was patron to Torah scholars and poets. In 1039 he was executed by the last of the Banu Tujib kings.

An ivory vessel from 10th-century Spain.
The original is in the museum of the Hispanic Society in New York.

RECONQUISTA:
THE RECONQUEST
Until the Middle of the Twelfth Century

Indecisive wars and battles were fought over a period of several hundred years between Muslim and Christian princes. Charlemagne helped the Christians create a frontier buffer zone, Marca Hispanica, between Muslim Spain and Carolingian France. Barcelona was one of the first cities in which Christian rule was consolidated. It was in this district that Jews developed extensive operations in commerce and in leasing of fields and vineyards. Landholding was either by outright ownership (*allodium*) or by tenancy. Jews often made land transactions with bishops or monastaries, and also with diocesan and parochial churches, the deeds of transfer being written in Hebrew or at least bearing a Hebrew signature.

Jews developed various spheres of economic activity in the city of Barcelona and in their own neighborhood, which came to an end during riots in 1391. In addition to the official writs of privileges which regulated Jewish life in Barcelona, there was a more ancient writ known as the Book of Usatges (Book of Usage) which defined the legal status of the Jews and was composed between 1053 and 1071. Among its many laws was one which stated that the punishment for doing bodily harm to a Jew or for killing him would be determined by the king. This meant that the Jews were dependent upon the good will of the ruler. The church councils of Gerona (1067–1068 and 1078) forced Jews who purchased land from Christians to pay a regular tithe to the church.

Ordoño I (850–866) invaded the region between Salamanca and Saragossa. He was very active in resettling the north of Spain and chose León as his capital. His son, Alfonso III (866–909), continued his father's policies and conquered territories in northern Portugal only to lose them to the Muslims. Internal dissension and factionalism forced him to halt the Christian advance. Perhaps he was also deterred by the Muslim king 'Abd al-Rahman III, who was then the ruler of Andalusia. During the reign of the King Ramiro II (931–950), Count Fernan González of Castile rebelled against the king and from this point the history of Castile actually begins. Ramiro concluded a pact with Tota, queen of Navarre (who negotiated with Hisdai ibn Shaprut). The Jews in Castile were also apparently dependent upon the good will of the ruler. Killing or wounding a Jew was punishable by a heavy fine payable to the ruler, as though the Jews were his property. In fact the regulations in this matter differed in each city

and district. The special circumstances of Jewish life are exemplified by the riot of the inhabitants of Castrojeriz in 1035. In order to develop the district King Sancho III the Great, encouraged the Jews to settle on the land, despite the opposition of the Christian population in the district. Upon his death in 1035 the Christian inhabitants of Castrojeriz broke into one of the king's estates in Burgos, killing sixty Jews. Jewish settlement in the rural districts not only required the approval of the ruler but was dependent upon his physical ability to protect these settlers. The settlements themselves were on royal lands and were known as *villa nova de Judaeis*. Such settlements were established in Navarre and Aragón.

Ferdinand I unified Castile, León and Galicia under one crown (1037), thus creating the largest kingdom in Spain. the reign of his second son, Alfonso VI (1065–1109), coincided with the momentous events in Europe during the First Crusade. During this period the behavior toward the Jews in Christian Spain was entirely different from that in the rest of Europe. Alfonso VI, who assumed the title of Emperor of All Spain, carried the battle standard against the Muslims. His preoccupation with the Reconquista, in which he employed French knights, was probably one of the reasons why the Jews were not massacred like their brethren in other parts of Europe.

The services rendered by the Jews to the ruling power stood them in good stead. The Jews of Spain, who were more numerous than their brethren in Ashkenaz (Franco-Germany), remained where they were after the Muslim retreat southward. Those Jews who occupied important posts in the local civil administration of the various Arab emirates were destined later to play a vital role in establishing the rule of the Christian victor.

Alfonso VI defeated the rulers of Seville, Badajoz and Granada and forced them to pay him tribute. He also conquered Coimbra in Portugal and assisted in establishing the Portuguese kingdom.

On 6 May 1085 he captured Toledo and in the terms of capitulation he promised the Muslims that he would honor their rights and their mosques. However, only two generations later the Muslims were forced to leave their dwellings in the city, and the main mosque was converted to a church (1102). Twelfth-century documents from Toledo attest to a sparse Muslim population. The Jews of the city continued to live in the southwest corner of the city which also contained a fortress. (Remains of Jewish edifices have been preserved to this day.)

The Jews were fortunate in having a personality like Joseph Nasi Ferruziel (called Cidellus). He held office in the royal court and was active on their behalf. He was born in Cabra in the kingdom of Granada, and became the physician of Alfonso VI, and *nasi* of all the Jews residing in Alfonso's kingdom. He assisted the Jews of Guadalajara when the city was captured by Alfonso and also aided the Jews who migrated from the south to the north. The large estates in and around Toledo that he owned were confiscated by the crown after his death. Extant royal documents bear his signature in Latin characters as a witness verifying the contents of the document. His signature also appears on a purely political document, *Privilegium immunitatis*, dated 1110, one year after the death of Alfonso VI. Joseph adopted a firm stand regarding internal politics and ruthlessly expelled the Karaites from Castile.

THE RECONQUEST

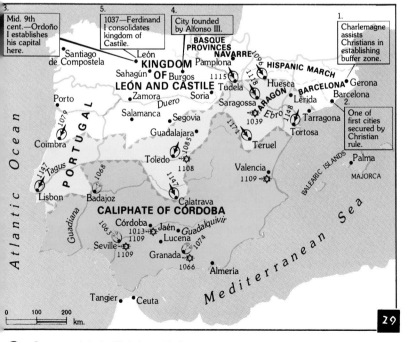

↔ Conquest of city by Christians, with date
↩ Tribute paid to Christians
✡ Massacres of Jews by Almohads and Almoravids

JEWISH COMMUNITIES IN ASHKENAZ
Up to 1096

Otto I "the Great" (936–973), the Holy Roman Emperor, and Otto II (973–983) were favorably disposed toward Jews settling in their empire. In fact these were the formative years of the German Jewish communities. Henry II (1002–1024) at first confirmed the rights of the Jews of Merseburg (1004) in their relations with the bishop of the city. However, in 1012 the Jews of Mainz were expelled. Some say this was due to the incident of the priest Wecelinus converting to Judaism; others relate it to the burning of the Church of the Holy Sepulcher in Jerusalem by the Fatimid caliph al-Hakim. The decree was soon revoked, apparently after the intervention of Rabbi Jacob b. Jekuthiel with Pope Benedict VIII (1012–1024).

Mainz was the capital of the state and it was natural that Jews should have dealings with the ruling authorities in many spheres and that these dealings should affect the Jews in other parts of the state. A Jewish community existed in Mainz in the tenth century and perhaps even slightly earlier. The arrival of Kalonymus and his Lucca family inaugurated a period of efflorescence.

Speyer was ideally situated, not only on the Rhine but also on an old Roman road. The official beginnings of its Jewish community date from the time of Bishop Ruediger (1073–1090), who granted the Jews privileges in 1084. Ruediger was a major supporter of Henry IV in the Investiture Controversy. His successor, Johann (1090–1104), continued his predecessor's policies in his relations with the Jews of Speyer.

The significance of Ruediger's privileges granted to the Jews of Speyer transcends their actual value for the community. They were approved in 1090 by the emperor Henry IV and eventually served as a model for many privileges granted to the Jews by other German rulers and in other European countries. The privileges determined the way of life of the Jews and their relations with their Christian neighbors. From what was allowed the Jews in the privileges we can infer what was forbidden. The Jews were obliged to pay a protection tax. In due course, their legal status was defined as belonging to the crown or the state treasury and this implied their subservience to the crown.

Worms was another important community. Construction of its synagogue began in 1014 and was completed in 1034. Shortly afterwards a Jewish neighborhood is mentioned in documents. The local Jews supported Henry IV in the investiture question and were rewarded, together with the other citizens of the city, with tax privileges. The commercial contacts of the Jews of Worms extended to Frankfurt, Goslar and other places. From the mid-eleventh century, Worms and Mainz were the Torah study centers of Ashkenaz.

The Jewish neighborhood in Cologne is first mentioned during the term of office of Archibishop Anno (1056–1075). Apparently the synagogue was built in the second decade of the eleventh century, though archaeological remains support a claim that the building is from the end of the tenth century. Relations between Jews and Christians in Cologne were

1. End 10th cent.—Emperors Otto I and Otto II issue edicts subordinating Jews to bishops. They are to reside in separate neighborhoods and enjoy certain privileges.

3. Rabbenu Gershom, c.960-1030, head of *yeshiva* and known as *Me'or ha-Golah* (Light of the Exile). Among his important *takkanot* (regulations) are a ban on bigamy and an order forbidding amending Talmudic texts.

4. Henry II expels Jews who refuse to convert. Among forcibly baptized is son of Rabbenu Gershom.

8. Prince Vratislav II (1061–1092) grants autonomy to Jews.

7. 1090 — Henry IV confirms privileges granted by Ruediger and grants additional ones.

5. Rashi (R. Solomon b. Isaac) studies at *yeshivoth* of Worms and Mainz. 1068—Returns to Troyes and establishes *yeshiva*. Composes commentary on Bible and Talmud.

6. 1084—Bishop Ruediger allocates special neighborhood to Jews; encloses it with wall; grants privileges. Group of Jews arrive from Mainz.

2. 982—Kalonymus, a Jew whose family moved to Mainz in 917, saves life of Otto II.

satisfactory during the eleventh century. Archbishop Anno seems to have used the services of Jewish moneylenders. It is known that many Jews brought their goods to the triannual trade fairs in Cologne. Apparently they had a privilege to do so and must have also had protection and exemption from travel tax.

There were smaller Jewish communities in the district like Trier and Metz. Many Jews in this region owned vineyards. Troyes was known for its leather industry and the Jews of that city were known for their manufacture of parchment.

The spring of 1096 saw a bustle of activity related to the march eastward. Peter the Hermit from Amiens was the chief agitator and preacher for launching the First Crusade. The march of the peasants was the factor that confronted the Jews with a choice between conversion and death. Rabbi Solomon b. Samson, a contemporary Jewish chronicler, describes the massacres of 1096, and cites the cries of the mob: "As they passed through towns where there were Jews they said to one another: 'We are going on a distant journey to seek the [Gentile] house of worship [reference to the Sepulcher of Christ] and to exact vengeance on the Ishmaelites. Yet here are the Jews dwelling in our midst whose forefathers slew him and crucified him without reason. First let us take vengeance on them and destroy them as a people, so that the name of Israel shall no longer be remembered, or so that they should be like us and submit to the son of depravity [Jesus].'"

The Jewish communities, in a state of dreadful apprehensiveness, circulated letters warning of the impending danger and advising on various measures of defense. Peter the Hermit arrived at Trier bearing a letter from the French Jewish communities requesting that their coreligionists in Germany give him and his crusaders money and provisions. The Trier community responded and was thus saved. Perhaps one could infer from this that there was a possibility of avoiding the tragic results by paying a suitable bribe to the leaders of the crusade. However, this could only have succeeded with a leader who had the power to control the mob. Such was not the case with the leader of another contingent of crusaders, Godfrey of Bouillon, who was destined to become the first ruler of the crusader kingdom in the Holy Land. A rumor spread that Godfrey had vowed to exact vengeance on the Jews for the blood of Jesus. The Jews of the Rhine communities turned to Kalonymus, the *parnas* of the Mainz Jewish community, asked him to intervene with Henry IV, who was in northern Italy at the time, and requested him to order Godfrey to desist from his plans. However, before Henry's orders reached him, the bloody events took place. Henry ordered his vassals to protect the Jews and guarantee their safety. The Jews of Mainz and Cologne appealed directly to Godfrey and payed him five hundred pieces of silver to dissuade him from his intentions. Godfrey, having succeeded in his extortion, informed the king that he had no intention of harming the Jews.

The first attack on the Jews of France was by Volkmar and his followers, who then went on to Prague, arriving while Vratislav II (1061–1092), king of Bohemia was fighting in Poland and Cosmas the bishop of Prague was acting as regent. Volkmar gave the Jews of the city a choice between apostasy or death. Many chose to die for *kiddush ha-Shem* (sanctification of God's name); the few that converted later returned to Judaism.

While the Jews of Prague were undergoing their terrible ordeal, the Jewish communities of the Rhine were faced with a similar trial. On 3 May 1096, William, viscount of Melun, surnamed the Carpenter, attacked Speyer at the head of his followers.

The Jewish community was saved by Bishop Johann, who sheltered the Jews in his palace. Those killed were "eleven holy souls who first sanctified their Creator on the holy Sabbath and did not desire to foul the air with their stench. And there was a graceful, prominent woman who slaughtered herself for *kiddush ha-Shem*. And she was the first of the slaughterers and slaughtered amongst all the communities" (*Sefer Gezerot*, p. 25). On 18 May, William and his cohorts arrived at Worms. Here too Bishop Alebrand attempted to protect the Jewish community by transferring some of them to his palace. Most of the Jews who were left in the city were massacred. After a week, William informed the

Jewish community that he could no longer lay siege to the city and demanded that they submit to baptism. Most of the community was destroyed. A week later William arrived at Mainz, linking up with Count Emich (Emicho) of Leisingen. Emich claimed that divine revelation ordered him either to convert the Jews or to destroy them. The brigands then forced their way into the palace of Archbishop Rothard, who was a relative of Emich. The tragic story of the Jewish community of Mainz is one of the great heroic chapters in the history of the Jewish people. Its members exemplified the ideology of *kiddush ha-Shem* and whole groups sacrificed themselves as one for their religion and their faith. They saw themselves as a generation chosen to be tested and they were proud to be able to pass the test.

Mainz was not the end of the tragic story. Emich and his followers next moved on to Würzburg and Nürnberg and then to Regensburg, where they arrived on 10 June 1096. Meanwhile, mixed bands of new crusaders composed of English, Flemings and Lotharingians gathered at Cologne, intending to attack the Jews. The archbishop of the city together with some of its citizens attempted to hide the Jews in the fortress and afterwards to disperse them in the surrounding villages. The brigands contented themselves with plundering Jewish property. For about three weeks the Jewish refugees from Cologne succeeded in finding shelter in their hiding places. However, on 23 June they were discovered in Wevelinghoven, on 24 June in Neuss, and on 30 June in Mörs. Those Jews who did not undergo baptism by force or by consent died for *kiddush ha-Shem*.

During this perod a band of French farmers who had attacked the Jews of Rouen at the end of May reached Cologne. In mid-June the Jewish communities of Trier and Metz were slaughtered.

The destruction of the Ashkenaz communities was almost total. Most of the scholars of Mainz and Worms, the two most important centers, were killed. This was the major reason for the transfer, during this period, of the Jewish cultural center to northern France.

The path of the crusaders was a bloody one. Their goal in the Holy Land was Jerusalem and it was there that the Jews, together with the Muslims of the city, fought for their lives. After losing the battle, the entire Jewish community was slaughtered.

THE MASSACRES OF 1096: "GEZEROT TATNU" (4856)

Columns of a synagogue in Worms.

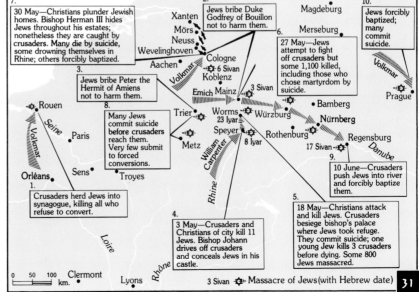

7.
30 May—Christians plunder Jewish homes. Bishop Herman III hides Jews throughout his estates; nonetheless they are caught by crusaders. Many die by suicide, some drowning themselves in Rhine; others forcibly baptized.

2.
Jews bribe Duke Godfrey of Bouillon not to harm them.

10.
Jews forcibly baptized; many commit suicide.

6.
27 May—Jews attempt to fight off crusaders but some 1,100 killed, including those who chose martyrdom by suicide.

3.
Jews bribe Peter the Hermit of Amiens not to harm them.

8.
Many Jews commit suicide before crusaders reach them. Very few submit to forced conversions.

9.
10 June—Crusaders push Jews into river and forcibly baptize them.

1.
Crusaders herd Jews into synagogue, killing all who refuse to convert.

4.
3 May—Crusaders and Christians of city kill 11 Jews. Bishop Johann drives off crusaders and conceals Jews in his castle.

5.
18 May—Christians attack and kill Jews. Crusaders besiege bishop's palace where Jews took refuge. They commit suicide; one young Jew kills 3 crusaders before dying. Some 800 Jews massacred.

Magdeburg • Merseburg • Xanten • Mörs • Neuss • Wevelinghoven • Aachen • Cologne • 6 Sivan Koblenz • Emich Mainz • 3 Sivan • Bamberg • Trier • Worms 23 Iyar • Würzburg • Nürnberg • Speyer • Rothenburg • Regensburg 17 Sivan • Rouen • Paris • Orléans • Sens • Troyes • Metz 8 Iyar • Clermont • Lyons • Prague • Volkmar • William Carpenter • Seine • Loire • Rhône • Rhine • Danube

0 50 100 km.

3 Sivan ✡ Massacre of Jews (with Hebrew date)

31

THE FIRST CRUSADE
1096 to 1099

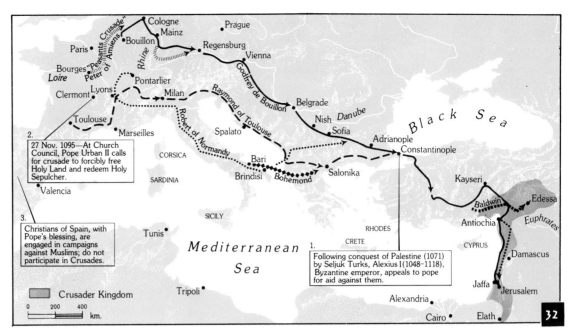

2. 27 Nov. 1095—At Church Council, Pope Urban II calls for crusade to forcibly free Holy Land and redeem Holy Sepulcher.

3. Christians of Spain, with Pope's blessing, are engaged in campaigns against Muslims; do not participate in Crusades.

1. Following conquest of Palestine (1071) by Seljuk Turks, Alexius I (1048–1118), Byzantine emperor, appeals to pope for aid against them.

Crusader Kingdom

0   200   400 km.

32

Crusaders

THE CRUSADER KINGDOM IN ERETZ ISRAEL

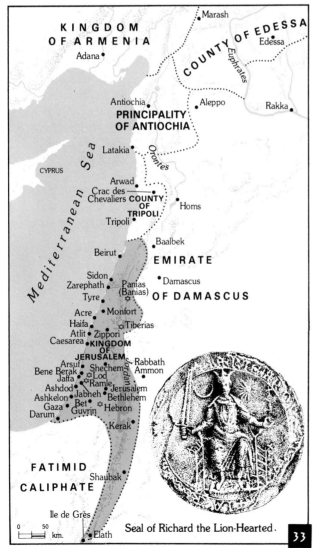

☆ Jewish town

"On Rosh Hodesh Sivan, The day the Israelites were summoned to Mount Sinai to receive the Torah, those who remained in the bishop's courtyard trembled; the enemies molested them as they had done to the first group, and then put them to the sword. The victims, fortified by the courage of their brethren, died for kiddush ha-Shem, extending their necks to the sword. There were some who took their own lives fulfilling the words of the prophet "when mothers and babes were dashed to death together;" and father fell upon his son. Each his brother did despatch, his kinsman wife and children, also the bridegroom his betrothed, and a merciful woman and her only child. And all with willing hearts accepted the heavenly judgment, making peace with their master they shouted Hear, O Israel! The Lord is our God, the Lord alone."

A.M. Habermann, Sefer Gzerot Ashkenaz ve-Tsarfat, *Jerusalem 1946, p. 29*

"While sundered children lay twitching in heaps,
They hasten to slaughter the others who wallow in their blood,
Strewn on the floor of Your Sanctuary,
They will seethe before Your eyes forever."

David b. Meshullam of Speyer: God! Be not silent on my blood, penitential hymn for eve of the Day of Atonement.

THE CAPTURE OF JERUSALEM
June 7th to July 15th, 1099

Seal of Richard the Lion-Hearted.

33

Seal of Emperor Frederick Barbarossa.

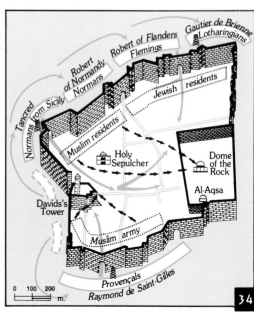

0   100   200 m.

34

40

FROM CRUSADE TO CRUSADES

One whole year elapsed after the fall of Edessa (1144) before a delegation arrived at the court of Pope Eugenius III (1145–1153) in Italy, with a request for aid. In December 1145 the pope issued a bull calling for a Second Crusade and promised those who answered the call an abeyance of their debts and cancellation of the interest. This cancellation particularly affected Jews engaged in moneylending. The pope also declared that participation in the crusade was equivalent to a "sacrament of repentance" and anyone joining a crusade who in his heart repented of his sins would be purified and absolved from the punishment due for those sins. However,

there was little response until Bernard of Clairvaux became active. He appeared before a large assembly of French nobles including King Louis VII at Vézelay on 31 March 1146. His rhetoric electrified the assembly, who soon pledged to take up the cross. He continued preaching the crusade for about a year in the Rhenish towns and in 1147 persuaded the German king Conrad III (1138–1152) to take up the cross. During this period a fanatical Cistercian monk called Rudolf was stirring the masses of the Rhineland to massacre Jews.

Once again the Jewish communities faced a repetition of the massacres of 1096. This time, however, the ecclesiastical and political heads of state intervened, fearing that unbridled mob violence might turn against them. They appealed to Bernard of Clairvaux as the person responsible for the crusade propaganda and as a man of stature and authority in the Christian world in general and in the Cistercian order — of which Rudolf was a member — in particular. They urged him to act responsibly and sagaciously in order to protect the Jews. Jewish sources express an appreciation for the religious feeling that motivated Bernard to protect the Jews. Unfortunately he did not succeed in saving many Jewish

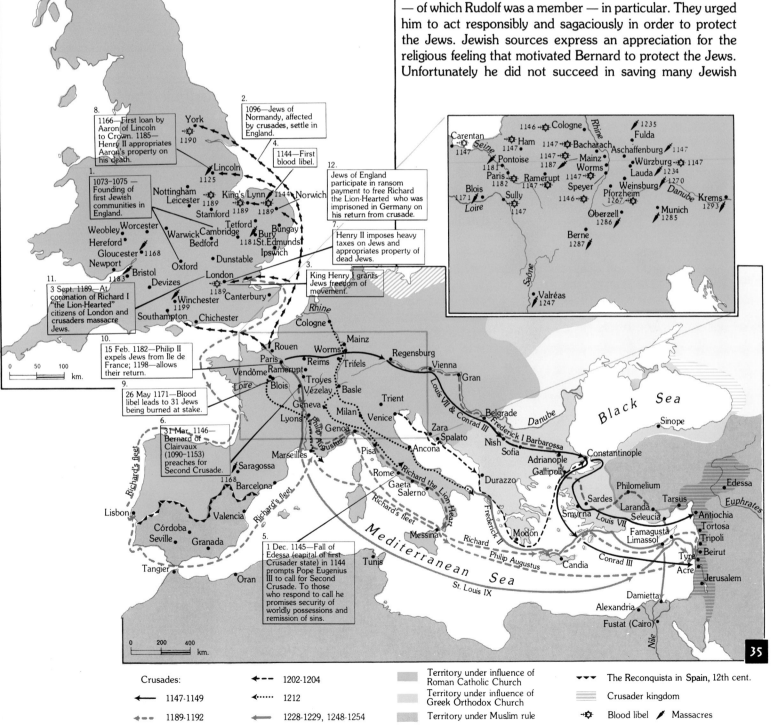

Crusades:

← 1147-1149	←-- 1202-1204
←--- 1189-1192	←···· 1212
	← 1228-1229, 1248-1254

Territory under influence of Roman Catholic Church
Territory under influence of Greek Orthodox Church
Territory under Muslim rule

▼▼▼ The Reconquista in Spain, 12th cent.
Crusader kingdom
⊹ Blood libel ⚡ Massacres

communities; the massacre of French Jewry (in the towns of Ham, Sully, Carentan and Ramerupt) had begun before the crusaders reached Germany. Rabbenu Tam (Jacob b. Meir Tam, c. 1100–1171) was among the wounded at Ramerupt. It was fortunate that Louis VII of France did not heed the counsel of Peter the Venerable, abbot of Cluny (c. 1092–1156), who, in a vitriolic and vituperative letter unprecedented even for the Middle Ages, called for the total annihilation of the Jews.

In England King Stephen (1135–1154) protected the Jews. In Germany the Jewish communities attacked were those of Cologne (only a few Jews were saved by hiding in the Wolkenburg fortress), Worms, Mainz, Bacharach, Würzburg and Aschaffenburg. The rioting against the Jews ended in the summer of 1147.

The Jewish communities of France continued to be persecuted in the period between the Second and Third crusades. An example was the blood libel against the Jewish community of Blois in 1171. In 1182 the Jews were expelled from the kingdom of France by King Philip Augustus (1179–1123). All debts owed by Christians to Jews were annulled and the Jews were forced to pay a fifth of the debt to the state treasury. In 1198 Philip Augustus authorized their return and established a special department in his treasury to deal with the Jews, as had been done in England.

The crusader defeat at the battle of Hittin (1178) and Saladin's capture of Jerusalem aroused enthusiasm for a new crusade (the Third). Popes Gregory VIII (1187) and Clement III (1187–1191) called for Christians to save the Holy Land. Once again the crusade had its preacher, Henry of Albano, a monk from the Clairvaux monastery, who was aided by the monk Joachim of Fiore, who spent the winter of 1190–1191 in Palestine. The Jews of Mainz, Speyer, Worms, Strasbourg and Würzburg, through which the crusaders were destined to pass, decided to abandon these towns for places removed from the crusader route. Frederick I Barbarossa (emperor 1152–1190) and his son Duke Frederick of Swabia protected the Jews. Even the church intervened on their behalf and undoubtedly both these factors were instrumental in saving the Jews.

In England the crusade was closely linked to the personality of King Richard I "the Lion Hearted" (1189–1199). During an eight-month period (in 1189–1190) the Jews of England suffered from a wave of massacres. Most of the London Jewish community was destroyed. In February–March 1190 most of the rural Jewish communities were destroyed. The massacres were well organized and presaged the eventual expulsion of the Jews from England.

The Fourth Crusade (1202–1204), initiated by Pope Innocent III (1198–1216), ended without achieving its goal.

Innocent had hoped that the crusade would bring the Greek Orthodox Church back into the Catholic fold. He saw it as "a return of Samaria to Zion," but his hopes were not fulfilled. This crusade set out for Constantinople but was redirected to Egypt by the Venetians in order to settle some political scores. After this crusade, Germany was endangered by the Children's Crusade (1212), which marched through northern France and the lower Rhineland. The crusade ended dreadfully, as unscrupulous merchants sold the children as slaves in Egypt.

The Fifth Crusade (April 1217–July 1221), the goal of which was to free the Christians in Muslim captivity, was also unsuccessful. Frederick II (1198–1250) and John of England (1199–1216) were both supposed to participate in the Sixth Crusade but only Frederick arrived in the Holy Land some years later (1228) and stayed in Jerusalem. In 1248 Louis IX (St. Louis, king of France 1226–1270) led the Seventh and last crusade which was also unsuccessful.

The Jews of Europe were no sooner free from the nightmare of the crusades than they found other disasters in store for them.

THE CITY OF NORWICH

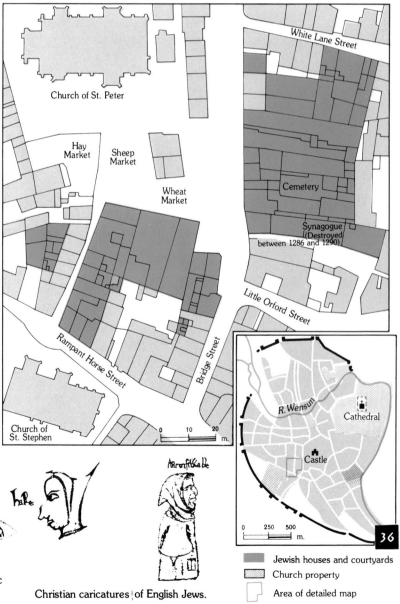

Caricature of English Jews from document dated 1233 showing Isaac son of Jurnet of Norwich (with crown) and members of his household.

Christian caricatures of English Jews.

Jewish houses and courtyards

Church property

Area of detailed map

36

UNTIL THE BLACK DEATH

Opening of the book of Numbers, *The Duke of Sussex Pentateuch*,
showing the four leading tribes of Israel camping around the
Tabernacle. Circa early 14th century, Ashkenaz.

BLOOD LIBELS

England had the first recorded case of blood libel, but it was closely followed by other European countries, and the notion even spread to Islamic countries. A libel case occurred in England in 1144 at Norwich where it was alleged that the Jews of the town bought a Christian child named William (who was apparently an epileptic and died after one of his fits) before Easter, allegedly tortured him and then killed him.

The number of libel incidents increased and the emperor of Germany, Frederick II finally decided to clarify the matter. Consulting with decent and learned Jewish converts to Christianity, he initiated an enquiry as to whether Jews used blood for ritual purposes. The council of the converts concluded that they did not, and Frederick published a statement to this effect. In 1247 Pope Innocent IV issued a bull denouncing blood libels against the Jews. However, the bull did not succeed in eliminating further occurrences.

Pope Gregory X (1271–1276) vigorously combatted blood libel adding a special clause to the Bull of Protection of 1272 (*Sicut Judaeis*).

In 1343 an attempt was made to sell a Christian child born out of wedlock to the head of the Jewish community in Brünn. A similar offer was made in 1699 to Meyer Goldschmidt, the Jewish court jeweler to the king of Denmark.

In 1540 Pope Paul III (1534–1549) issued a bull (*Licet Judaeis*) addressed to the bishops of Poland, Bohemia and Hungary, in which he rejected the allegation that Jews used the blood of Christian children.

There were two major blood libels whose repercussions spread far beyond the place at which they occurred. One concerned Simon of Trent (1475) who was beatified in the eighteenth century and whose beatification was canceled in 1965 by Pope Paul VI. The second libel was that of the "Holy Child of Laguardia" in Spain (1490–1491) whose body was never found. In this libel Jews and conversos were accused of attempting to bring about the annihilation of Christianity, the Inquisition and the inquisitor Tomás de Torquemada by means of the sorcerous use of a child's heart.

Another form of libel was the desecration of the host; Jews were accused of stealing the holy wafer and using it in sorcerous ritual in order to destroy Christianity. Such a libel occurred in 1168 at Saragossa, Spain.

The poisoning of drinking wells was another accusation levelled at the Jews (1320–1321). Europe was rife with these libels, all of which ended tragically for the Jewish people.

THE TRAVELS OF BENJAMIN OF TUDELA   1160 to 1173

Benjamin of Tudela was a merchant-traveler who set out on a journey to Palestine either in 1159 or in 1160, returning to Spain in 1172–1173. His book *Sefer ha-Massa'ot* ("Book of Travels") contains a vivid description of his travels. In every city that he visited he sought out the Jewish community, enquiring about the life of the Jews in the East, and his account became a major source for the history of that community. Benjamin visited the Holy Land during the period of Crusader rule, meeting a number of Jews, some of them in Jerusalem. After Benjamin had shown the way, and until the time of Judah al-Harizi, a considerable number of Jewish pilgrims from Spain and Ashkenaz visited Palestine, their courage bolstered by a passionate yearning for the Holy Land and the belief that their pilgrimage would hasten the coming of the Redemption. A pupil of the Ramban (Nahmanides, 1194–1270) wrote: "Children of Israel — Torah scholars and pious men of action from all four points of the compass, this one from a city, the other from a family — every man whose heart was prompted to generosity, to a spirit of sanctity and purification and affection for all that is holy — comes to Eretz Israel, and to them the Messiah will reveal himself... And now, many are awakened and volunteer to go to Eretz Israel. And many think that we are approaching the coming of the Redeemer" (A. Yaari: *Massa'ot Eretz Israel*).

Memorial plaque to R. Benjamin in the city of Tudela.

Decorated opening pages of the portion *Shelah Lekha* (Num. 13–15). Egypt, 11th century.

THE TRAVELS OF BENJAMIN OF TUDELA:

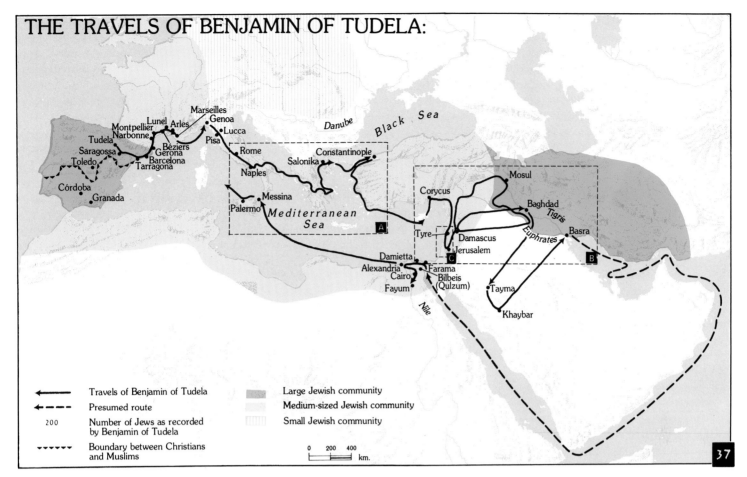

Marseilles
Genoa
Lunel
Montpellier
Narbonne
Arles
Lucca
Tudela
Béziers
Pisa
Saragossa
Gerona
Barcelona
Rome
Toledo
Tarragona
Salonika
Constantinople
Córdoba
Naples
Granada
Messina
Palermo

Mediterranean Sea

Danube
Black Sea

Corycus
Mosul
Baghdad
Tigris
Tyre
Damascus
Euphrates
Basra
Jerusalem
Damietta
Alexandria
Farama
Cairo
Bilbeis
Fayum
(Qulzum)
Nile
Tayma
Khaybar

→ Travels of Benjamin of Tudela
--→ Presumed route
200 Number of Jews as recorded by Benjamin of Tudela
vvvv Boundary between Christians and Muslims

Large Jewish community
Medium-sized Jewish community
Small Jewish community

0 200 400
km.

37

IN ITALY, GREECE AND TURKEY

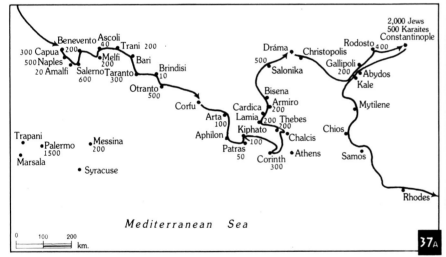

Benevento
Ascoli
200
40
Trani 200
300 Capua
Melfi
Dráma
Christopolis
Rodosto
2,000 Jews
500 Karaites
Constantinople
500 Naples
200
500
400
20 Amalfi
Salerno
Taranto
Bari
Salonika
Gallipoli
600
300
Brindisi
200
Abydos
Otranto
10
Kale
500
Bisena
Corfu
Cardica
Armiro
Mytilene
Arta
Lamia
200
100
200
Thebes
Aphilon
Kiphato
200
Chios
Patras
100
Chalcis
Trapani
50
Corinth
Athens
Palermo
Messina
300
Samos
1500
200
Marsala
Syracuse

Rhodes

Mediterranean Sea

0 100 200
km.

37A

Call greeting unto daughters and kindred,
Peace to brothers and to sisters,
From the captive of hope who is possessed
By the sea, and hath placed his spirit in the hand of the winds,
Thrust by the hand of the west into the hand of the east:
This one passeth to lead on, and that one to thrust back.
Between him and death is but a step,
Aye, between them but the thickness of a plank;
Buried alive in a coffin of wood,
Upon no floor, with no four cubits of earth, nor even with less.
He sitteth—he cannot stand upon his feet,
He lieth down—he cannot stretch them forth;
Sick and afraid because of the heathen
And because of the marauders and the winds.
The pilot and the mariner, and all their rabble—
They are the rulers and captains there.

A section of a sea-poem of Judah Halevi, describing the hardships en route to the Holy Land. Translated by Nina Salaman, Selected Poems of Judah Halevi, *Philadelphia 1924.*

IN THE HOLY LAND

IN THE NEAR EAST

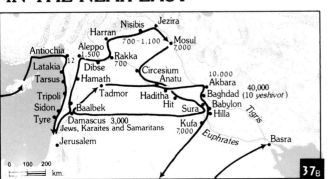

Nisibis
Jezira
Harran
700-1,100
Mosul
Antiochia
Aleppo
7,000
12
1,500
Rakka
Latakia
Dibse
700
Tarsus
Hamath
Circesium
Anatu
10,000
Akbara
Tripoli
Tadmor
Haditha
Baghdad
40,000
Sidon
Hit
(10 *yeshivot*)
Tyre
Baalbek
Sura
Babylon
Damascus 3,000
Hilla
Jerusalem
Jews, Karaites and Samaritans
Kufa
Tigris
7,000
Euphrates
Basra

0 100 200
km.

37B

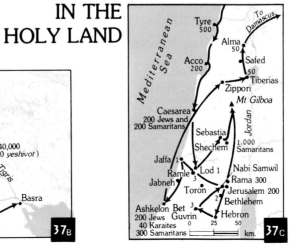

Mediterranean Sea
Tyre
500
To Damascus
Alma
50
Acco
200
Safed
50
Zippori
Tiberias
Mt Gilboa
Caesarea
200 Jews and
200 Samaritans
Sebastia
Jordan
Shechem
1,000
Samaritans
Jaffa 1
Nabi Samwil
Ramle
Lod 1
Rama 300
Jabneh
3
Jerusalem 200
Toron
2
Bethlehem
Ashkelon
Bet
3
Hebron
200 Jews and
Guvrin
40 Karaites
0   25   50
300 Samaritans
km.

37C

Depiction of a sea voyage.

45

1.
Judah Halevi received with great
honor and admiration. Lodges in
Alexandria with *dayyan* Aaron
Alamani; in Damietta with his friend
Halfon ha-Levi; and in Cairo with
nagid Abu Manzur.

2.
Trip to city
in Persia
and a visit
to tombs of
prophets
Ezekiel,
Nahum the
Elkoshite,
and Baruch
b. Neriah.

The synagogue established by Nahmanides upon his arrival
in Jerusalem (apparently a Crusader structure).

Interior of the Nahmanides synagogue with restored pillars.

JEWISH COMMUNITIES IN THE HOLY LAND   Twelfth to Fourteenth Centuries

The continuous arrival of Christians from Europe did not substantially alter the life style of the country, since they did not
establish permanent settlements. The land was desolate and
even the crusaders' seignorial system was unable to provide
adequate livelihood. During the crusader period there were
a number of rural Jewish settlements which had probably
already been established during or before the Arab period.
In the second half of the twelfth century Jews were living in
Tiberias, the capital of the "Principality of Galilee," and in
Safed, the important stronghold of Galilee. Both these cities
were surrounded by Jewish villages.

Until Saladin's conquest of Jerusalem, Jews, with the ex-
ception of a few families, were forbidden to reside in the city.
Nevertheless, when Benjamin of Tudela visited Jerusalem he
found Jews engaged in the craft of dyeing, for which they had
purchased a monopoly from the king. These Jews resided
either near the king's palace or near the Citadel (David's
Tower).

Tyre, Sidon and Ashkelon had the largest Jewish communities in the country. According to Benjamin of Tudela,
about five hundred Jews resided in Tyre and two hundred
in Ashkelon. Karaites and Samaritans also resided in these
cities. Acre, Beirut and Caesarea also had a substantial
Jewish populations. The crusader conquest opened a period
of economic development from which the Jews benefited.
Various crafts constituted their major source of income. (In
Tyre, for instance, Jews manufactured glass and were trades-
men.) The settlers in the reconstituted *yishuv* (the Jewish
population in Eretz Israel) continued to maintain contact
with their countries of origin, from where they had come in
the wake of the crusaders. The importance of Rabbi Judah
Halevi's *aliyah* (immigration) lies not only in its indication of
a yearning for Eretz Israel but also in its illustration of the
possibility of putting that yearning into practice.

Benjamin of Tudela was the first Jewish traveler to reach

the Holy Land in the 1160s. In about 1175 Pehthahiah of Regensburg set out on his journey to Eretz Israel. The *aliyah* in 1209 of a group of rabbis and their pupils, headed by Rabbi Samson b. Abraham of Sens, gave a considerable impetus to the revival of the *yishuv*. In 1216 Judah al-Harizi was on a visit to the Holy Land and met "the group who came from France," headed by Rabbi Joseph b. Baruch of Clisson and his brother Meir. The Disputation of Paris (1240) and the public burning of the Talmud caused Rabbi Jehiel of Paris and his son to migrate, while the Barcelona Disputation in 1263 caused the Ramban (Nahmanides) to migrate in 1267.

When Rudolf I of Hapsburg, king of Germany, attempted to assert royal authority over the Jews through additional taxation, thousands of Jews, led by the Maharam (Rabbi Meir b. Baruch of Rothenburg), decided to leave Germany. In 1286 Rudolf issued orders to prevent this emigration; the Maharam was arrested while attempting to leave and delivered to Rudolf who had him imprisoned. Rudolf demanded a huge ransom for the Maharam. But the latter refused to be ransomed on the grounds that this would serve as a precedent for the authorities to imprison rabbis and leaders of the community in order to extort large sums of money from them. He died in prison in 1293.

Jews also migrated to the Holy Land from North Africa and Egypt. Ashkelon was the focus for this *aliyah*.

In 1209–1210 the Babylonian exilarch visited Eretz Israel (possibly David b. Zakkai II, exilarch in Mosul). From his visit we learn that Safed was a "state," that is, the center of Jewish settlement in the Galilee. Little is known about the Jewish community in Tiberias; Benjamin of Tudela described it as having "about fifty Jewish families." An old tradition relates that the disciples of Maimonides, who died in Fustat in 1204, brought his remains for reburial in Tiberias. Tiberias had favorable conditions for Jews to settle and for the revival of its *yishuv*.

The beginning of the thirteenth century saw a strengthening of the Jewish community in Jerusalem. Rabbi Jehiel b. Isaac ha-Zarefati resided there and maintained contact with the Jewish community of Fustat. Controversies within the community were not resolved until 1240. In 1244 the city was sacked and destroyed by the Khwarizmi Turks.

When the Ramban came to Jerusalem in 1267 he found it in a state of ruin. The *minyan* (quorum) of Jews who gathered for prayers on the Sabbath were "the *she'ar yashuv*" (the remnant that returned — cf. 1 Samuel 7:3). He had a Torah scroll brought from Shechem and renovated a building for use as a synagogue. In 1268 he moved to Acre, where he died in 1270.

Acre was a large and important Jewish center in the thirteenth century. It had a Jewish quarter and a "Jews' house" in 1206. When the newly crowned king of Jerusalem, John of Brienne, visited Acre, he was received by representatives of the Frankish and Greek communities and by members of the Jewish community holding a Torah scroll. Judah Al-Harizi described the community as ignoramuses "not a man among them who could stand in the breach," and this despite the arrival of three hundred rabbis from France and England in 1211.

The Muslims conquered the city in 1291 and massacred its Christian and Jewish inhabitants. One of the survivors who reached Spain, Rabbi Isaac of Acre, described the destruction. Among those killed was Rabbi Solomon, the grandson of Rabbi Simon of Sens. The Jewish captives were apparently brought to Egypt where they were ransomed by the community.

The impoverished state and status of the *yishuv* continued until the immigration waves of the fourteenth century inaugurated a process of regeneration.

IMMIGRATION TO THE HOLY LAND Thirteenth to Early Fourteenth Century

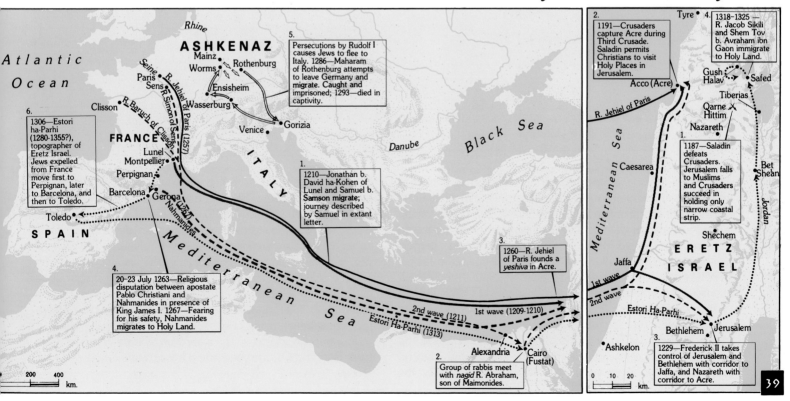

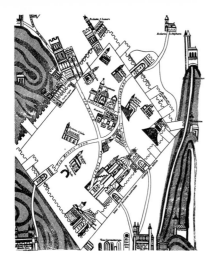

Jerusalem in 12th century (From: J. Prawer, *A History of the Crusader Kingdom*, Hebrew ed., Jerusalem 1963, p. 138.)

THE JEWS OF ITALY
Thirteenth Century

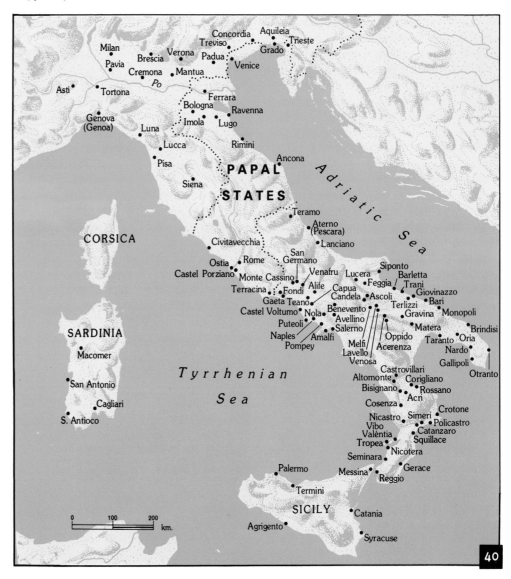

Jewish life in Italy in the twelfth and thirteenth centuries was determined by a constantly fluctuating political climate, with the church promulgating anti-Jewish laws. Most of the Jewish population was located from the center of the Italian Peninsula southward. Rome was an important Jewish center, while cities such as Lucca, Pisa and Venice had sparse Jewish populations. Jehiel Anav, a relative of Nathan b. Jehiel, supervised the finances of Pope Alexander III (1159–1181).

The significant political events of this period were the Hohenstaufen rule in Sicily, the Angevin invasion of Italy at the invitation of Pope Boniface VIII (1294–1303), and the wars of the Aragonese dynasty over the rule of south-central Italy. Jews gave financial aid to the war campaigns of the Aragonese.

For its part, the church had already established its attitude toward Jews: at the Third Lateran Council (1179) and the Fourth Lateran Council (1215) a number of anti-Jewish edicts were issued, among them a decree that Jews must dress so as to be easily distinguished from Christians. The distinction soon became institutionalized in the Jewish badge. The council also limited the maximum rate of interest that Jews could charge Christians. This period is also noted for the blood libels in Trani, where in 1290 one such libel resulted in four synagogues being converted into churches.

The popularization of the *kabbalah* in Italy began to bear fruit; Bari and Otranto becoming important centers of Torah study.

JEWISH COMMUNITIES IN SPAIN AND THE RECONQUEST
Thirteenth and Fourteenth Centuries

The reign of King James I (1213–1276), over the kingdom of Aragón saw the continuation of the Reconquest, which affected Spanish Jewry. King James encouraged Jews from Marseilles and North Africa to settle in his kingdom, and many Jews supported his campaigns of conquest of the Balearic Islands and Valencia. In order to settle and develop the conquered territories, he granted land and property to the Jews and they in turn enjoyed the status of settlers in frontier areas. He exempted communities from payment of taxes and reestablished the Jewish community of Perpignan, which at that time belonged to the kingdom of Aragón. Many of the communities which developed enjoyed preferential status in commerce. Jews held key positions in the court administration, including that of manager of the king's personal property.

It would be accurate to say that the major royal administrative posts were held by Jews who were also prominent in the Jewish community. Among the more outstanding of these were Nahmanides of Gerona; the brothers Solomon and Bahya Alconstantini of Saragossa, who assisted the king in his campaigns of conquest and were destined to take part in the controversy regarding the writings of Maimonides; Don Judah (ibn Lavi) de la Cavalleria, who is mentioned from 1257 onwards as being the royal treasurer and bailiff of Saragossa.

From 1260 Don Judah controlled all the crown revenues, judiciously managing royal expenditure. Nevertheless, from 1260 on, a decline in Jewish power and influence was already apparent.

Despite the prominence of Jews under James, their status in Aragón was not one of total security or welfare. Though no official action was directed against them nor was any specific anti-Jewish policy promulgated, certain changes did occur. During the reign of James I, the laws and edicts of Popes Innocent III and Gregory IX were activated. In 1228, James decreed laws relating to Jews: a fixed 20 percent maximum interest permitted on loan, identical to that of the Christian merchants of Florence; a Jewish oath could not serve as evidence in a court of law; and Jews were excluded from state administrative posts. Although the king was in no way involved, the first instance of a blood libel in Spain, concerning a Christian boy allegedly murdered by Jews, was circulated in Saragossa in 1250.

These events are indicative of the change that took place in the lives of Spanish Jewry. The Barcelona Disputation in 1263, with the participation of Nahmanides and in the presence of James I, was undoubtedly instigated by the church, particularly by the Dominicans, who were fervent advocates of a militant church policy. In many respects James's policy

▼▼▼	Extent of the Reconquest, 1147
▼▼▼	Extent of the Reconquest, 1344

41

regarding Jews vacillated between two courses of action: while he used them for his own purposes and had need of many Jews for royal adminstration, he was nevertheless guided by those church principles and policies that argued for conversion, degradation and limitation. It was church policy that eventually triumphed, although it is difficult to determine the precise date at which this occurred.

The reign of James's son and successor Peter III (1276–1285) is an important chapter in the history of the Jews in the kingdom of Aragón. The first Spanish ruler to acquiesce to the pressures of Jew-haters, he enacted numerous limitations on them. However, he too was compelled to use the services of Jews in carrying out his foreign and domestic policies. Thus we find Moses Alconstantini and the Abravalia family of Gerona among his courtiers. Their involvement in state administration and finances was reminiscent of the Reconquest period. One of the members of the Abravalia family accompanied Peter on his Sicilian campaign in 1282. During the latter part of his reign Peter himself actively repressed the Jews, removing them from all positions of influence. His son and successor, Alfonso III (1285–1291), heeded the complaints of the urban nobility against the Jews; dark clouds were beginning to gather in Aragón, foreboding days of retrogression and deterioration that would end in the persecutions of 1391.

The reign of James I in Aragón was contemporary with that of two kings of Castile–Leon — Ferdinand III the Saint (1217–1252) and Alfonso X the Wise (1252–1284). During James I's conquest of the Balearic Islands (1224–1233) and Valencia (1238), Ferdinand III conquered most of the cities of Andalusia (Córdoba in 1236 and Murcia in 1243) thereby opening an outlet to the Mediterranean that severed the Aragonese advance to the south. Thereafter the military campaigns were Castilian: Jaén in 1246 and Seville in 1248.

After Alfonso's completion of his father's campaigns, there followed a truce of about two hundred years in the Reconquest. During its final campaigns in the reign of Ferdinand and Isabella, Jews did not take part in settling the frontier areas; they were only required to pay a special war tax.

Under Alfonso X known as a lawmaker, continuing the work of Ferdinand III, a code of laws in the spirit of Roman and canon law, was prepared for his country. Called *Las siete partidas* because of its division into seven parts, it went into effect about the middle of the fourteenth century. The prime characteristic of the code was its attempt to organize Spanish society according to the contemporary spirit of Christianity. In the general section of the code (part seven) the regulation requiring modesty of dress applied also to the Jews. The code fixed a maximum rate of interest of 33⅓ percent for loans extended by Jews to Christians; it established the formula of the Jewish oath, but also forbade breaking in to a synagogue. In the fourteenth and fifteenth centuries, the code served as a basis for legal corroboration, but otherwise had little impact on Jewish life. The code was only imperfectly implemented in matters of state appointment and the employment of the services of Jewish physicians. Christians were unhappy with the code because it contained a measure of protection for the Jews. However, the Jewish communities still had the privileges granted to them by Alfonso's predecessors.

Alfonso did not restrict the communal autonomy of Castilian Jewry. The Jewish judiciary remained independent and Jewish judges dispensed justice according to the laws of the Torah. However, the litigants were allowed right of appeal to the king's tribunal. The king also had the right to appoint a Jew as chief justice who would be in charge of Jewish judicial matters in any particular community. He was to act as chief justice of appeals and was known as Rab de la Corte.

Be advised that we (that is, the *kahal* of Barcelona), the *kahal* of Villafranca del Penedès, the *kahal* of Tarragona, and the *kahal* of Montblanch, maintain a common chest and a common purse for the payment of taxes and imposts levied upon us by the crown. Whenever they wish to pass new regulations governing the assessment of taxes either by the tax-assessors or by the submission of memoranda or by individual declaration, to meet the requirements of the king, we do not impose our will upon them, even though we are in the majority and the city is supreme in all matters. If we should take action without their counsel, they would not heed us. Sometimes we send our men to them, and other times their representatives come to us with their resolutions. Only if they fail to do either of these things at our request do we compel them by the arm of the government to come to us or to adopt in their communities the measures that are in force in ours. In other places however the head community decrees for its dependencies and subjects them to its will.

(Solomon b. Abraham Adret, Responsa III No. 411) from Y. Baer, A History of Jews in Christian Spain, Vol. 1. Translated from the Hebrew by Louis Schoffman, Philadelphia, 1961, pp. 216–217.

Drawing of the key given to Ferdinand III by the Jews of Seville to commemorate his conquest of the city (23 Nov. 1248). The tongue of the key reads: *Dios abrirá, Rey entrará* (God opens and the King enters).

THE COLLECTA ORGANIZATION

The Collecta was a regional organization of Jewish communities based on tax districts; its purpose was to create a single, central fund for a group of communities, in which a major community extended its authority over a number of smaller satellites. This organizational structure created a mutual alliance based not only on geographical proximity but on a network of relations between large and small communties. Despite the dependence of the smaller communities, the larger were not always able to impose their will upon the smaller dependencies.

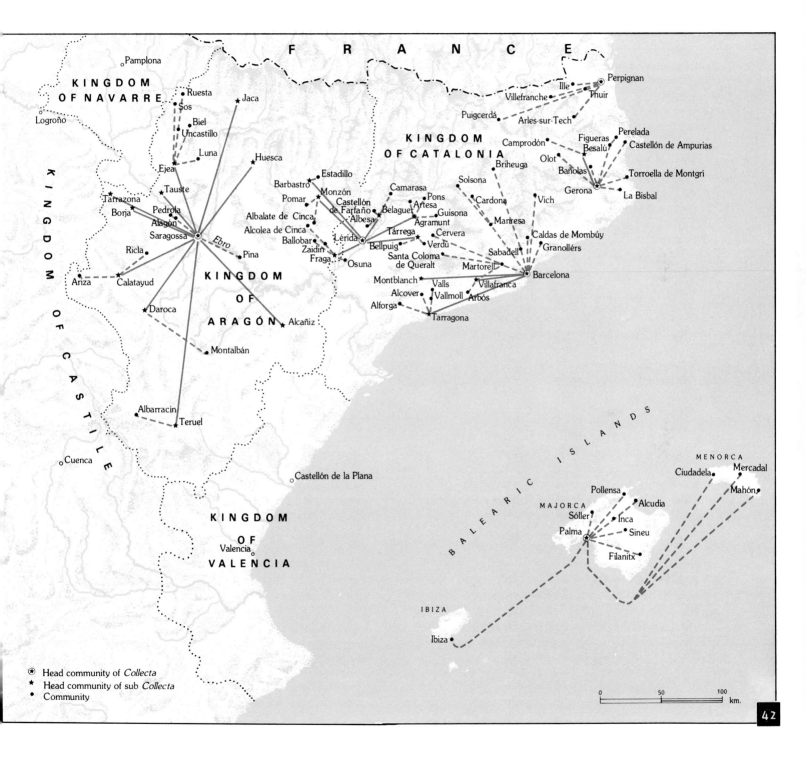

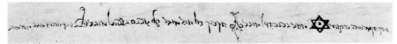

Signature of Jews on a bill of sale from 1248. The Magen David forms part of the witness's signature.

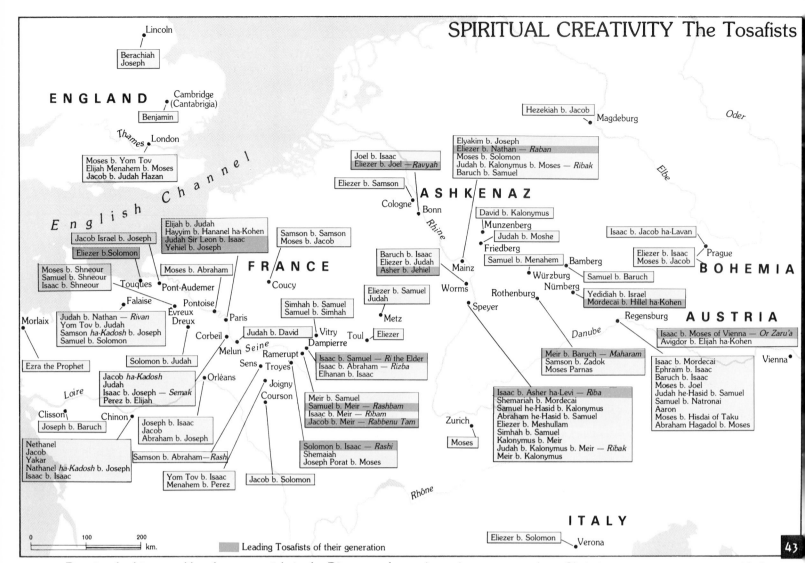

Lincoln
Berachiah
Joseph

E N G L A N D

Cambridge
(Cantabrigia)
Benjamin

Thames London

Moses b. Yom Tov
Elijah Menahem b. Moses
Jacob b. Judah Hazan

Hezekiah b. Jacob — Magdeburg

Oder

Elyakim b. Joseph
Eliezer b. Nathan — Raban
Moses b. Solomon
Judah b. Kalonymus b. Moses — Ribak
Baruch b. Samuel

A S H K E N A Z

Joel b. Isaac
Eliezer b. Joel — Ravyah

Eliezer b. Samson

Cologne Bonn

David b. Kalonymus
Munzenberg
Judah b. Moshe
Friedberg

Isaac b. Jacob ha-Lavan

Elbe

E n g l i s h   C h a n n e l

Jacob Israel b. Joseph
Eliezer b. Solomon

Elijah b. Judah
Hayyim b. Hananel ha-Kohen
Judah Sir Leon b. Isaac
Yehiel b. Joseph

Moses b. Abraham

F R A N C E

Samson b. Samson
Moses b. Jacob

Rhine

Eliezer b. Isaac
Moses b. Jacob

Prague

B O H E M I A

Moses b. Shneour
Samuel b. Shneour
Isaac b. Shneour

Touques

Pont-Audemer

Coucy

Baruch b. Isaac
Eliezer b. Judah
Asher b. Jehiel

Samuel b. Menahem
Bamberg

Mainz
Würzburg
Nürnberg

Samuel b. Baruch

Yedidiah b. Israel
Mordecai b. Hillel ha-Kohen

Morlaix

Falaise

Judah b. Nathan — Rivan
Yom Tov b. Judah
Samson ha-Kadosh b. Joseph
Samuel b. Solomon

Pontoise
Evreux
Dreux

Paris

Eliezer b. Samuel
Judah

Metz

Worms

Speyer

Rothenburg

Danube

Regensburg

A U S T R I A

Isaac b. Moses of Vienna — Or Zaru'a
Avigdor b. Elijah ha-Kohen

Ezra the Prophet

Corbeil

Seine

Melun

Solomon b. Judah

Loire

Jacob ha-Kadosh
Judah
Isaac b. Joseph — Semak
Perez b. Elijah

Orléans

Sens

Ramerupt
Troyes

Vitry
Dampierre

Toul

Eliezer

Judah b. David

Joigny
Courson

Isaac b. Samuel — Ri the Elder
Isaac b. Abraham — Rizba
Elhanan b. Isaac

Meir b. Baruch — Maharam
Samson b. Zadok
Moses Parnas

Isaac b. Mordecai
Ephraim b. Isaac
Baruch b. Isaac
Moses b. Joel
Judah he-Hasid b. Samuel
Samuel b. Natronai
Aaron
Moses b. Hisdai of Taku
Abraham Hagadol b. Moses

Vienna

Clisson
Chinon
Joseph b. Baruch

Joseph b. Isaac
Jacob
Abraham b. Joseph

Meir b. Samuel
Samuel b. Meir — Rashbam
Isaac b. Meir — Ribam
Jacob b. Meir — Rabbenu Tam

Isaac b. Asher ha-Levi — Riba
Shemariah b. Mordecai
Samuel he-Hasid b. Kalonymus
Abraham he-Hasid b. Samuel
Eliezer b. Meshullam
Simhah b. Samuel
Kalonymus b. Meir
Judah b. Kalonymus b. Meir — Ribak
Meir b. Kalonymus

Zurich

Moses

Nethanel
Jacob
Yakar
Nathanel ha-Kadosh b. Joseph
Isaac b. Isaac

Samson b. Abraham — Rash

Yom Tov b. Isaac
Menahem b. Perez

Jacob b. Solomon

Solomon b. Isaac — Rashi
Shemaiah
Joseph Porat b. Moses

Rhône

I T A L Y

Eliezer b. Solomon
Verona

0   100   200   km.

Leading Tosafists of their generation

43

Despite the bitter and burdensome trials in the Diaspora, the spiritual creativity of the Jewish people never ceased. Their spheres of creativity were diverse and their contribution to the world of ideas of the Middle Ages and the subsequent generations was great. In Spain Jews participated in the translation from Arabic to Latin of classical works of philosophy. They thus served as a bridge between the culture of the ancient world and that of the Middle Ages.

The specifically Jewish aspects of this creativity had many facets ranging from biblical exegesis to *kabbalah*. Jewish sages and scholars in various countries added their contribution to the spiritual edifice of the people and in a few European countries, between the eleventh and the fourteenth centuries, their achievements were unique. If one country was famous for having the great Bible commentator, Rashi, another was well known for being the cradle of *kabbalah*, and still another for being the home of philosophical and ethical literature. All these achievements became precious assets of the Jewish people.

An examination of the intellectual climate in which the *tosafot* ("additions," i.e., collections of comments on the Talmud) were compiled reveals similar, scholarly activity in the fields of Latin literature of the Middle Ages, Roman and canon law and Christian biblical exegesis. Despite the differences between and the barrier that separated Jews and Christians, they were nevertheless both affected by the same intellectual climate. They not only confronted one another in religious disputations but also met in order to

learn from one another. Christian commentators were aided by Jews in deciphering difficult biblical passages and the phrase *Hebraeus meus dicit* ("a Jew told me") is frequently found in the writings of Andreas, the pupil of Abelard, in the twelfth century.

Although the *tosafot* were a collective compilation, like the Mishnah and Talmud, nevertheless one can discern different methodologies and local distinctions between France, Germany, England and other places. Rashi's pupils expanded, elaborated, developed and completed his commentary, ushering in a new period of exegesis. The transitional period is represented by Shemaiah of Troyes (Rashi's responsa) and Simhah b. Samuel of Vitry. However, the most significant work was done by Rashi's two sons-in-law: Judah b. Nathan (Rivan), the father of a family of scholars, who checked Rashi's Talmud commentary, added glosses to it and even composed independent commentaries for most of the Talmud tractates. He frequently used the commentaries of the sages of Mainz and did not refrain from criticizing Rashi. The other son-in-law, Meir b. Samuel of Ramerupt, was sometimes known as "the father of the rabbis." (His sons were Samuel b. Meir — Rashbam, Isaac b. Meir and Jacob b. Meir — Rabbenu Tam, who called his father's commentaries *tosafot*.)

These sages witnessed the persecutions and massacres of French Jewry during the crusades and their expulsion from Île de France in 1182. It was they who issued the call to immigrate to the Holy Land. In the towns of France and Ashkenaz they attracted many pupils who then continued their method of learning and it is, therefore, not surprising that Moses b. Jacob of Coucy was able to compile his monumental work *Sefer Mitzvot Gadol* (*Se Ma G*) which became a basic reference book for the study of the *halakhah*.

The works of the tosafists reached Bohemia; pupils from Prague (Eliezer b. Isaac and Isaac b. Jacob ha-Lavan — brother of the famous traveler, Pehthahiah of Regensburg) came to Ramerupt to study with Rabbenu Tam. Some of these scholars were active in Ashkenaz and others in Bohemia and Russia. The tosafist Peter b. Joseph of Carinthia in Austria participated in editing *Sefer ha-Yashar* by his teacher, Rabbenu Tam, adding his own glosses. He died a martyr during the Second Crusade. In Hungary there were two tosafists: Abraham the Proselyte and his son Isaac the Proselyte.

Ramerupt, Regensburg and Dampierre were important tosafist centers, the Regensburg school having such scholars as Joel b. Isaac ha-Levi and his son Eliezer b. Joel ha-Levi (known as Ravyah). The head of the school in Dampierre was Isaac b. Abraham (known as Rizba), who was a grandson of Samson b. Joseph of Falaise and had been privileged to study with Rabbenu Tam. The Rizba was a great halakhist and rabbinical judge (*posek*), whose decisions were accepted by scholars of many generations. Among those who sought his opinion on aspects of Jewish law was Jonathan b. David ha-Kohen of Lunel, an admirer of Maimonides (Rambam). The Rizba was probably familiar with the Rambam's writings, since he was the recipient of one of the letters sent by Meir b. Todros Abulafia of Toledo to the rabbis of southern France regarding the Rambam's doctrine of resurrection. His younger brother was Samson b. Abraham of Sens who was particularly noted for his commentary on several orders of the Mishnah and for his use of the Jerusalem Talmud as a source for halakhic decisions. Little is known of his life but his literary legacy is greater than that of the other tosafists. The bulk of his work has been preserved in his own language and not reworked by his pupils. He emerges from his work as a great scholar whose world was steeped in the *halakhah*.

After Samson of Sens immigrated to the Holy Land at the beginning of the thirteenth century, Paris became the center of Torah study in northern France. Its school was headed by Judah b. Isaac (known as Judah Sir Leon of Paris, 1166–1224), pupil and relative of Isaac b. Samuel of Dampierre (known as Ha-Zaken). The school was closed in 1182, when the Jews were expelled from the kingdom of France by King Philip II Augustus, but was reopened in 1198, when the Jews were allowed to return. Jehiel of Paris, Moses of Coucy and Isaac of Vienna studied and were active in this school. Asher b. Jehiel (Rosh, 1250–1327) was an outstanding scholar and leader of German Jewry, who, in 1303, left Germany for Spain to take up a position as rabbi in Toledo. He introduced the system of study of Ashkenazic tosafists into Spain.

Jewish creativity in France declined after the Disputation of Paris (1240) and the burning of the Talmud (1242). With the destruction of the French Jewish villages and their expulsion in 1306, this great spiritual achievement came to an end.

The Ashkenazic Hasidic movement developed in Germany during the twelfth and thirteenth centuries. Samuel b. Kalonymus he-Hasid of Speyer and his son Judah he-Hasid of Regensburg (c. 1150–1217) were the founders of the movement and their most important work was *Sefer Hasidim*, a book of pragmatic true-to-life ethical teachings which reflect the contemporary life of German Jewry in their Christian environment. The book preaches spiritual revival and instructs the pious on avoiding sin and on leading a righteous life that will ensure his salvation in the life to come. Various weltanschauungen are expressed in the book and scholars believe that some of these were influenced by ideas prevalent in the area; even the languages of the text, German and French, indicate such influences. The Hasid, the protagonist, is portrayed as the ideal — in his conduct, his full Jewish life, and in his relations with his Christian neighbors. While he is fully aware of the grim realities which surround his people, he is called upon to bear the burden of the community and lead it along the true path.

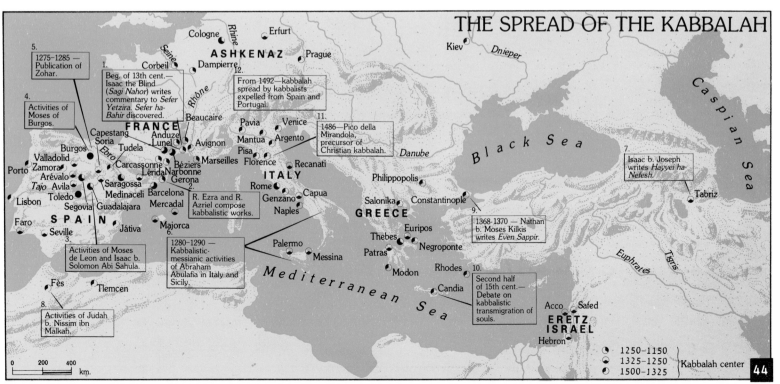

THE SPREAD OF THE KABBALAH

5. 1275–1285 — Publication of Zohar.

1. Beg. of 13th cent.— Isaac the Blind (*Sagi Nahor*) writes commentary to *Sefer Yetzira*. *Sefer ha-Bahir* discovered.

12. From 1492—kabbalah spread by kabbalists expelled from Spain and Portugal.

4. Activities of Moses of Burgos.

11. 1486—Pico della Mirandola, precursor of Christian kabbalah.

7. Isaac b. Joseph writes *Hayyei ha-Nefesh*.

2. R. Ezra and R. Azriel compose kabbalistic works.

9. 1368-1370 — Nathan b. Moses Kilkis writes *Even Sappir*.

3. Activities of Moses de Leon and Isaac b. Solomon Abi Sahula.

6. 1280-1290 — Kabbalistic-messianic activities of Abraham Abulafia in Italy and Sicily.

10. Second half of 15th cent.— Debate on kabbalistic transmigration of souls.

8. Activities of Judah b. Nissim ibn Malkah.

ASHKENAZ — FRANCE — ITALY — GREECE — SPAIN — ERETZ ISRAEL — Mediterranean Sea — Black Sea — Caspian Sea

- 1250–1150
- 1325–1250
- 1500–1325
Kabbalah center

44

THE SPREAD OF THE KABBALAH

Jewish mysticism in its various guises was another manifestation of spiritual creativity. It was rooted in theosophy as expressed by the creation, the revealed Shekhinah and the promised redemption in time to come. The Kabbalah with all its social and historical implications for the people of Israel, held a special place among all the mystical philosophies. A prolific literature created a world of values which found expression in *Sefer ha-Zohar*, the greatest book of Kabbalah, and in the literature which developed around it, for example, *Tikkunei Zohar* and *Ra'aya Meheimna* ("The Faithful Shepherd"). At the beginning of the thirteenth century, kabbalistic works flourished in southern France and northeastern Spain, eventually spreading even beyond the Spanish border. According to Isaac b. Samuel of Acre, who arrived in Spain in 1305, *Sefer ha-Zohar* was written by Moses de Leon between 1275 and 1285.

Kabbalistic literature gives further expression to a protest against the moral decline in a Jewish society which must mend its ways, as *Sefer ha-Zohar*, *Tikkunei ha-Zohar* and *Ra'aya Meheimna* do. In this literature, with its wealth of symbols, Jewish sages sought solutions to the problems of *galut* (being dispersed in the Diaspora), apprehension of the Shekhinah and even practical instruction on hastening the redemption (see Map 86 for details of the Lurianic Kabbalah in Safed of the seventeenth century).

Two pages from a compendium of religious laws from the Rashi school, c. 13th century.

THE MAIMONIDEAN CONTROVERSY

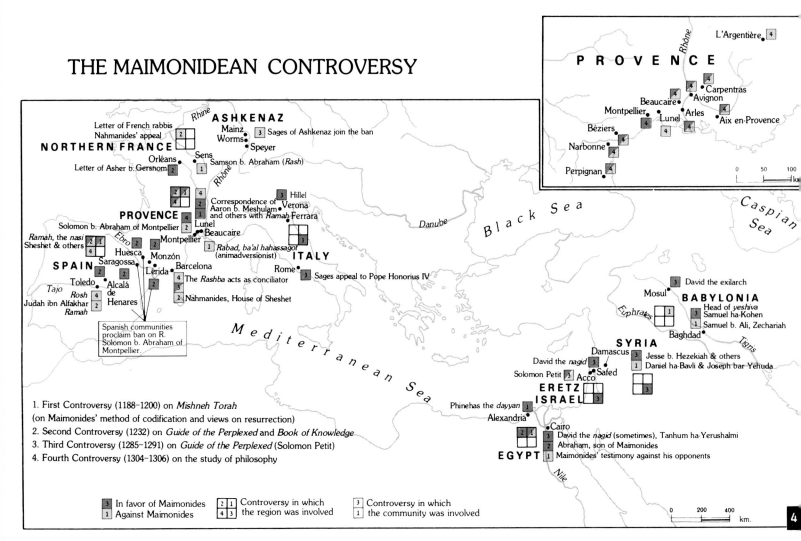

PROVENCE (inset map)
L'Argentière · Carpentras · Avignon · Beaucaire · Montpellier · Lunel · Arles · Aix en-Provence · Béziers · Narbonne · Perpignan

ASHKENAZ
Mainz · Worms · Speyer · Sens · Orléans
Letter of French rabbis / Nahmanides' appeal
Sages of Ashkenaz join the ban
Samson b. Abraham (*Rash*)
Letter of Asher b. Gershom

NORTHERN FRANCE

PROVENCE
Solomon b. Abraham of Montpellier
Correspondence of Aaron b. Meshulam and others with *Ramah*
Hillel · Verona · Ferrara
Lunel · Beaucaire · Montpellier

SPAIN
Ramah, the *nasi* Sheshet & others
Huesca · Monzón · Saragossa · Lérida · Barcelona
Toledo · Alcalá de Henares
Rosh · Judah ibn Alfakhar · *Ramah*
Spanish communities proclaim ban on R. Solomon b. Abraham of Montpellier
Rabad, ba'al hahassagot (animadversionist)

ITALY
Rome
The *Rashba* acts as conciliator
Nahmanides, House of Sheshet
Sages appeal to Pope Honorius IV

Black Sea · Caspian Sea · Danube · Mediterranean Sea

BABYLONIA
David the exilarch · Mosul
Head of *yeshiva* Samuel ha-Kohen
Samuel b. Ali, Zechariah · Baghdad

SYRIA
Damascus · Safed · Acco
David the *nagid*
Solomon Petit
Jesse b. Hezekiah & others
Daniel ha-Bavli & Joseph bar Yehuda

ERETZ ISRAEL
Phinehas the *dayyan* · Alexandria

EGYPT
Cairo
David the *nagid* (sometimes), Tanhum ha-Yerushalmi
Abraham, son of Maimonides
Maimonides' testimony against his opponents

1. First Controversy (1188–1200) on *Mishneh Torah*
(on Maimonides' method of codification and views on resurrection)
2. Second Controversy (1232) on *Guide of the Perplexed* and *Book of Knowledge*
3. Third Controversy (1285–1291) on *Guide of the Perplexed* (Solomon Petit)
4. Fourth Controversy (1304–1306) on the study of philosophy

In favor of Maimonides / Against Maimonides
Controversy in which the region was involved
Controversy in which the community was involved

Drawing of a personal seal belonging to Nahmanides, found in 1972 near Acre. The text reads: *Moshe b'Rabbi Nahman, Nuah Nefesh, Gerondi Hazak* Moses the son of Rabbi Nahman of restful soul the Gerundian Be Strong!

The writings and activities of Moses b. Maimon (Rambam, 1135–1204) encompassed all aspects of contemporary Jewish life, extending even beyond his lifetime and domicile.

The range of his writings was wide and varied, covering commentaries, *halakhah* (*Mishneh Torah*), medicine, responsa, epistles, philosophy and science. In the *Guide of the Perplexed* he attempted to formulate a complete philosophical system for the interpretation of Jewish scripture. The book set out to grapple with the weltanschauungen of both Christianity and Islam and the threat they posed to the spiritual and physical survival of the Jewish people.

The Rambam's halakhic approach and his views on resurrection caused a furious controversy which almost divided the Jewish people, lasting about a hundred years and which engulfed Jews in the east and west, in Islamic countries and in Christian Europe.

The four controversies associated with the Rambam's methods, philosophy and writings, were in fact merely stages in an ongoing polemic which emerged during the Rambam's lifetime, at the end of the twelfth century. The first controversy arose from reservations regarding the *Mishneh Torah*, the Rambam's system of defining *halakhot*, and his views on resurrection. The second (1232) was associated with the *Guide of the Perplexed* and *Sefer ha-Madda*; in the third (end of the thirteenth century), an attempt was made to ban the *Guide*; while the fourth dealt with the study of philosophy, with the Rambam's writings assuming a secondary role. The second controversy was the bitterest polemic, occurring at a time when there were spiritual and religious conflicts in Christianity and Islam as well. (In those days a savage crusade was taking place in southern France against the Albigensian heretics.) This second controversy, in which the greatest Jewish scholars of the age were involved, had far-reaching ramifications regarding the nature of Jewish education. In 1232, Solomon b. Abraham of Montpellier and his two pupils David b. Saul and Jonah b. Abraham Gerondi with the support of the rabbis of northern France issued a ban on the study of the Rambam's philosophical works. A counterban against Solomon of Montpellier and his pupils was issued in the summer of 1232 by the Aragonese *aljamas* (communities) and David Kimhi, a pro-Maimonist, tried to enlist support from the elders of Toledo for this counterban. Nahmanides attempted to reach a compromise by proposing an educational program for the study of the philosophical writings geared to different age groups and communities. His prime concern was to avoid a schism in Jewry. One of the consequences of this polemic was the drawing of the papal Inquisition's attention to Jewish religious matters and writings.

The third controversy involved a number of Jewish sages from the Islamic countries. Solomon b. Samuel (Petit), one of the important kabbalists in Acre, tried to revive the ban on the *Guide of the Perplexed* by enlisting the support of rabbis in Ashkenaz, France and Italy. He failed, arousing the opposition of the heads of the community of Damascus and Mosul, and that of the *nagid* David b. Abraham, the grandson of the Rambam. In Italy, Hillel b. Samuel of Verona (c. 1220–c. 1295), and in Spain, Solomon b. Abraham Adret (Rashba) tried to mediate between the antagonists.

The last controversy occurred at the beginning of the fourteenth century in Provence and Spain. Abba Mari of Montpellier (b. Moses b. Joseph of Lunel) induced the Rashba to issue a ban on the study of science and metaphysics by anyone under twenty-five years of age. The Rambam's writings were not specifically mentioned in the ban and gradually the polemic abated.

Autographed responsum of Maimonides.

Statue of Maimonides in the Tiberias Plaza in Córdoba.

HEBREW MANUSCRIPTS OF ASHKENAZ, FRANCE AND SPAIN

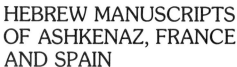

Illuminated page of prayer for Yom Kippur in second volume of Worms Mahzor, Germany, c.1270.

In various Jewish communities scribes were engaged in copying books required for study and reference. The profession developed as patrons employed scribes to copy books especially for them.

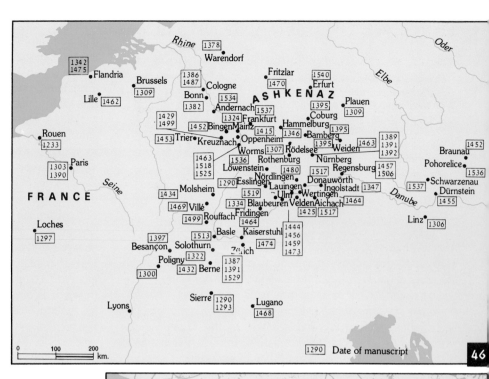

ASHKENAZ / FRANCE

Warendorf 1378
Flandria 1342 1475
Brussels 1386 1487
Cologne 1309
Lille 1462
Bonn 1382
Andernach 1534
Bingen 1452
Frankfurt 1324
Mainz 1415
Trier 1453
Kreuznach
Worms 1307
Oppenheim
Rödelsee
Rothenburg
Nürnberg 1480
Regensburg 1517
Fritzlar
Erfurt 1540 1470
Plauen 1395
Coburg 1309
Hammelburg 1346
Bamberg 1395
Weiden 1463 1391 1392
Braunau 1452
Pohorelice
Schwarzenau 1536
Dürnstein 1537
Linz 1306
Rouen 1233
Paris 1303 1390
Worms 1463 1518 1525
Löwenstein 1536
Esslingen 1290
Nördlingen 1519
Lauingen
Ulm
Velden 1457 1506
Donauwörth
Ingolstadt 1347
Wertingen
Aichach 1464
Molsheim 1434
Villé 1469
Rouffach 1499
Fridingen 1334
Blaubeuren 1464
Basle 1513
Kaiserstuhl
Zürich 1474
Besançon 1397
Solothurn
Poligny 1322
Berne 1432
Sierre 1290 1293
Lugano 1468
Lyons
Loches 1297
1444 1456 1459 1473
Berne 1387 1391 1529
Poligny 1300

1290 Date of manuscript

SPAIN / PORTUGAL / PROVENCE

La Rochelle 1215 1216
Lyons 1386
Taillebourg 1279
Crest 1296
Tallard 1304
Sisteron 1433
Provence
1337 1389 1437
Digne 1296 1310
Lalbenque 1340
Orange 1284 1323 1331 1395
Avignon 1390
Tarascon
L'Isle 1343
Montpellier 1386
Cavaillon
Arles 1202 1291 1295 1418 1431 1454 1467
Salon
Trets 1369
Revel 1476
Mèze
Marseilles 1336 1332
1406 1466
Narbonne 1282
1299 1355
Perpignan 1378 1391 1395 1396 1397 1406 1416 1419 1429 1453 1467 1487
Tarascon 1408
La Coruña 1299 1471 1477
Miño 1342
Lugo 1383
Agra 1207
Feás 1442
Maceda
Laguna de Negrillos
Aguilar de Campóo 1454
Villadiego 1476 1481 1491
Burgos 1480 1483 1487
Fromista
Benavente
Villalón de Campos 1485
Valladolid 1436 1457
Zamora
Almeida 1484 1494
San Felices de los Galiegos 1471
Salamanca 1462 1483 1516
Alba 1487
Guarda
Almeida 1484 1494
Seia 1346
Béjar 1461 1477
Echalar 1442 1491
Miranda 1463
Pamplona 1403
Villadiego 1381
Uncastillo 1289
Tudela 1284 1304 1306 1312
Tarazona 1207 1260 1272 1488
Soria 1449
Peñafiel 1480
Montemayor de Pililla 1458 1479
Medina del Campo 1463
Segovia
Buitrago 1467
Huete 1470 1487 1491
Avila 1478 1482 1487 1491
Guadalajara 1483
Alcalá de Henares 1470
Santa Olalla
Maqueda 1470 1484
Ocaña 1491
Toledo 1191 1222 1239 1241 1256 1260 1272 1277 1300 1307 1334 1346 1355 1364 1366 1381 1477 1480 1492
Huesca 1472
Monzón 1474
Saragossa 1329
Albalate de Cinca 1444
Agramunt
Camprodón 1384 1388
Perelada
Castellón de Ampurias
Gerona 1184 1188 1305 1348 1396
Solsona 1408
Cervera 1299 1347
Barcelona 1264 1278 1325 1347 1368 1380
Tarragona 1311
Tortosa 1484
La Almunia 1397
Calatayud 1379 1461 1469 1471 1474 1475 1476
Pina 1473
Alcolea de Cinca 1400
Alcarrás 1383
Falset 1347
Almazán 1489
Albalate 1263 1341 1355 1495
Alcañiz 1408
Calaceite 1455
Teruel 1491
Soria 1481
Porto 1496
Almeida 1436 1457
Leiria 1478
Castelo Branco 1494
Trujillo 1360
Torres Vedras 1398
Lisbon 1278 1409 1469 1470 1473 1475 1482 1484 1487 1489 1490 1495
Setúbal 1390
Elvas 1467
Évora 1494
Badajoz 1483
Berlanga 1455
Beja
Moura 1470
Córdoba
Montemayor 1489
Seville
Lucena
Almagro 1483
Alcaraz 1400
Úbeda 1290
Agramón 1444
Fortuna 1509
Murcia 1333
Cúllar de Baza
Granada 1349 1435 1479 1480
Valencia 1290
Játiva 1481
Benitachell 1483
MAJORCA 1332 1352
Faro 1481 1489
Málaga 1472
1340 1386 1454 1466 1468 1471 1472 1474
Beja 1284
Guarda 1524 1393 1275
Huesca 1300
Tauste 1409 1352 1356 1404

MEDITERRANEAN SEA

46

47

THE JEWS OF ENGLAND UP TO THE EXPULSION

The history of the Jews in England in the thirteenth century can be described as one of persecutions and oppression by the state and the population at large. The state and the English church had, from the beginning, intended to convert the Jewish community to Christianity and for this purpose a home for converted Jews (*domus conversorum*) was established in London in 1232.

The tax policy toward the Jews was one of merciless exploitation. King Edward I (1272–1307) approved the church's attempts at converting Jews. Many towns expelled the Jews, while others received priviliges permitting them "not to tolerate Jews." (Leicester was the first to receive such a privilege in 1231.) The Jews moved to towns owned by Edward I after being expelled in 1275 by Eleanor, the queen mother, from the towns in her possession. However, local expulsions did not cease.

In 1275 Edward I issued a decree, *Statutum de Judaismo*, in which he endeavored to change the occupations of his Jewish subjects from moneylending and usury to crafts and agriculture. The attempt failed because by that time the Jewish community was completely impoverished. Pressured by the townspeople he ordered the *archae* (chirograph chests) containing records of their debts to the Jews to be closed. It soon became clear that there was nothing left to extort from the Jews.

On 18 July 1290 Edward issued an edict for the banishment of the Jews from England by the beginning of November. The Jews were allowed to take only their personal possessions; the rest of their property was confiscated. To replace the loss of income the crown was authorized by parliament to levy a tithe on ecclesiastical property and a 15 percent tax on the property of the nobles and citizens. These taxes were but a pittance in comparison to those paid by Jews a hundred years earlier. The number of Jews expelled has been estimated at four thousand, most of them going to France and Ashkenaz.

A Hebrew quitclaim of Jose son of Elias, Jose son of Moses, and Judah the Frenchman. H. Loewe, Starrs and Jewish Charters Preserved in the British Museum, London 1932, Plate IX.

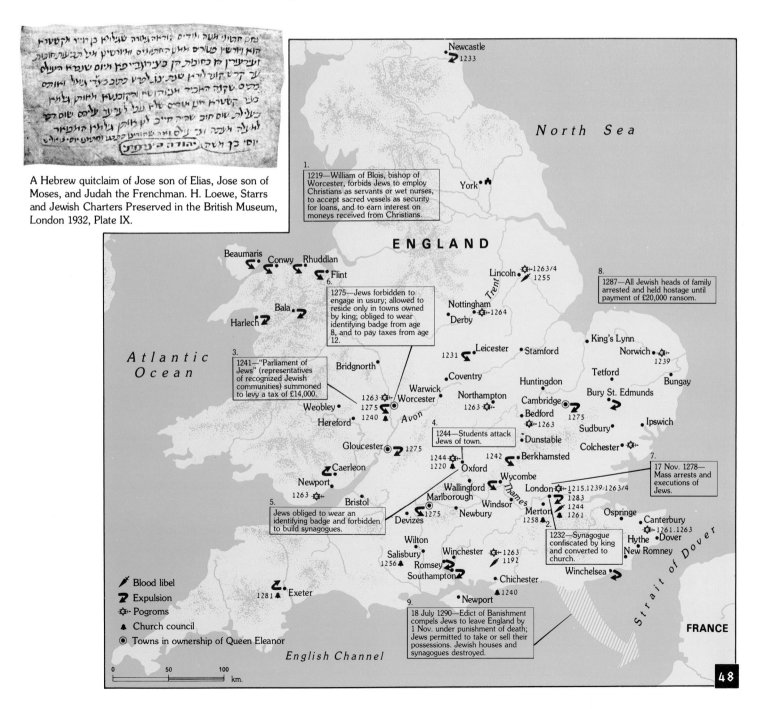

1. 1219—William of Blois, bishop of Worcester, forbids Jews to employ Christians as servants or wet nurses, to accept sacred vessels as security for loans, and to earn interest on moneys received from Christians.

8. 1287—All Jewish heads of family arrested and held hostage until payment of £20,000 ransom.

2. 1275—Jews forbidden to engage in usury; allowed to reside only in towns owned by king; obliged to wear identifying badge from age 8, and to pay taxes from age 12.

3. 1241—"Parliament of Jews" (representatives of recognized Jewish communities) summoned to levy a tax of £14,000.

4. 1244—Students attack Jews of town.

7. 17 Nov. 1278—Mass arrests and executions of Jews.

5. Jews obliged to wear an identifying badge and forbidden to build synagogues.

2. 1232—Synagogue confiscated by king and converted to church.

9. 18 July 1290—Edict of Banishment compels Jews to leave England by 1 Nov. under punishment of death; Jews permitted to take or sell their possessions. Jewish houses and synagogues destroyed.

Legend:
- ✗ Blood libel
- ⇗ Expulsion
- ✡ Pogroms
- ▲ Church council
- ◉ Towns in ownership of Queen Eleanor

North Sea
ENGLAND
Atlantic Ocean
FRANCE
English Channel
Strait of Dover

0   50   100 km.

48

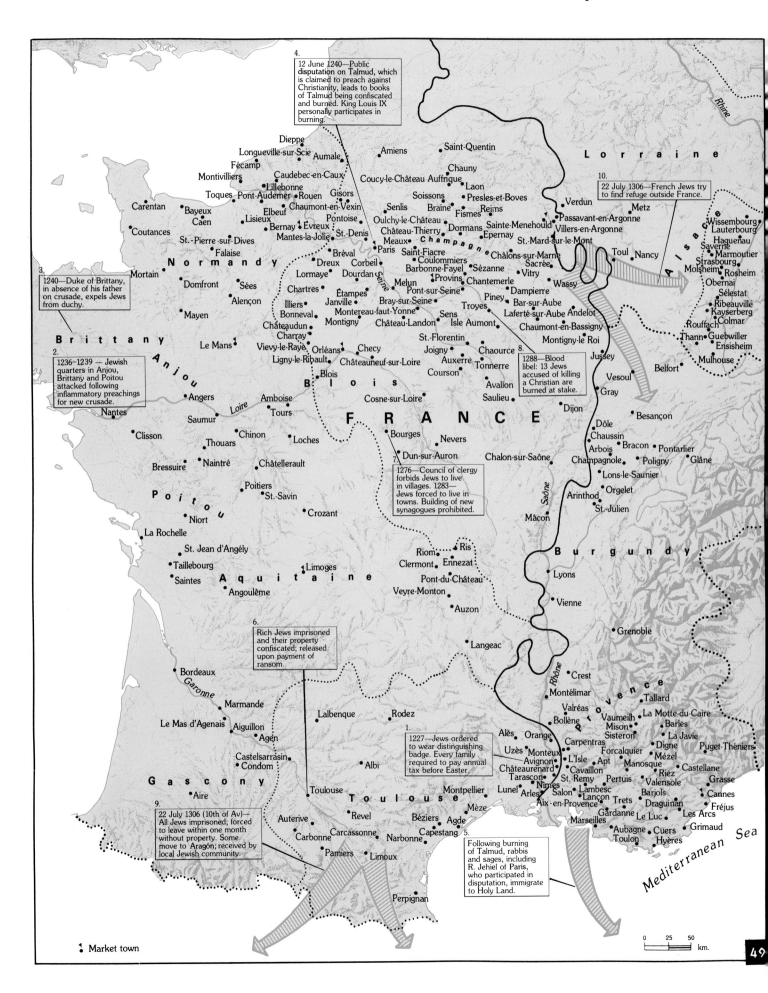

THE JEWISH COMMUNITIES OF FRANCE Thirteenth Century

4. 12 June 1240—Public disputation on Talmud, which is claimed to preach against Christianity, leads to books of Talmud being confiscated and burned. King Louis IX personally participates in burning.

10. 22 July 1306—French Jews try to find refuge outside France.

3. 1240—Duke of Brittany, in absence of his father on crusade, expels Jews from duchy.

2. 1236–1239 — Jewish quarters in Anjou, Brittany and Poitou attacked following inflammatory preachings for new crusade.

8. 1288—Blood libel: 13 Jews accused of killing a Christian are burned at stake.

7. 1276—Council of clergy forbids Jews to live in villages. 1283—Jews forced to live in towns. Building of new synagogues prohibited.

6. Rich Jews imprisoned and their property confiscated; released upon payment of ransom.

1. 1227—Jews ordered to wear distinguishing badge. Every family required to pay annual tax before Easter.

9. 22 July 1306 (10th of Av)— All Jews imprisoned; forced to leave within one month without property. Some move to Aragón; received by local Jewish community.

5. Following burning of Talmud, rabbis and sages, including R. Jehiel of Paris, who participated in disputation, immigrate to Holy Land.

Lorraine

Alsace

Rhine

Champagne

Normandy

Brittany

Anjou

Blois

FRANCE

Poitou

Aquitaine

Burgundy

Saône

Rhône

Provence

Gascony

Garonne

Toulouse

Mediterranean Sea

Dieppe · Longueville-sur-Scie · Aumale · Amiens · Saint-Quentin · Chauny · Coucy-le-Château Auffrique · Laon · Verdun · Metz · Wissembourg · Lauterbourg
Fécamp · Caudebec-en-Caux · Montivilliers · Lillebonne · Soissons · Presles-et-Boves · Reims · Passavant-en-Argonne · Villers-en-Argonne · Haguenau · Saverne · Marmoutier
Toques · Pont-Audemer · Rouen · Gisors · Senlis · Braine · Fismes · Sainte-Menehould · Epernay · St.-Mard-sur-le-Mont · Strasbourg · Molsheim · Rosheim
Carentan · Bayeux · Chaumont-en-Vexin · Pontoise · Oulchy-le-Château · Château-Thierry · Dormans · St.-Mard-sur-le-Mont · Toul · Nancy · Obernai
Coutances · Caen · Elbeuf · Lisieux · Bernay · Evreux · St.-Denis · Meaux · Paris · Saint-Fiacre · Châlons-sur-Marne · Sélestat
St.-Pierre-sur-Dives · Mantes-la-Jolie · Bréval · Coulommiers · Sacrée · Vitry · Ribeauvillé · Kayserberg · Colmar
Mortain · Falaise · Dreux · Corbeil · Barbonne-Fayel · Sézanne · Wassy · Rouffach · Thann · Guebwiller
Domfront · Sées · Lormaye · Chartres · Dourdan · Melun · Provins · Chantemerle · Dampierre · Bar-sur-Aube · Andelot · Ensisheim
Mayen · Alençon · Illiers · Janville · Etampes · Pont-sur-Seine · Troyes · Piney · Laferté-sur-Aube · Chaumont-en-Bassigny · Jussey · Mulhouse
Bonneval · Montereau-faut-Yonne · Bray-sur-Seine · Sens · Isle Aumont · Montigny-le-Roi
Châteaudun · Montigny · Château-Landon · St.-Florentin · Chaource · Belfort
Le Mans · Charray · Vievy-le-Rayé · Orléans · Checy · Joigny · Auxerre · Tonnerre · Vesoul
Ligny-le-Ribault · Châteauneuf-sur-Loire · Courson · Avallon · Dijon · Gray
Blois · Cosne-sur-Loire · Saulieu · Besançon
Angers · Amboise · Dôle · Chaussin · Bracon · Pontarlier
Saumur · Tours · Bourges · Nevers · Chalon-sur-Saône · Arbois · Champagnole · Poligny · Glâne
Clisson · Chinon · Loches · Dun-sur-Auron · Lons-le-Saunier · Orgelet
Thouars · Arinthod · St.-Julien
Bressuire · Naintré · Châtellerault · Mâcon
Poitiers · St.-Savin
Niort · Crozant
La Rochelle · Riom · Ris
St. Jean d'Angély · Clermont · Ennezat · Lyons
Taillebourg · Limoges · Pont-du-Château
Saintes · Angoulême · Veyre-Monton · Vienne
Auzon · Grenoble
Langeac
Bordeaux · Crest · Montélimar · Tallard
Marmande · Lalbenque · Rodez · Valréas · Vaumeilh · Mison · La Motte-du-Caire · Barles
Le Mas d'Agenais · Aiguillon · Bollène · Sisteron · Digne · La Javie
Agen · Alès · Orange · Carpentras · Forcalquier · Mézel · Puget-Théniers
Castelsarrasin · Condom · Uzès · Monteux · Avignon · L'Isle · Apt · Manosque · Riez · Castellane
Albi · Châteaurenard · Cavaillon · Pertuis · Valensole · Grasse
Aire · St. Remy · Nîmes · Salon · Lambesc · Lançon · Trets · Draguignan · Cannes
Toulouse · Montpellier · Lunel · Arles · Aix-en-Provence · Barjols · Le Luc · Les Arcs · Fréjus
Revel · Béziers · Mèze · Gardanne · Grimaud
Auterive · Agde · Marseilles · Aubagne · Cuers · Hyères
Carbonne · Carcassonne · Narbonne · Capestang · Toulon
Pamiers · Limoux
Perpignan

Market town

0 25 50 km.

49

Thirteenth-century France underwent a process of centralization and the increased power of the king caused a worsening in the condition of the Jews. The years 1236 to 1239 were characterized by a revival of anti-Jewish feeling together with preachings for a new crusade. Jewish quarters in Anjou, Poitou and Brittany were attacked, prompting an order from Pope Gregory IX in 1236 to the bishops of France to denounce the assaults, despite his usually unfavorable attitude toward the Jews.

The expulsion of the Jews from England made a profound impression in France. Philip IV the Fair ordered the expulsion of the Jews in 1291 and again on 6 June 1299, but his orders were not implemented. The crown forbade the expelled Jews from Gascony (an English possession) and England to enter France and, judging by Philip's policies and extortionary methods, Jewish expulsion from France was inevitable. Thus in 1306 Philip ordered their expulsion from all districts under his control. This order and its purpose were similar to the expulsion of 1182, except that in 1182 it was ordered by a boy king (Philip Augustus) who depended upon irresponsible advisers, while in 1306 it was a well-calculated decision. The 1182 expulsion encompassed a relatively small area of France while that of 1306 covered all the areas of the king's domain, which was most of France. Philip the Fair hoped to achieve great financial gain from the expulsion of the Jews and the seizure of their property.

A small number of those expelled moved to Gascony while the majority were welcomed by the kingdoms of Aragón (including Provence) and Navarre (Barcelona took in sixty families). In 1315 they were allowed to return, only to be finally expelled in 1394.

King David, from an illuminated manuscript, eastern France, 1280.

THE RINDFLEISCH MASSACRES 1298

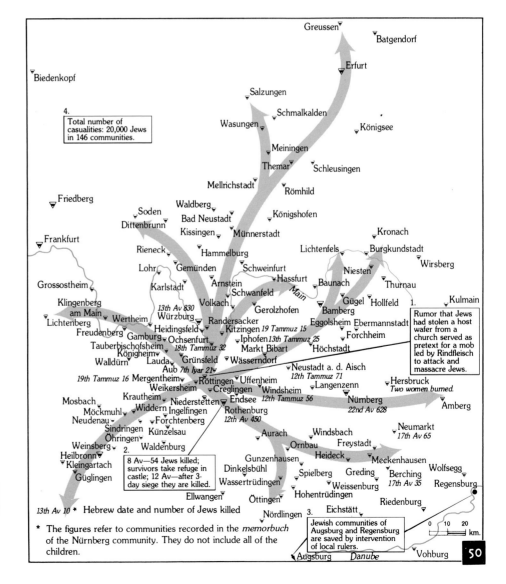

4.

Total number of casualities: 20,000 Jews in 146 communities.

1.

Rumor that Jews had stolen a host wafer from a church served as pretext for a mob led by Rindfleisch to attack and massacre Jews.

2.

8 Av—54 Jews killed; survivors take refuge in castle; 12 Av—after 3-day siege they are killed.

3.

Jewish communities of Augsburg and Regensburg are saved by intervention of local rulers.

13th Av 10 * Hebrew date and number of Jews killed

* The figures refer to communities recorded in the *memorbuch* of the Nürnberg community. They do not include all of the children.

0 10 20
km.

50

Depictions of Jewish figures of the 13th century.

PERSECUTIONS IN ASHKENAZ
Thirteenth and Fourteenth Centuries

During the second half of the thirteenth century anti-Jewish propaganda seriously affected the Jewish communities in Germany. On 20 April 1298 a massacre instigated by a host-desecration libel spread from the Franconian town of Röttingen to many other areas. The inflamed mob, led by a German knight called Rindfleisch, went from town to town inciting the population of Franconia, Swabia, Hesse and Thuringia to slaughter the Jews. This they did with extreme cruelty, destroying entire Jewish communities. Among those killed in Nürnberg were Rabbi Mordecai b. Hillel and his family.

Between 1336 and 1339 a group of lawless German bands known as Armleder (so-called after the leather armpiece they wore) attacked Jewish communities in Franconia and Alsace leaving slaughter and destruction behind them. Of particular note was the massacre of Jews in the communities of Rouffach, Ensisheim, Ribeauvillé and Mülhausen (Mulhouse). In Colmar the local population massacred the Jews. When the Armleder began to menace the general peace and security, a number of towns concluded a ten-year armistice with John Zimberlin, one of the Armleder leaders in Alsace.

The local authorities tried to restore calm by concluding additional agreements in the Rhine and other areas but the armistice was shortlived. The Armleder massacres were portents of and preludes to the destruction of European Jewry during the Black Death.

1. 1287—Rumors of Jews torturing child called Werner the Good to death and subsequently light radiating from his body result in mass pilgrimage and massacre of Jews. 1288—Emperor Rudolph orders body of child burned.

6. 16 May 1338—Emperor Ludwig orders burghers of Limburg to receive expelled Jews, return their property and protect them.

2. 29–31 July 1336—Christian mobs called *Judenschlaeger* (Jew-killers) attack Jews; massacres spread to other districts.

3. 30 Sept. 1337—Desecration of host accusation instigates massacre of Jews, seizure of property and burning of houses. 4 Oct. 1337—Heinrich, Duke of Bavaria, approves burning of houses; cancels Christian debts to Jews and authorizes retention of seized Jewish property.

5. 23 Apr. 1338—Following discovery of host wafer in Jewish home, Christians kill all Jews in nearby towns.

4. 1337–1338—Judenschlaeger join Armleder bands in sweep through Alsace. Many Jews take refuge in Colmar but are besieged by *Armleder*. Emperor Ludwig of Bavaria routs bands, who later return and renew siege. 1339—Armistice concluded with Armleder.

7. Armleder massacres result in death of 5,000 Jews from 100 communities.

0   50   100
km.

MASSACRES IN THE RHINE DISTRICTS

Emmerich
Kleve
Rees
Goch
Wesel
Xanten
Rheinberg
Dinslaken
Geldern
Mülheim a.d. Ruhr
Essen
Dortmund
Kempen
Duisburg
Iserlohn
Ruhr
Dülken
Uerdingen
Kaiserswerth
Wolfhagen
ladbach
Neuss
assenberg
Wevelinghoven
Erkelenz
Dormagen
krevenbroich
Monheim
Rödingen
Kaster
Stommeln
Bergheim
Mülheim
Jülich
Lövenich
Idenhoven
Cologne (Köln)
Düren
Kerpen
Biedenkopf
Lechenich
Siegburg
Siegen
Nideggen
Brühl
Bonn
Beuel
Sieg
Zülpich
Heimerzheim
Münstereifel
Euskirchen
Königswinter
Hachenburg
Marburg
Remagen
Linz am Rhein
Westerburg
Giessen
Gerolstein
Ahrweiler
Altenahr
Sinzig
Heinbach
Grünberg
Andernach
Siershahn
Wetzlar
Münzenberg
Mayen
Kobern
Koblenz
Montabaur
Nidda
Münstermaifeld
Diez
Limburg
Weilnau
Friedberg
Alken
Braubach
Assenheim
Büdingen
Cochem
Ehrenburg
Kamp
Gelnhausen
Karden
Boppard
Königstein
Kronberg
Mülheim
Beilstein
Oberwesel
Kaub
Frankfurt
Hanau
Krov
Bacharach
Lorch
Eltville
Offenbach
Steinheim
Wittlich
Trarbach
Rheinböllen
Mainz
Seligenstadt
Aschaffenburg
Bernkastel
Kirchberg
Bingen
Babenhausen
Neumagen
Bretzenheim
Langenlonsheim
Grossostheim
Trier
Kirn
Sobernheim
Kreuznach
Oppenheim
Dieburg
Obermoschel
Lichtenberg
Klingenberg am Main
Saarburg
Alzey
Bensheim
Freudenberg
Rockenhausen
Worms
Miltenberg
Heppenheim
Amorbach
St. Wendel
Kusel
Altleiningen
Weinheim
Waldürn
Kaiserslautern
Dürkheim
Schriesheim
Buchen
Wachenheim
Ladenburg
Eberbach
Deidesheim
Heidelberg
Mosbach
Neustadt an der Weinstrasse
Speyer
Wiesloch
Möckmühl
Neudenau
Hornbach
Landau in der Pfalz
Germersheim
Weinsberg
Saargemund
Bruchsal
Eppingen
Zabern
Kleingartach
Heilbronn
Wissembourg
Bretten
Güglingen
Woerth
Lauterbourg
Neuwiller
Haguenau
Seltz
Pforzheim
Bischwiller
Sinzheim
Leonberg
Stuttgart
Saverne
Herrlisheim
Weil der Stadt
Esslingen
Wolfsheim
Strasbourg
Herrenberg
Molsheim
Oberkirch
Rosheim
Enheim
Offenburg
Erstein
Benfeld
Rhinau
Lahr
Châtenois
Ettenheim
Haslach
St. Hippolyte
Sélestat
Bergheim
Kenzingen
Ribeauvillé
Riquewihr
(Rappoltsweiler)
Marckolsheim
Hornberg
Kaysersberg
Turckheim
Rottweil
Munster
Endingen
Sulzbach
Colmar
Waldkirch
Herrlisheim
Breisach
Freidburg
Villengen
Guebwiller
Rouffach
Thann
Soultz
Ensisheim
Masevaux
Wattwiller
Sentheim
Rougemont
Mulhouse
Überlingen
Belfort
Altkirch
Radolfzell
Delle
Waldshut
Säckingen
Constance
Ailingen
Ferrette
Rheinfelden
Diessenhofen
Friedrichshafen
Basle
Baden
Winterthur

10 20 km.

52

THE PASTOUREAUX AND "LEPERS" MASSACRES 1320–1321

A popular religious movement of Pastoureaux ("shepherds") in the town of Agen in southern France soon turned into a crusade bent on storming Granada and freeing the last portion of Christian European soil from Muslim rule. Along their route they turned first on Jewish communities in southern France and then on communities across the Pyrenees in the kingdoms of Aragón and Navarre. Pope John XXII opposed the crusaders and so did James II of Aragón, who, in order to protect the communities of northern Iberia, dispatched his son, crown prince Alfonso, to suppress them. This is one of the rare instances of a movement for liberating Christian soil from Muslim domination being destroyed by the party it wished to serve.

As if this were not enough, the Jews of Chinon (in central France) were, in 1321, accused of poisoning wells in conspiracy with the lepers (who lived as outcasts from society).

Orléans
Tours
Chinon
Loire

6. 1321—During lepers massacres, 120 of town's Jews burned at stake in one day.

Atlantic Ocean

FRANCE

1. 'Shepherds' wreak havoc in about 120 Jewish communities.

Narbonne
Lyons

2. Jews flee from Toulouse, barricade themselves in tower of Narbonne. Viscount of Toulouse orders arrest of Pastoureaux, whereupon Jews leave tower, Pastoureaux freed by town priests; massacre 150 Jews.

Bordeaux
Garonne
Castelsarrasin
Agen
Albi
Rhône

4. Rich Jews are killed by Christian guides whom they paid to help them flee to Spain.

Marsan
Condom
Verdun-sur-Garonne
Toulouse
Arles
Carcassonne

3. Jewish survivors in Toulouse convert to Christianity.

Lourdes
Bagnères-de-Bigorre
Pamplona
Luz
NAVARRE
Jaca
Montclus
Gerona

Burgos
Jaca
Montclus
Huesca

CASTILE
Tudela
Ebro
Saragossa
ARAGÓN
Barcelona

Mediterranean Sea

5. Pastoureaux checked in attempt to reach Granada.

Tarragona

Madrid
Tajo

0 50 100 km.

53

▽ Jewish community

▽ Major community (before 1239)

▽ Massacres before 1298 (excluding that of Werner the Good)

● Werner the Good blood libel, 1287

● Rindfleisch massacres, 1298

▽▽ Armleder massacres, 1336–1339

THE BLACK DEATH   1348

Many countries — from Spain in the southwest to Poland in the east — were hard hit by the great bubonic plague that reached Europe in 1348. The non-Jewish population accused the Jews of causing the plague by poisoning the wells. While Jewish casualties of the plague were relatively low in proportion to those of the Christians, the number of Jewish dead was swelled by the massacres. Jews were cruelly tortured in order to extract confessions that they were responsible for disseminating the plague. In many places they were burned at the stake. Pope Clement VI (1342–1352), recognizing the absurdity of the allegations against the Jews, issued a bull from the papal court at Avignon in 1348 denouncing the allegations.

Charles IV, emperor of Germany, and King Peter IV of Aragón tried to protect their Jewish communities, but, nonetheless, Jewish casualties were great.

The Black Death and its aftermath proved a critical turning point for the Jewish communities. In Spain it represents the beginning of a decline for the communities in Castile and Aragón, not only in numbers but also politically, culturally and economically.

Woodcut depicting the burning of Jewish martyrs in Ashkenaz. From Schedel's *Weltchronik*, 1493.

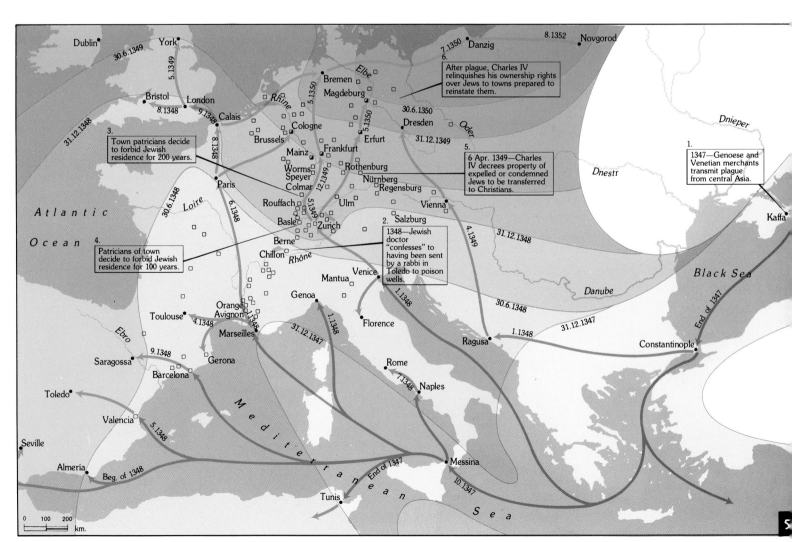

After plague, Charles IV relinquishes his ownership rights over Jews to towns prepared to reinstate them.

1347—Genoese and Venetian merchants transmit plague from central Asia.

Town patricians decide to forbid Jewish residence for 200 years.

6 Apr. 1349—Charles IV decrees property of expelled or condemned Jews to be transferred to Christians.

Patricians of town decide to forbid Jewish residence for 100 years.

1348—Jewish doctor "confesses" to having been sent by a rabbi in Toledo to poison wells.

1.1348 Progression of the Black Death (month & year)

Spread of the Black Death at six-month intervals

□ Jewish community stricken by massacre

■ Jewish community which defended itself

UNTIL THE EXPULSION FROM SPAIN

Burning of books by Pedro Berruguette. Saint Dominic supervises the burning. The book in the air is the New Testament.

DESTRUCTION OF THE JEWISH COMMUNITY IN FRANCE
Fourteenth Century

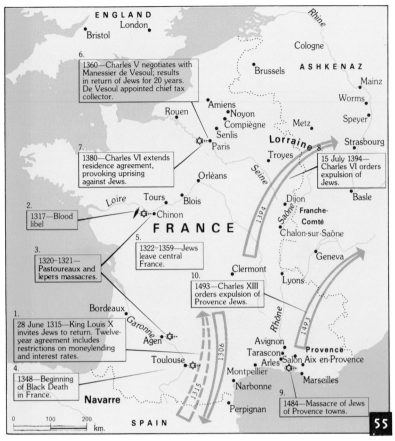

ENGLAND
London
Bristol

6.
1360—Charles V negotiates with Manessier de Vesoul; results in return of Jews for 20 years. De Vesoul appointed chief tax collector.

Rouen
Amiens
Noyon
Compiègne
Senlis
Paris

7.
1380—Charles VI extends residence agreement, provoking uprising against Jews.

Orléans

Loire Tours Blois

2.
1317—Blood libel

Chinon

FRANCE

3.
1320-1321—Pastoureaux and lepers massacres.

5.
1322-1359—Jews leave central France.

Clermont

10.
1493—Charles XIII orders expulsion of Provence Jews.

Bordeaux

1.
28 June 1315—King Louis X invites Jews to return. Twelve-year agreement includes restrictions on moneylending and interest rates.

Garonne Agen

Toulouse

4.
1348—Beginning of Black Death in France.

Navarre

Montpellier
Narbonne
Perpignan

Avignon
Tarascon
Arles Salon Aix en-Provence
Provence
Marseilles

9.
1484—Massacre of Jews of Provence towns.

Rhine
Cologne
Brussels
ASHKENAZ
Mainz
Worms
Speyer
Lorraine
Strasbourg
Troyes

8.
15 July 1394—Charles VI orders expulsion of Jews.

Dijon
Franche-Comté
Chalon-sur-Saône
Basle
Geneva
Lyons
Rhône

Seine Saône

0 100 200 km.

SPAIN

55

In 1365 and 1366 certain factions tried to influence the crown to expel the Jews. Charles V (1364–1380) did in fact sign a decree to this effect on 6 January 1367, but it was never implemented. The king also ordered an inventory of Jewish property. Similar decrees were issued in 1368 and 1370. When Charles V died in 1380, the population attacked the Jews, killing many. They died as martyrs and their children were kidnapped. In Paris, the provost Hugues Aubriot tried to thwart the rioters, even returning kidnapped children to their parents, but was dismissed and imprisoned. Aubriot and the Jews were both casualties of the anti-crown riots of 1382. Charles VI succumbed to popular pressure and on 15 July 1394 decreed the expulsion of the Jews from France by 3 November — seven years short of the twenty-year period granted in the charter of resettlement issued by his father Charles V.

The Jews were also expelled from Toulouse on 7 December 1394. (There were twelve families and an additional seven from the environs of Toulouse.) Jewish communities remained in Franche-Comté, Lorraine in the north, Provence and Navarre. In 1481, when Provence was annexed to France, the edict of expulsion was applied there as well; however, the king acquiesced to the plea of the Jews of Marseilles, Arles, Aix-en-Provence, Tarascon and Salon-de-Provence and re-newed their privileges. In 1484 there was an outbreak of riots in the towns of Provence (except Salon) and on 19 August 1484 Charles VIII (1483–1498) forbade Jewish settlement in Arles. In 1486 the town council turned to its representatives in the Assembly of Estates demanding the expulsion of the Jews, a similar demand being made in Marseilles. Anti-Jewish feelings were particularly strong after the Spanish expulsion (1492) and Charles finally yielded to the pressure. At the end of July 1493 he ordered all Jews to either convert or leave Arles within three months.

The Jews of Arles and Marseilles succeeded in obtaining a number of postponements of the decree but in 1500–1501 the remnant were forced to leave. Only a few Jews remained in the French papal territories. The renewal of Jewish settlement in southwest France became the task of the conversos who fled the Iberian Peninsula, but many years were to pass before they were allowed to live openly as Jews.

The Hundred Years War (between England and France, 1337–1453) further impoverished France. An attempt was made between the years 1359 and 1361 to renew Jewish settlement in the country. Privileges of protection were extended to the Jews and, for a period of twenty years, they were even allowed to charge a high rate of interest on loans.

THE BEGINNING OF JEWISH SETTLEMENT IN POLAND

It was only in the thirteenth century that the Jews of Poland began to enjoy privileges, although there is evidence of Jews in Poland at an earlier period. In 1264 King Boleslav V the Pious of Kalisz, granted the Jews privileges, being influenced by those granted them by the emperors of Germany. The first privilege was to ensure protection against blood libels. It also recognized the status of the Jews as the *servi camerae regis* ("servants of the royal chamber").

In 1334 Casimir III the Great conferred privileges upon the Jews of Poland, ratifying these privileges in 1336 for other parts of his kingdom — Lesser Poland (western Galicia with Cracow, its capital) and Red Russia (Ruthenia, eastern Galicia with Lvov, its capital). After the unification of Poland and Lithuania in 1386, Grand Duke Vitold granted the same privileges to Lithuania (1388).

In the fourteenth and fifteenth centuries many Jewish refugees from Germany arrived in Poland. The Polish nobles and townspeople wanted to expel the Jews and consequently, during the reign of Ladislaus (Władysław) II Jagiellon (1386–1434), the Jews were persecuted.

A blood libel in 1399 in Poznań resulted in the massacre of the Jews and the looting of their neighborhood. In 1407 there was an anti-Jewish outbreak in Cracow by the students of the university (founded in 1400).

There is little information about early Jewish communities in Lithuania. The important centers were Brest Litovsk, Troki, Grodno and perhaps Lutsk. In Volhynia the Jewish community of Ludmir (Vladimir in Volhynia) was already known in the thirteenth century. (Volhynia was annexed to Lithuania in 1336.) Many Lithuanian Jews were farmers, but the nobles from time to time attempted to drive them off the land. Slowly, Jewish urban settlement developed, with

Jews engaged in operating lease concessions, an activity that in due course extended over all of Poland, Lithuania and the Ukraine.

In 1441 Casimir IV Jagiellon recognized the Karaite community, granting them equal rights with Christians.

The expulsion of the Jews from Spain in 1492 also had repercussions in Poland and Lithuania, and in 1495 the Jews were expelled from Lithuania and Cracow. (However, they were allowed to reside in Kazimierz, a suburb of Cracow.)

Interior of a synagogue in the Jewish neighborhood of Toledo, founded in 13th century. After the riots of 1391, it was converted into Santa Maria La Blanca church.

Baltic Sea

8. 1441—Casimir IV Jagiellon grants Karaites autonomy.

PRUSSIA

Troki • Vilna

6. 1399—Blood libel; Jews accused of stealing the host.

3. 1264—Boleslav of Kalisz grants privileges to Jews of his kingdom.

Gdansk (Danzig)

Grodno

5. 1388—After unification of Poland and Lithuania (1386), Duke Vitold grants privileges to Jews of Lithuania.

EMPIRE

Great Poland

Poznan • Gniezno
Kościan • Konin
Gostyn
Kalisz
Łęczyca

Wloclawek • Plosk
Wyszogrod

Lomza
Pultusk
Warsaw

LITHUANIA

Brest
Pinsk
Pripyat

POLAND

Beg. 12th cent.—Following persecutions of Crusades, many Jews flee Germany for Poland.

Kazimierz
Lublin • Chelm
Vladimir (Ludmir) • Lutsk
Kovel
Rovno

Liegnitz
Breslau

SILESIA

Hrubieszów
Sandomierz
Dubno • Ostrog

BOHEMIA

Prague

Nysa

Cracow • Tarnów
Bochnia • Jaslo
Krosno
Little Poland
Drogobych

Jaroslav
Przemyśl
Lúbaczów
Lvov
Zhidachov
Galich • Buchach

MORAVIA

Brno

Red Russia

Kamenets Podolskiy

7. 1407—University students massacre Jews.

2. End 12th cent.— Mstislav, Prince of Cracow, imposes heavy fine on perpetrators of violence against Jews.

GERMAN

Vienna

Sopron

Danube • Esztergom

Ofen HUNGARY

4. 1334—Casimir III the Great renews privileges to Polish Jewry. 1364—Privileges extended to Lesser (Little) Poland and Red Russia.

0 50 100 km.

56

THE JEWS OF SPAIN UP TO THE MASSACRES OF 1391

The Black Death, which reached Aragón in 1348 brought with it a wave of murderous attacks on Jews, who were accused of causing the plague. The kingdom of Castile underwent a radical decline in population during the second half of the fourteenth century, not so much as a result of the plague as of a general increase in mortality and of population migration. The Jews were not held responsible for these factors. Thus, the 1354 attack on the Jews of Seville which seemed a distant echo of the Black Death, proved to have had a local cause — an accusation of a host desecration.

The rule of Peter the Cruel (1350–1369) king of Castile was contested by his half-brother Henry of Trastámara and during their bitter struggle many Jewish communities suffered. Henry was the first ruler to use an anti-Jewish line as the basis of his political policy, declaring that he was waging war against his brother in order to free Castile from the harmful influence of Peter's Jewish advisers. Toledo was one of the first communities to be affected when in the spring of 1355 some of Henry's forces entered the town attacking and looting the small Jewish quarter of Alcana. According to the contemporary Spanish historian Pedro López de Ayala, more than one thousand Jews were killed in Alcana. The attackers were not able to penetrate the larger Jewish quarter of Toledo, which was protected by mercenaries hired by the Jewish community.

Other Jewish communities in Castile were also attacked. In 1360 Henry advanced from northern Castile, attacking Jewish communities and populations along the way. In April 1366 Henry took the town of Burgos, demanding one million maravedis from the Jewish community in ransom money; in May when he entered Toledo, he made the same demand of its Jewish community, which had to sell the Torah crowns in order to pay the ransom. A year later Henry again entered Burgos, forcing the Jews to pay a further ransom of one million maravedis. The first rioters were French and English mercenary troops enlisted by Peter and Henry in their civil war. They were responsible for the destruction of most of the Jewish communities of Castile. Even the southern communities were not spared; Peter, the avowed protector of the Jews, allowed the Muslims of Granada, who aided him, to sell the Jews of Jaén into slavery.

The persecutions of 1391 were preceeded, in 1378, by the confiscation of synagogues in Seville, instigated by the anti-Jewish agitation of the archdeacon of Écija, Ferrant Martínez. On 4 June 1391 anti-Jewish disorders broke out in Seville spreading through the other Jewish communities of Andalusia and subsequently through most of the communities in Spain. Clergy, nobles, townspeople and peasants all participated in the riots. At the beginning of July news of the attacks reached Aragón, causing general agitation.

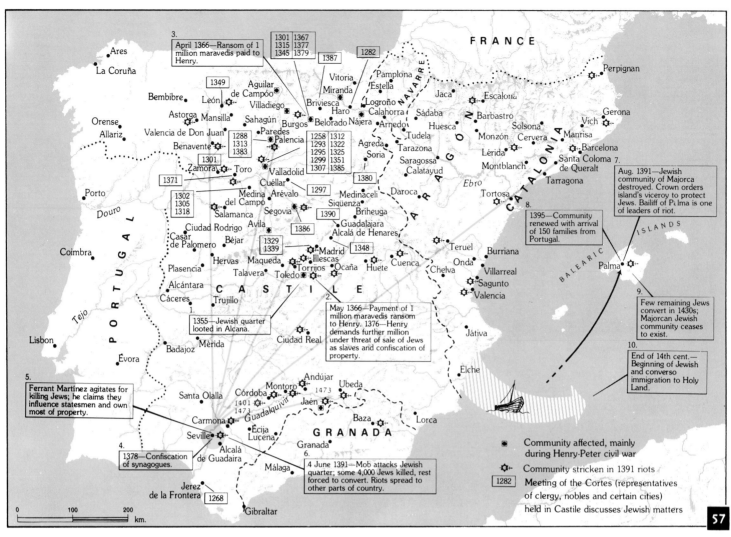

3.
April 1366—Ransom of 1 million maravedis paid to Henry.

1301 1367
1315 1377
1345 1379

1387

1282

1349

1288
1313
1383

1301

1371

1258 1312
1293 1322
1295 1325
1299 1351
1307 1385

1297

1302
1305
1318

1329
1339

1380

1390

1386

1348

FRANCE

Ares
La Coruña
Bembibre
Orense
Allariz
Astorga Mansilla
Valencia de Don Juan
Benavente
Zamora Toro
Porto
Coimbra
Ciudad Rodrigo
Casar de Palomero
Plasencia
Alcántara
Cáceres
Trujillo
Lisboa
Badajoz Mérida
Évora

León
Aguilar de Campóo
Villadiego
Sahagún
Paredes
Palencia
Burgos
Valladolid
Cuéllar
Medina del Campo Arévalo
Salamanca Segovia
Béjar Ávila
Hervás Madrid
Maqueda Illescas
Talavera Torrijos Ocaña
Toledo
Ciudad Real

Vitoria
Miranda
Briviesca
Belorado Nájera
Pamplona
Estella
Logroño
Calahorra
Arnedo
Agreda
Soria
Medinaceli
Sigüenza
Briheuga
Guadalajara
Alcalá de Henares
Huete
Cuenca

Jaca
Escalona
Sádaba
Huesca
Tudela
Tarazona
Saragossa
Calatayud
Daroca

NAVARRE

ARAGON

Ebro

Barbastro
Monzón
Solsona
Cervera
Lérida
Montblanch

Gerona
Vich
Manrisa
Barcelona
Santa Coloma de Queralt
Tarragona

CATALONIA

Perpignan

7.
Aug. 1391—Jewish community of Majorca destroyed. Crown orders island's viceroy to protect Jews. Bailiff of Palma is one of leaders of riot.

8.
1395—Community renewed with arrival of 150 families from Portugal.

9.
Few remaining Jews convert in 1430s; Majorcan Jewish community ceases to exist.

10.
End of 14th cent.— Beginning of Jewish and converso immigration to Holy Land.

Tortosa
Teruel
Onda
Burriana
Villarreal
Sagunto
Valencia
Chelva
Elche
Játiva

BALEARIC ISLANDS
Palma

CASTILE

1.
1355—Jewish quarter looted in Alcana.

2.
May 1366—Payment of 1 million maravedis ransom to Henry. 1376—Henry demands further million under threat of sale of Jews as slaves and confiscation of property.

5.
Ferrant Martínez agitates for killing Jews; he claims they influence statesmen and own most of property.

4.
1378—Confiscation of synagogues.

6.
4 June 1391—Mob attacks Jewish quarter; some 4,000 Jews killed, rest forced to convert. Riots spread to other parts of country.

Santa Olalla
Carmona
Écija
Lucena
Seville
Alcalá de Guadaira
Málaga
Jerez de la Frontera
1268
Gibraltar

Andújar
Montoro
Córdoba
1401
1473
Jaén
1473
Úbeda
Baza
Granada
Lorca

GRANADA

Guadalquivir

PORTUGAL
Douro
Tejo

⊙ Community affected, mainly during Henry-Peter civil war
✡ Community stricken in 1391 riots
1282 Meeting of the Cortes (representatives of clergy, nobles and certain cities) held in Castile discusses Jewish matters

0   100   200 km.

57

THE JEWISH QUARTER IN TOLEDO

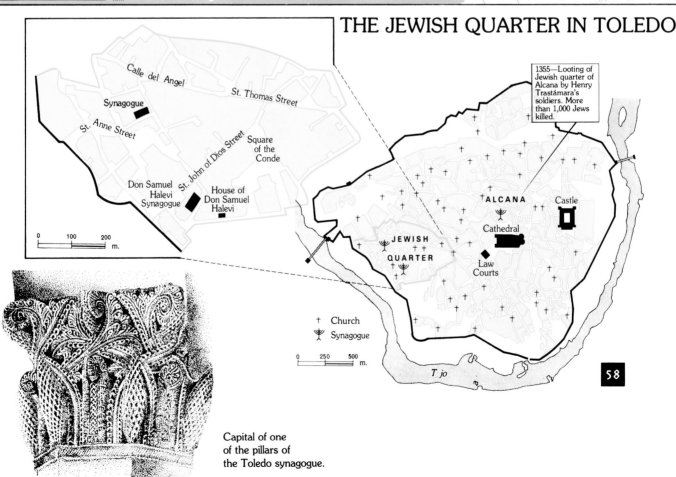

Calle del Angel
St. Thomas Street
Synagogue
St. Anne Street
St. John of Dios Street
Square of the Conde
Don Samuel Halevi Synagogue
House of Don Samuel Halevi

0   100   200 m.

1355—Looting of Jewish quarter of Alcana by Henry Trastámara's soldiers. More than 1,000 Jews killed.

ALCANA
Cathedral
Castle
JEWISH QUARTER
Law Courts

† Church
✡ Synagogue

0   250   500 m.

Tajo

58

Capital of one of the pillars of the Toledo synagogue.

In Catalonia, where most of the Jewish communities were destroyed, the riots were accompanied by a revolt of the indentured artisans and peasants against their lords. However, this revolt was only a secondary factor in the crusade against the Jews, although the authorities were wary of its side effects. The crown took advantage of the disturbances: the king of Aragón, John I (1387–1395) ordered an inventory of the property of Jews killed in the riots who had no heirs, since it was the custom in those days for the crown to inherit such property.

Two communities in the kingdom of Aragón were unharmed — those of Saragossa, the capital and royal residence, and Perpignan. In Saragossa Rabbi Hasdai Crescas was active and instrumental in organizing the defense of the town's Jews, collecting money to hire one of the nobles, Francisco d'Aranda, and his troops for this purpose. At the end of 1391 the king left Saragossa to tour the kingdom and pacify the population. Every place he visited he began negotiations

on the size of fines to be paid and the procedures for procuring a royal pardon. The population of a number of towns succeeded in placing the blame for the riots on the Jews.

Very few Castilian Jewish communities were spared; even the large ones disappeared as if they had never existed. Only Navarre escaped almost unscathed from the riots. But the Jews were attacked during the riots of 1328.

Many Spanish Jews saved their lives by apostasy, so that entire communities together with their leaders were obliterated. Even great Jewish personalities converted prior to the riots of 1391, some of them under the influence of Friar Vincent Ferrer. This gave rise to a new phenomenon: the creation of a community of conversos who wished to return to Judaism and who secretly practiced Jewish observance alongside openly professing Jewish communities that began to recuperate and rebuild their lives during the fifteenth century.

JEWISH SETTLEMENT IN PORTUGAL
Thirteenth and Fourteenth Centuries

Ever since Portuguese independence, during the reign of Afonso III (1248–1279), the Jewish communities of Portugal developed their own unique organizational structure. The crown appointed a single head of all the Jews in Portugal called the *arrabi môr*, who in turn appointed seven regional heads, or *arrabi menors*, each heading one of the seven regional divisions of Portugal. The *arrabi môr* had a wide range of authority in supervising Jewish communal life. He was the intermediary between the crown and the community; he represented the latter before the crown and conveyed the crown's wishes to the community. He also advised the crown on matters of taxation and obligations imposed on the Jewish community. However, he was not a "chief rabbi" in the conventional sense, but rather a crown administrator.

The fourteenth century was relatively tranquil for the Jews of Portugal notwithstanding anti-Jewish agitation and church pressure, for example, with regard to the wearing of identifying badges and restriction of residence. Although the anti-Jewish atmosphere fomented by the church resulted in the massacres of 1449, Jewish communal life continued to function unperturbed.

Hebrew printing press.

Four Jewish quarters in existence; Alfama is most notable one.

✡ Jewish community in 13th cent. (1279-1325)
✿ New Jewish settlement in reign of Afonso IV, 1325-1357
✦ New Jewish settlement in reign of Pedro, 1357-1467
✶ New Jewish settlement in reign of Ferdinand, 1367-1383
— Boundary of regional organization under *arraby mor*
▢ Regional capital

67

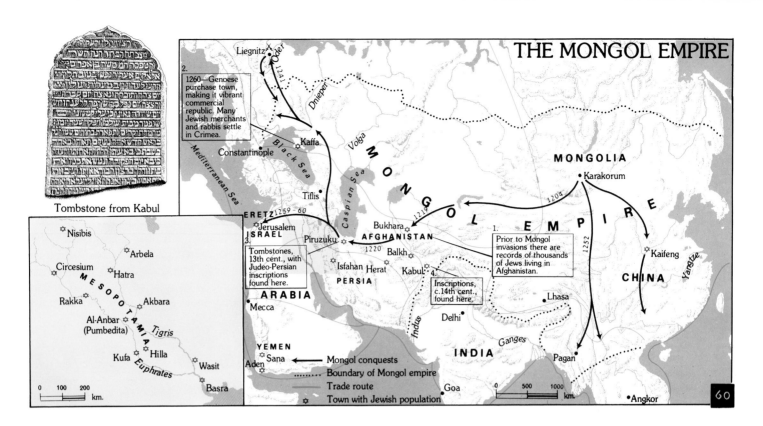

Tombstone from Kabul

2. 1260—Genoese purchase town, making it vibrant commercial republic. Many Jewish merchants and rabbis settle in Crimea.

1. Prior to Mongol invasions there are records of thousands of Jews living in Afghanistan.

3. Tombstones, 13th cent., with Judeo-Persian inscriptions found here.

4. Inscriptions, c.14th cent., found here.

← Mongol conquests
••••• Boundary of Mongol empire
—— Trade route
✡ Town with Jewish population

| 0 | 100 | 200 |
| km. | | |

| 0 | 500 | 1000 |
| km. | | |

60

THE MONGOLIAN INVASIONS OF PALESTINE

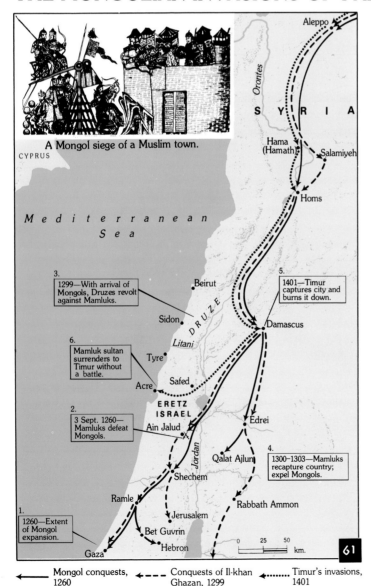

A Mongol siege of a Muslim town.

3. 1299—With arrival of Mongols, Druzes revolt against Mamluks.

6. Mamluk sultan surrenders to Timur without a battle.

5. 1401—Timur captures city and burns it down.

2. 3 Sept. 1260— Mamluks defeat Mongols.

4. 1300–1303—Mamluks recapture country; expel Mongols.

1. 1260—Extent of Mongol expansion.

| 0 | 25 | 50 |
| km. | | |

61

← Mongol conquests, 1260   ■ ■ ■ Conquests of Il-khan Ghazan, 1299   ••••• Timur's invasions, 1401

The Mongol invasion of Europe and the Middle East from the end of the twelfth century brought radical changes to those areas. Nations were destroyed and whole populations annihilated. The world was engulfed by a powerful wave of conquest the like of which it had never known before.

Before the death of Genghis Khan (1227) the Mongols had reached the Dnieper in Europe and in 1421 they crossed the Oder, annihilating a German and Polish army in a battle near Liegnitz. In 1258 the Mongols, led by Il-khan Hülegü, conquered Mesopotamia, from which they proceeded to Palestine, reaching Gaza in 1260. In September 1260, at the battle of Ain Jalud (Ein Harod) in the Valley of Jezreel, they were decisively defeated by Baybars and the Mamluk army, thus ensuring Mamluk rule over Palestine. In 1299, under the leadership of Il-khan Ghazan, they launched an invasion with the aid of an Armenian army and Druzes from the Lebanon. At the end of the fourteenth century the Tartar prince Timur (Tamerlane) revived the Mongol empire and in 1401 conquered and set fire to Damascus. Palestine surrendered without battle, accepting the Tartar yoke until the death of Timur in 1405.

The Mongol campaigns directed against Muslims in the east as well as their expansion in Europe caused great dread both in the east and in the west. The Muslims in the east were the chief victims of these campaigns although in the course of events the Mongols became closer to Islam, some even converting. The Jewish communities were saved in a number of places, including Baghdad (1258), Aleppo (in 1260 Jews found asylum in the central synagogue, which was left untouched) and Damascus. The Mongol invasions aroused messianic hopes for an imminent redemption among the Jews of Italy and Spain. Some believed the Mongols to be descendants of the ten tribes. In Christian Europe some Jewish communities were suspected of contact with the Mongols, and accused of being associated with their invasions and devastations. The Jewish communities in Silesia and Germany suffered from the Mongol advance westward.

IMMIGRATION TO THE HOLY LAND
Fourteenth and Fifteenth Centuries

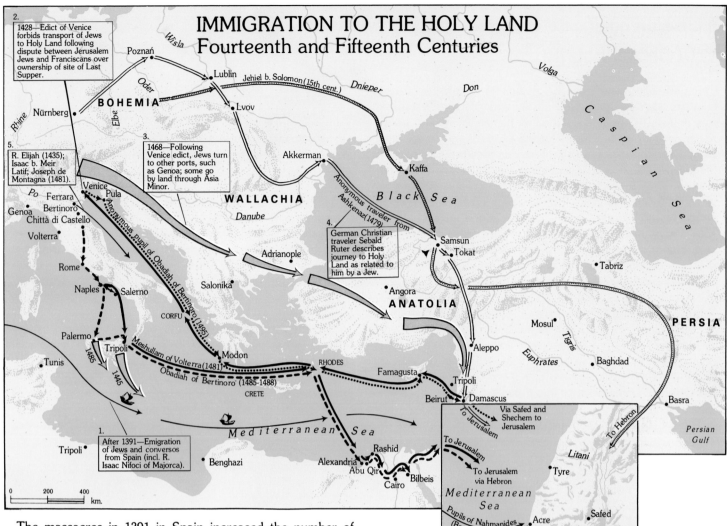

2. 1428—Edict of Venice forbids transport of Jews to Holy Land following dispute between Jerusalem Jews and Franciscans over ownership of site of Last Supper.

5. R. Elijah (1435); Isaac b. Meir Latif; Joseph de Montagna (1481).

3. 1468—Following Venice edict, Jews turn to other ports, such as Genoa; some go by land through Asia Minor.

4. German Christian traveler Sebald Ruter describes journey to Holy Land as related to him by a Jew.

1. After 1391—Emigration of Jews and conversos from Spain (incl. R. Isaac Nifoci of Majorca).

Meshullam of Volterra (1481)

Obadiah of Bertinoro (1485-1488)

Anonymous pupil of Obadiah of Bertinoro (1495)

Anonymous traveler from Ashkenaz (1479)

0   200   400 km.

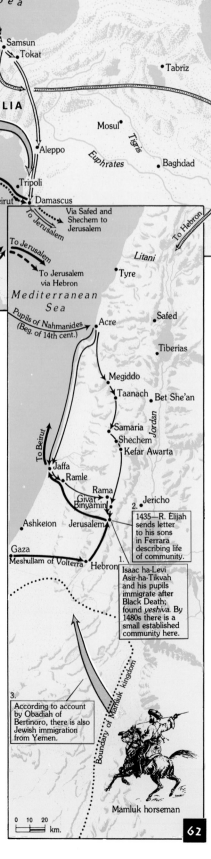

Via Safed and Shechem to Jerusalem

To Jerusalem

To Jerusalem via Hebron

To Hebron

Pupils of Nahmanides (Beg. of 14th cent.)

To Beirut

2. 1435—R. Elijah sends letter to his sons in Ferrara describing life of community.

1. Isaac ha-Levi Asir-ha-Tikvah and his pupils immigrate after Black Death; found *yeshiva*. By 1480s there is a small established community here.

3. According to account of Obadiah of Bertinoro, there is also Jewish immigration from Yemen.

Mamluk horseman

62

The massacres in 1391 in Spain increased the number of immigrants to Eretz Israel. Among the newcomers, of whose travels we do not have details, were many conversos, such as Isaac Nifoci of Majorca. They went to Palestine despite the difficult living conditions and the persecutions of the Mamluk regime. Jews came not only from Spain but also from Ashkenaz. Two important personalities from Italy came in the 1480s: Meshullam of Volterra (1481) and Obadiah of Bertinoro (1485). The involvement of the latter in the life of the Jerusalem community was both considerable and significant. Every traveler had to choose his own way from among the existing routes to Palestine, a particularly difficult task after the Venetian edict against transporting Jewish travelers to the Holy Land.

Some travelers wrote reports on their journey, describing not only the communities of Jerusalem and Safed but also those encountered on the way, thus leaving noteworthy accounts of Jewish life in Eretz Israel and the Diaspora.

Wood engraving of a map of Jerusalem by Erhard Reuwich, 1486.

THE BEGINNINGS OF THE OTTOMAN EMPIRE

Ottoman incursions into the Byzantine Empire occurred over an extended period, gradually undermining Byzantine rule in Asia Minor and the Balkan peninsula. Region upon region was wrenched from Byzantium, even by Venice and Genoa, which took control over various islands in the eastern Mediterranean. It was in these regions that Jewish life was revived. The Turks captured Gallipoli in 1354 and Adrianople in 1361. From this point the way was open to additional conquests in Europe and the course of the wars between 1361 and 1430 determined the fate of Macedonia. Salonika held out after being under Venetian rule from 1423 until it was occupied by the Turks in 1430. From that date the Ottoman Empire became a serious threat to the Christian states of Europe.

In the fourteenth century there were few Jewish settlements in Asia Minor or in the areas ruled by Byzantium. Constantinople had a small Jewish community as well as a Karaite one. The Romaniot (Byzantine Jews) failed to develop a rich cultural or spiritual life under the Byzantines and after the Ottoman conquest they integrated with the newly established communities.

The fall of Constantinople to Mehmed (Muhammad) II

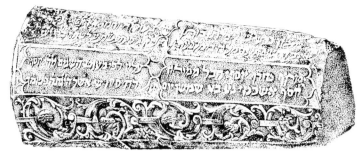

Jewish tombstone found in cemetery near Istanbul.

in 1453 was seen by Jewry as a second fall of Rome. Constantinople epitomized hatred of Jews in all its dreadful manifestations. Its conquest became associated with messianic hopes for the beginning of the redemption, arousing Jews and conversos to leave Spain for the east, the Holy Land and other places under Ottoman rule; in the words of the emigres "to be taken under the wings of the Shekhinah (divine presence)."

After the conquest of Constantinople the Ottomans established their capital there (also called Kosta by the Jews) and repeopling the almost deserted city by the forcible transfer of Jews and other populations from Salonika, Adrianople and other towns.

In 1470 the first group of Jewish emigrants from Ashkenaz settled in Salonika, followed by a large number of Sephardic

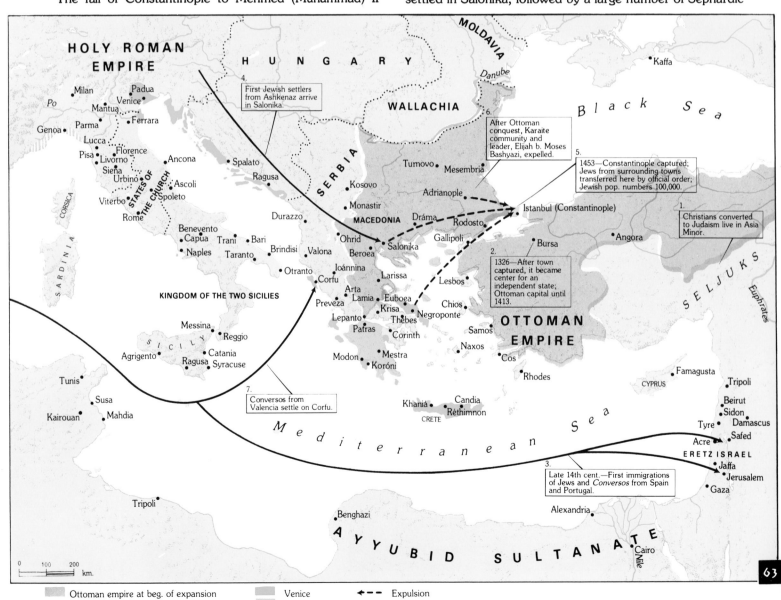

4. First Jewish settlers from Ashkenaz arrive in Salonika.

6. After Ottoman conquest, Karaite community and leader, Elijah b. Moses Bashyazi, expelled.

5. 1453—Constantinople captured; Jews from surrounding towns transferred here by official order; Jewish pop. numbers 100,000.

1. Christians converted to Judaism live in Asia Minor.

2. 1326—After town captured, it became center for an independent state; Ottoman capital until 1413.

7. Conversos from Valencia settle on Corfu.

3. Late 14th cent.—First immigrations of Jews and *Conversos* from Spain and Portugal.

| | Ottoman empire at beg. of expansion | | Venice | ◄--- Expulsion |
| | Genoa | | Byzantium | |

refugees from Spain, after the Expulsion (1492), Portugal, Sicily, Calabria and Naples. The city soon became a thriving Jewish center along with Constantinople, Adrianople, Bursa and other places.

The conquest of Damascus and Aleppo in 1516 and the Ottoman subjugation of Palestine (1516) and Egypt (1517) opened new horizons for the Jews of the Diaspora.

The volunteers and the Venetian and Catalonian residents of the city's trading cantons were unable to withstand the Ottoman siege. The Jewish Romaniot community was dispersed and its quarter destroyed.

THE FALL OF CONSTANTINOPLE

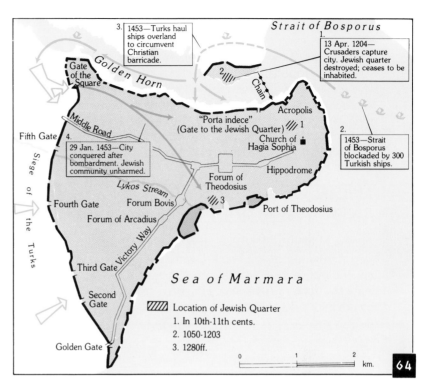

3. 1453—Turks haul ships overland to circumvent Christian barricade.

13 Apr. 1204—Crusaders capture city. Jewish quarter destroyed; ceases to be inhabited.

29 Jan. 1453—City conquered after bombardment. Jewish community unharmed.

2. 1453—Strait of Bosporus blockaded by 300 Turkish ships.

"Porta indece" (Gate to the Jewish Quarter)

Location of Jewish Quarter
1. In 10th-11th cents.
2. 1050-1203
3. 1280ff.

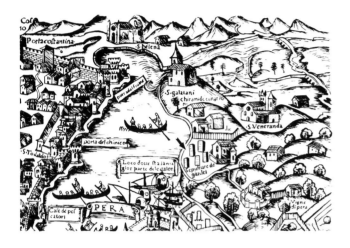

Detail from a woodcut of Constantinople (1520). Jewish cemetery in center indicated by an arrow.

COMMERCE IN THE MEDITERRANEAN BASIN
Fourteenth to Fifteenth Centuries

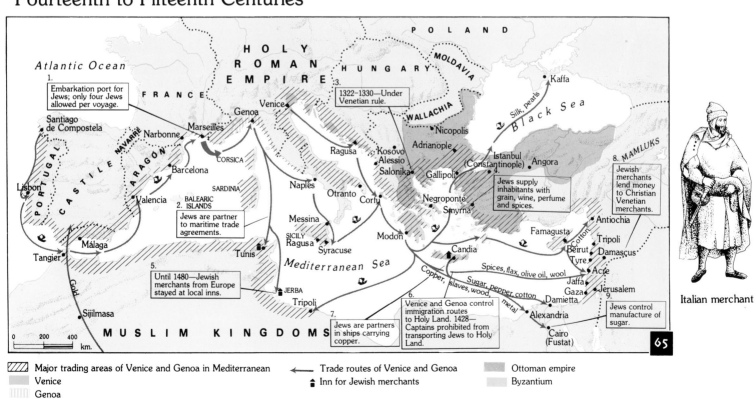

1. Embarkation port for Jews; only four Jews allowed per voyage.

3. 1322-1330—Under Venetian rule.

4. Jews supply inhabitants with grain, wine, perfume and spices.

8. MAMLUKS
Jewish merchants lend money to Christian Venetian merchants.

2. Jews are partner to maritime trade agreements.

5. Until 1480—Jewish merchants from Europe stayed at local inns.

6. Venice and Genoa control immigration routes to Holy Land. 1428—Captains prohibited from transporting Jews to Holy Land.

7. Jews are partners in ships carrying copper.

9. Jews control manufacture of sugar.

Spices, flax, olive oil, wool
Sugar, pepper, cotton
Copper, slaves, wood, metal

Italian merchant

Major trading areas of Venice and Genoa in Mediterranean
Venice
Genoa
Trade routes of Venice and Genoa
Inn for Jewish merchants
Ottoman empire
Byzantium

71

Jewish economic activity in the Mediterranean basin in the fourteenth and fifteenth centuries covered a variety of commercial fields including maritime trade to many countries. Jews were partners to trade agreements with ship captains. The captain carried out the commercial transaction and the Jew financed the merchandise. Sometimes special joint ventures would be organized between Jewish and Christian merchants, including Jewish residents of Muslim countries who would lend the Venetian Christian merchants money for payment of customs duty on the goods they were delivering. A number of ports (e.g. on Crete) had special inns for Jewish travelers. Many Jews served as agents in the trade between Europe and Muslim countries.

Jewish commercial activity was considerable despite many restrictions: Jewish passengers were limited to four per ship per voyage; some captains refused to carry Jewish passengers to Egypt; Venice forbade sea captains to carry Jewish passengers bound for the Holy Land; and Mamluk rulers in Syria and Egypt generally oppressed their Jewish citizens.

European trade in the fourteenth and fifteenth centuries developed considerably in comparison with that of the Radhanites in the ninth to the eleventh centuries. Credit facilities and methods of finance improved, and trade routes were shorter and safer. Jews in their various places of residence played an important role in this trade.

THE JEWS OF GERMANY IN THE SHADOW OF EXPULSIONS AND MASSACRES   Fourteenth and Fifteenth Centuries

Although the Jewish communities were persecuted even before the period of the Black Death, neither the massacres nor the plague itself and its consequences were able to eliminate the Jews of Ashkenaz. However, conditions within the communities deteriorated; in some places Jewish residence was limited to ten years. Only a few communities were able to recuperate, but by the middle of the fifteenth century the network of Jewish communities had grown despite the continued harrassment of the population. The Jews of Prague who were saved during the Black Death were massacred in

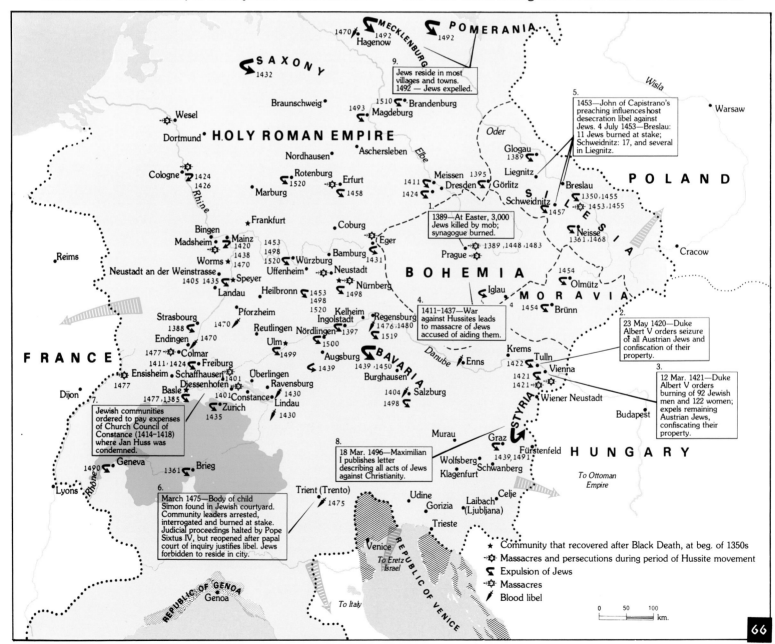

5. 1453—John of Capistrano's preaching influences host desecration libel against Jews. 4 July 1453—Breslau: 11 Jews burned at stake; Schweidnitz: 17, and several in Liegnitz.

9. Jews reside in most villages and towns. 1492 — Jews expelled.

1. 1389—At Easter, 3,000 Jews killed by mob; synagogue burned.

4. 1411–1437—War against Hussites leads to massacre of Jews accused of aiding them.

2. 23 May 1420—Duke Albert V orders seizure of all Austrian Jews and confiscation of their property.

3. 12 Mar. 1421—Duke Albert V orders burning of 92 Jewish men and 122 women; expels remaining Austrian Jews, confiscating their property.

7. Jewish communities ordered to pay expenses of Church Council of Constance (1414–1418) where Jan Huss was condemned.

8. 18 Mar. 1496—Maximilian I publishes letter describing all acts of Jews against Christianity.

6. March 1475—Body of child Simon found in Jewish courtyard. Community leaders arrested, interrogated and burned at stake. Judicial proceedings halted by Pope Sixtus IV, but reopened after papal court of inquiry justifies libel. Jews forbidden to reside in city.

★ Community that recovered after Black Death, at beg. of 1350s
✡ Massacres and persecutions during period of Hussite movement
Ϛ Expulsion of Jews
✡ Massacres
⚡ Blood libel

0   50   100
km.

66

1389. In the 1380's a long list of expulsions from various places were added to the list of massacres.

During the second half of the fifteenth century John of Capistrano preached in German cities, inciting people against the Jews. Many of the expulsions in the fifteenth century were initiated by the townspeople. The Jewish privilege of temporary residence in Cologne was not renewed. King Sigismund requested that the expulsion be postponed and Duke Adolf was appointed as a judge-arbitrator. In his judgment of 24 July 1425 he asserted that the city was entitled to carry out its decision, but the Jews had already been expelled in October 1424. The refugees settled in a region adjacent to the archbishop's diocese, but a dispute between the archbishop and the townspeople of Mainz led to the expulsion of the Jews from the diocese. Albert III, elector of Brandenburg (1470–1486), wrote in 1462 "Every ruler is entitled to appropriate Jewish property, even to kill them, except for those few who must be allowed to live as a testimony. The Jews can avert this fate by giving one-third of their property to every ruler upon his investiture." Albert slightly altered this text in 1463 but basically it remained the same.

The Emperor Maximilian I (1493–1519) adopted the same tactic of expelling the Jews, publishing an edict of expulsion of the Jews of Styria on 18 March 1496, in which he enumerates *all* the Jewish offences against Christianity such as kidnapping and killing of Christian children, thus giving official sanction to the legendary lies and superstitions current among Christians. Maximilian did leave an opening for Jews to return to Styria, but the local authorities obtained extensions of the expulsion order. He refrained from molesting the Jews of Moravia and Bohemia and opposed their expulsion from Regensburg.

One would have thought that upon the election of Charles I of Spain as emperor of the Holy Roman Empire (Charles V [1519–1556]) he would have treated the Jews of Ashkenaz in as harsh a way as did his grandparents Ferdinand and Isabella. However, he made a distinction between his Jewish policy in the two realms, particularly since he was preoccupied with the problems of Lutheranism in Germany. At Charles' court the Jew Joseph (Joselmann) b. Gershon of Rosheim (c. 1478–1554) was successfully active as the *shtadlan* (intercessor) for the Jews of Germany. There was very little change in conditions for the Jews of Germany in the sixteenth century, the Ashkenazic center of gravity moving to Poland-Lithuania, Bohemia and Moravia. Already in the fourteenth and particularly in the fifteenth and sixteenth centuries there were the beginnings of Jewish immigration to northern Italy and in the direction of the Ottoman Empire, including Palestine. The persecutions, massacres and expulsions took their toll on the Jews of Germany and sapped their creative strength.

CENTERS OF DISSEMINATION OF HATRED OF THE JEWS

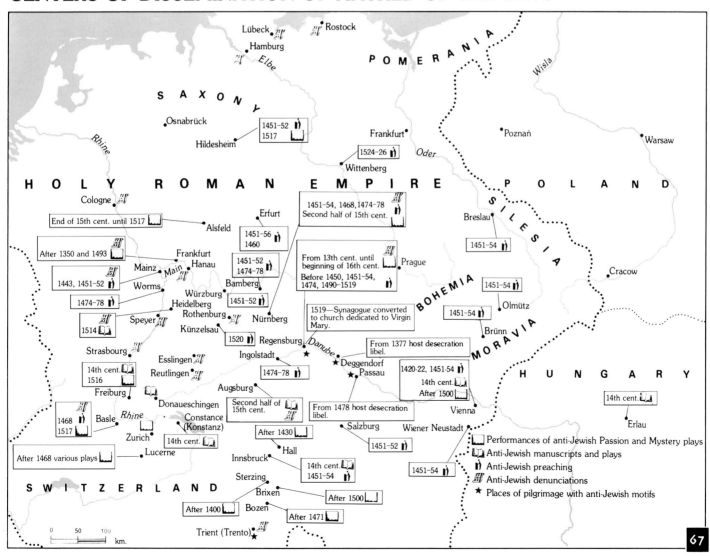

THE JEWS OF SWITZERLAND   Thirteenth to Fifteenth Centuries

The oldest Jewish community in Switzerland seems to have been in Basle, where Jews are first mentioned in 1213. Additional communities in the area in the thirteenth century were in Constance, Lucerne, Berne, Zurich, Geneva and Lausanne. Although most of their members were engaged in moneylending there were also merchants, tailors, metal craftsmen and owners of vineyards and orchards. The Jews of these towns, who came mainly from Alsace and Germany, were soon destined to be persecuted and expelled from Switzerland. Among other things they were accused of caus-

ing the Black Death and the Jews of Chillon were accused of poisoning wells. The fate of the Jews of Geneva, Lucerne and Berne was similar; many were expelled or burned at the stake.

Jewish life in Switzerland was reconstituted on a small scale toward the end of the fourteenth century, a few Jewish doctors being given permits of residence. It was only in the German-speaking areas that a number of communities took root. The scholar Moses of Zurich was known for his notes and additions on the *Semak* (*Sefer Mitzvot Katan*).

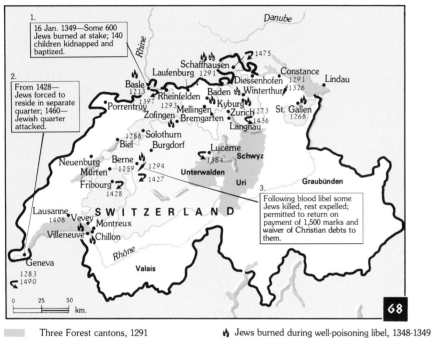

Three Forest cantons, 1291

Cantons that joined Confederation, till 1353

Cantons that joined Confederation, till 1513

1384 Jewish community founded

🔥 Jews burned during well-poisoning libel, 1348-1349

🔥 Burning of Jews in 1401

✗ Blood libel

↗ Expulsion

1. 16 Jan. 1349—Some 600 Jews burned at stake; 140 children kidnapped and baptized.

2. From 1428—Jews forced to reside in separate quarter; 1460—Jewish quarter attacked.

3. Following blood libel some Jews killed, rest expelled; permitted to return on payment of 1,500 marks and waiver of Christian debts to them.

A 15th century woodcut depicting Jews bleeding the child Simon — subject of a blood libel in 1475.

THE JEWS OF SPAIN ON THE EVE OF THE EXPULSION   Fifteenth Century

The expulsion of Spanish Jews in 1492 had its roots in the persecutions of 1391, when a large Jewish population of about two hundred thousand was forcibly converted and continued to live alongside both the surviving Jewish community, to which they no longer belonged, and the Christian community, which had not accepted them. The apostates Pablo de Santa María in Castile (formerly Solomon ha-Levi, rabbi of Burgos) and Jerónimo de Santa Fé (formerly the doctor Joshua ha-Lorki of Alcañiz) became prominent figures within the Christian community, both working actively against their former coreligionists, each in his own way inducing the authorities to convert the remaining Jewish population. Upon the advice of Jerónimo, the antipope Benedict XIII in 1413 convened a religious disputation in Tortosa, inviting twelve rabbis from the kingdom of Aragón to participate. The disputation, which continued for about two years (1413 and 1414) caused considerable stress among the Aragonese communities, bereft of their rabbis and leaders, who were struggling with the apostates in Tortosa. These years were characterized by much apostasy. The Dominican friar Vincent Ferrer traveled from place to place preaching conversion and exerting pressure on the Jewish population.

Only at the beginning of the 1430s could signs of recuperation be discerned among the communities of Castile, particularly in their attempt to establish a nationwide Jewish organization with a code of regulations. In 1432 Abraham Benveniste of Soria, "Rab de la Corte," convened representatives of the Castilian Jewish communities in order to reestablish the Jewish judicial and educational systems, determine methods of tax collection, combat informers and establish norms for a more modest life style in Jewish society.

Unlike those of Castile, the large Jewish communities in Aragón were not revived after the persecutions of 1391, and in the 1430s the Jewish communities of the Balearic Islands ceased to exist.

The riots against the conversos in 1449 in Toledo and Ciudad Real must be viewed against the background of an antagonistic Christian society unwilling to accept the "new Christians" and their descendants. The instigator of the riots in Toledo was Pedro Sarmiento, appointed by King John II of Castile as commander of the fortress. A heavy war tax imposed on the city, to be collected by the converso tax farmers, served as the pretext for the riots which were directed against the conversos and did not affect the Jews.

SPANISH JEWISH COMMUNITIES

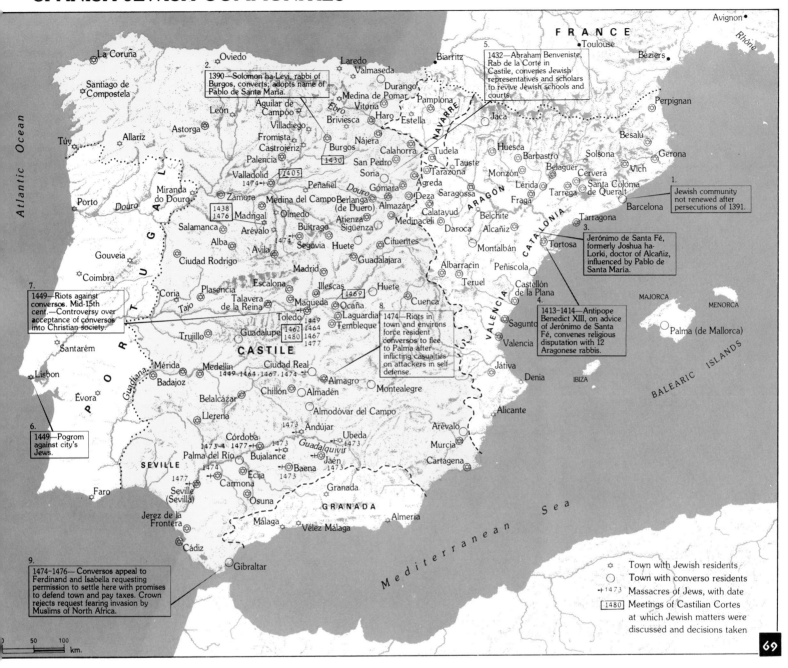

2. 1390—Solomon ha-Levi, rabbi of Burgos, converts; adopts name of Pablo de Santa María.

5. 1432—Abraham Benveniste, Rab de la Corte in Castile, convenes Jewish representatives and scholars to revive Jewish schools and courts.

1. Jewish community not renewed after persecutions of 1391.

3. Jerónimo de Santa Fé, formerly Joshua ha-Lorki, doctor of Alcañiz, influenced by Pablo de Santa María.

4. 1413–1414—Antipope Benedict XIII, on advice of Jerónimo de Santa Fé, convenes religious disputation with 12 Aragonese rabbis.

7. 1449—Riots against conversos. Mid-15th cent.—Controversy over acceptance of conversos into Christian society.

8. 1474—Riots in town and environs force resident conversos to flee to Palma after inflicting casualties on attackers in self defense.

6. 1449—Pogrom against city's Jews.

9. 1474-1476—Conversos appeal to Ferdinand and Isabella requesting permission to settle here with promises to defend town and pay taxes. Crown rejects request fearing invasion by Muslims of North Africa.

☆ Town with Jewish residents
○ Town with converso residents
✛1473 Massacres of Jews, with date
[1480] Meetings of Castilian Cortes at which Jewish matters were discussed and decisions taken

69

Riots recurred against the conversos in Toledo in 1467 and in the towns of Andalusia in 1473–1474.

The status of the conversos in the intensely religious environment of a militant Christian state striving for religious unification became the subject of considerable polemical literature. The disputes between those favoring integration and those opposing it, gave rise to anti-Jewish as well as anticonverso literature. Alfonso de Espina, a Franciscan friar, published a major work around 1460 in which he argued that the continued observance of Mosaic law by the conversos resulted from their contact with Jews and could be remedied only by the expulsion of the Jews. Alfonso was also the principal originator of the idea of the national Spanish Inquisition.

The ascent of Ferdinand and Isabella to the throne of Castile in 1474 and of the united kingdoms of Castile and Aragón in 1479 raised hopes for a respite among the Jews. In 1474 the converso request to settle in Gibraltar, on a promise of fidelity to Christianity, was rejected out of hand by Ferdinand and Isabella. The Catholic Monarchs conceived

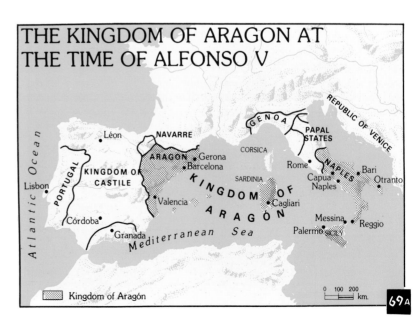

THE KINGDOM OF ARAGON AT THE TIME OF ALFONSO V

▒ Kingdom of Aragón

69A

a plan for the organization of the united kingdom to be implemented in stages: stabilizing their rule by creating a calm atmosphere and preventing revolts of the nobles and townspeople; establishing a national Spanish Inquisition to deal with the problem of converso fidelity to Christianity; the conquest of Granada, the last Muslim foothold in western Europe and the Expulsion of the Jews. By these methods they intended to create a united Christian kingdom of Castile and Aragón of "one flock and one sword." The crown's first step in 1475–1476 was to quell the revolt of the marquis of Villena that supported the union of Portugal and Castile through the marriage of crown princess Joana, daughter of Henry IV of Castile, to Afonso V, king of Portugal. Ferdinand and Isabella then turned to deal with the "Jewish heresies" of the conversos.

In 1477 they appealed to Pope Sixtus IV for permission to establish a national Inquisition in Spain, which was granted in 1478, and in 1480 two Dominican monks, Miguel de Murillo and Juan de San Martín, were appointed as the first inquisitors. They began their activities on 1 January 1481 in Seville for the whole of Andalusia and Spain. In 1483 an expulsion order was issued against all Jews of Andalusia giving them one month to leave. During that time the Dominican Tomás de Torquemada was appointed inquisitor-general of the Spanish kingdom, and it was he who was responsible for the Andalusian and other expulsions — Saragossa and Albarracín in 1486. The latter, postponed at the request of Ferdinand, did not take place until the general expulsion of 1492. Inquisition tribunals were systematically established throughout Spain.

During the war against Granada the Jewish communities of Castile were heavily taxed, the amounts increasing each year. On 25 November 1491 Granada, the last Muslim foothold in the Iberian Peninsula, capitulated. On 6 January the Catholic Monarchs entered the city in a triumphal procession and on 31 March 1492 they signed the Edict of Expulsion of the Jews from the whole of Spain. The edict specifically stated that the reason for the act was religious, namely that so long as Jews continued to reside in Spain there would be no hope for the integration of the conversos with Christianity. There is no doubt that the ideas embodied in the edict were those of Torquemada, who based his anti-Jewish ideology on the writings of Alfonso de Espina.

THE CONQUEST OF GRANADA
1 January 1492

3. 1482–1491—Heavy war tax on Jewish communities; collected annually according to a tax map.

4. 1483—Expulsion of Andalusian Jews.

2. Pope Sixtus IV approves establishment of Inquisition tribunal when Catholic Monarchs undertake to conquer Granada (1478).

6. Granada, last Muslim stronghold in Europe, falls to Christians; some of Muslims leave for North Africa. 2 Jan. 1492—Catholic Monarchs enter city.

5. 1487—After capture of Málaga, Jews of city held prisoners of war; ransom of 20 million maravedis demanded for their release.

1. 1477—Ferdinand and Isabella request permission from pope to establish Inquisition tribunal; 1478—permission granted; 1480—Miguel de Morillo and Juan de San Martín first inquisitors; Jan. 1481—begins functioning.

0 50 100 km.

1492 Conquest and date

Expulsion

70

70A

← Christian attacks
◄ Moslem attacks

ANNUAL TAXES PAID IN 1474 BY JEWS OF CASTILE AND WAR TAX PAID IN 1491 FOR THE CONQUEST OF GRANADA

TOWN	1474	1491			
Alaejos	—	3,770	Jerez de la Frontera	1,500	—
Alcalá	5,000	45,000	León	2,600	44,870
Alfara	1,000	15,120	Lorca	—	11,785
Almagro	800	—	Madrid	1,200	11,825
Almansa	1,100	5,200	Madrigal	4,000	42,120
Almazán	4,500	76,234	Medina del Campo	8,500	64,000
Arnedo	3,000	—	Merida	2,500	38,000
Avila	1,200	83,750	Miranda	2,000	13,350
Ayllón	2,000	33,120	Olmeda	500	5,800
Badajoz	7,500	65,750	Palencia	2,000	14,500
Belvis	—	13,539	Plasencia	5,000	53,400
Benavente	3,500	16,000	Salamanca	4,800	51,020
Briviesca	2,500	38,550	Saldaña	2,000	23,970
Burgos	700	28,350	Segovia	11,000	140,000
Cáceres	8,200	42,775	Seville	2,500	—
Cartagena	—	3,742	Talavera de la Reina	2,500	52,000
Castrojeriz	1,100	6,120	Toledo	3,500	107,560
Córdoba	1,200	—	Toro	2,000	16,070
Coria	3,300	25,030	Trujillo	7,500	111,400
Escalona	1,000	4,000	Valladolid	5,500	60,120
Estadillo	1,800	12,600	Vitoria	3,000	30,870
Guadalajara	6,500	90,620	Zamora	6,500	100,650
Huete	4,000	44,750			

(In 1474 the tax was paid in maravedis. The war tax in gold coins (castellanos; 1 castellano=485 marevedis.)

VIOLENT ATTACKS AGAINST THE CONVERSOS OF CÓRDOBA 1473

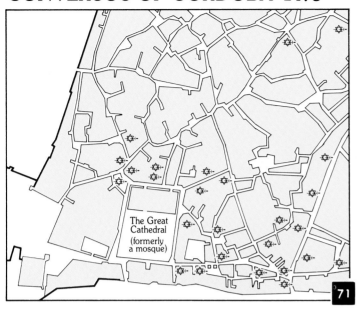

The Great
Cathedral
(formerly
a mosque)

71

The Israelites battle with Amalek. A drawing from a manuscript of Moses Arragel's Spanish translation of the Bible (1422–1430).

Illustration from a Hebrew illuminated manuscript, *Arba'ah Turim* by Jacob b. Asher, Mantua, Italy, 1435.

JEWISH COMMUNITIES IN ITALY
Fourteenth to Sixteenth Centuries

The distribution of Jews in Italy underwent a change after the Black Death, beginning with emigration from the south and the arrival in northern Italy of Jews, some of whom had been expelled from Germany. Communities were founded where previously there had been none. The changing political climate in the Italian Peninsula also created favorable conditions for Jewish settlement. Jewish loan-bankers gave great impetus to Jewish settlement in northern Italy and greatly assisted in the development of town and rural centers. Settlement was facilitated by the founders of banks receiving a *condotta* (privilege) for a period of time adequate for the establishment of a community.

Among the popes who reigned at the end of the fourteenth century it was Urban V (1362–1370) who issued a bull of protection for the Jews, as did Boniface IX (1389–1404) after him. The antipope Benedict XIII (1394–1417) was extremely hostile toward the Jews, his animosity reaching its peak during the Disputation of Tortosa (1413–1414). He was deposed in 1417; his successor Martin V (1417–1431) issued two bulls favorable to the Jews and also attempted to restrain the anti-Jewish agitation of the Franciscan friars. Other popes were either indifferent to the Jews or assisted in their persecution. Calixtus III (b. Alfonso de Borgia, 1455–1458), the Spanish pope, showed his disdain for Judaism when he intentionally dropped a Torah scroll given him by the Jews of Rome at his election. Another pope, Sixtus IV (1471–1484), was instrumental in establishing the national Spanish Inquisition and in 1475 a papal court of inquiry justified the Trent libel, which the pope endorsed in a bull of 1478. Rodrigo Borgia, later elected as Pope Alexander VI (1492–1503), had a considerable influence upon late fifteenth-century popes while he held the post of vice chancellor of the papal curia.

The expulsion from Spain also caused changes in Italy, particularly in the territories under Aragonese rule — Sicily, Sardinia and southern Italy — since Jews were also expelled from those territories. Until the end of April 1492 no expulsion order similar to that of Spain had been published. Furthermore, on 23 May the municipality of Palermo declared that it was forbidden to harm the Jews. However, on 9 June Ferdinand and Isabella forbade emigration from Sicily and the transfer of money to the Ottoman Empire. Jews were obliged to prepare an inventory of their possessions and deposit their bills of exchange with notaries. On 18 June the expulsion order was published, causing a wave of protest. On 20 June the citizens of Messina warned the king of the harm that would be done to the city if the Jews left. Palermo argued that the exodus of Jewish craftsmen would affect arms and agricultural supplies. At the request of the Jews the governor issued an order for their protection, continuing to protect them even though he was compelled to rescind the order. The Jews succeeded in postponing the expulsion until 12 January 1493. In the interim period there were continuous attempts to persuade the crown to rescind the order. Ferdinand, however, insisted that all Jews leave, including those of Malta and Sardinia.

About forty thousand Jews left Sicily alone. The numbers expelled from Sardinia were comparatively small. Pope Alexander VI did not prevent the refugees from residing in districts of the Papal States. Others went to the Ottoman-dominated Balkans and still others to the kingdom of Naples, where refugees from Spain had arrived.

In 1503 the kingdom of Naples was won by the Spanish and on 25 November 1510 an order was issued for the expulsion of the Jews, the date of implementation being fixed for the end of March 1511. By this order the Jews were forbidden ever to return. The expulsion order enabled the conversos of Apulia and Calabria and those who were tried and condemned in absentia by the Inquisition to put their affairs in order and leave the kingdom within a few months. They were allowed to take all their movable possessions other than gold and silver. Despite the edict, two hundred families were allowed to remain on condition that they annually paid three thousand ducats to the crown. Most of the Jews left the kingdom and in 1541 a total expulsion was ordered which included the conversos.

THE CITY OF ROME

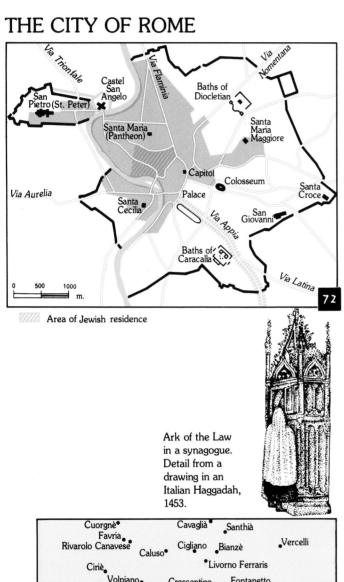

////// Area of Jewish residence

Ark of the Law in a synagogue. Detail from a drawing in an Italian Haggadah, 1453.

THE JEWISH COMMUNITIES OF ITALY

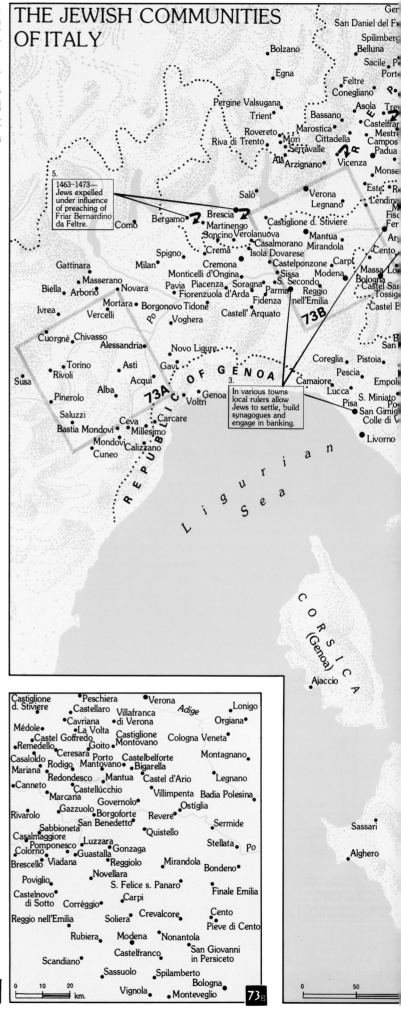

5. 1463–1473—Jews expelled under influence of preaching of Friar Bernardino da Feltre.

3. In various towns local rulers allow Jews to settle, build synagogues and engage in banking.

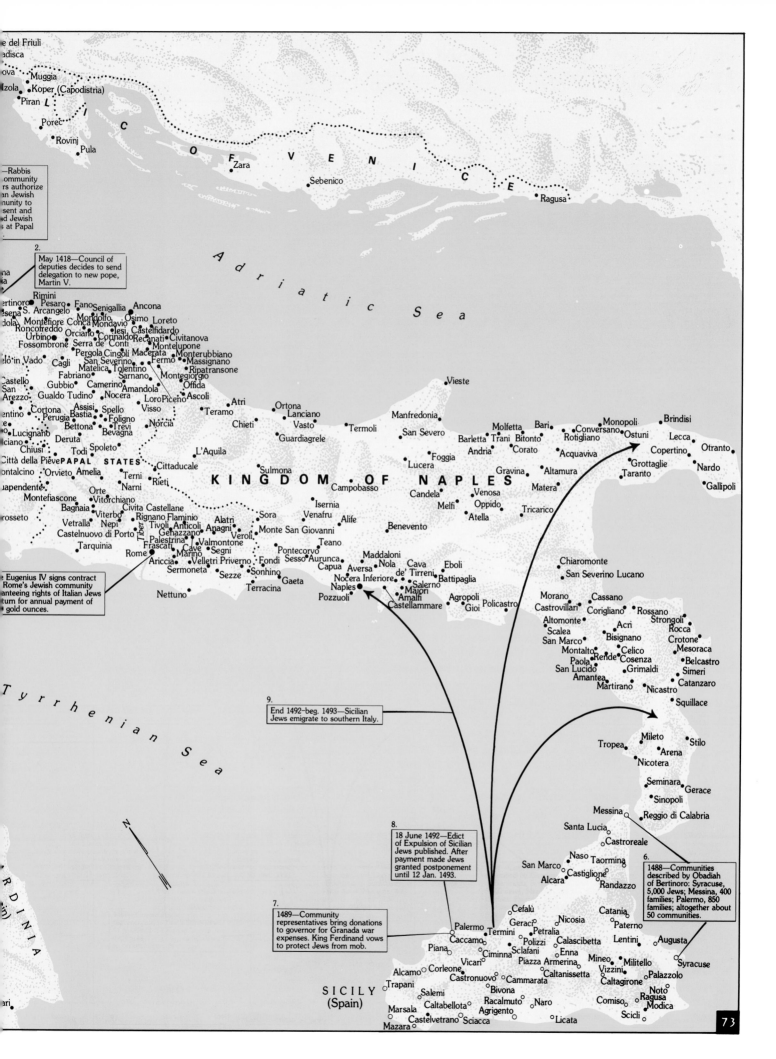

Muggia
Koper (Capodistria)
Piran
Porec
Rovinj
Pula
Zara
Sebenico
Ragusa

L I C
O F   V E N I C E

A d r i a t i c   S e a

2.
May 1418—Council of
deputies decides to send
delegation to new pope,
Martin V.

Rimini
Bertinoro Pesaro Fano Senigallia Ancona
esena S. Arcangelo Mondavio Osimo Loreto
dola Montefiore Conca Mondolfo Loreto
Roncofreddo Orciano Iesi Castelfidardo
Fossombrone Urbino Corinaldo Recanati Civitanova
elo'in Vado Serra de' Conti Montelupone
Cagli Pergola Cingoli Macerata Monterubbiano
San Severino Massignano
Fabriano Matelica Tolentino Sarnano Ripatransone
San Gubbio Camerino Amandola Montegiorgio
Arezzo Gualdo Tudino Nocera Offida
Assisi LoroPiceno Ascoli
Cortona Perugia Bastia Spello Visso Atri
tino Bettona Foligno Norcia Teramo
Lucignano Deruta Bevagna Ortona
Chiusi Todi Spoleto Norcia Chieti Lanciano
Città della Pieve **PAPAL STATES** Vasto
ontalcino Orvieto Amelia Guardiagrele
apendente Terni Rieti Cittaducale **KINGDOM · OF · NAPLES**
Montefiascone Narni L'Aquila
Bagnaia Orte Vitorchiano Sulmona
Vetralla Viterbo Civita Castellane Campobasso
Castelnuovo di Porto Rignano Flaminio Sora Isernia
Tarquinia Nepi Alatri Anticoli Venafru Alife
Palestrina Anagni Monte San Giovanni Benevento
Rome Genazzano Valmontone Veroli
Ariccia Cave Segni Teano
Frascati Marino Velletri Priverno Pontecorvo Maddaloni
Sermoneta Sezze Fondi Sesso Aurunca Nola
Nettuno Sonhino Capua Aversa Cava
Gaeta Nocera Inferiore de' Tirreni Eboli
Terracina Naples Salerno Battipaglia
Pozzuoli Amalfi Agropoli
Castellammare Gioi Policastro
Majori

Vieste
Manfredonia
Termoli San Severo
Molfetta Bari Monopoli Brindisi
Barletta Trani Bitonto Conversano Ostuni Lecca
Andria Corato Rotigliano Copertino Otranto
Lucera Foggia Acquaviva Grottaglie Nardo
Candela Gravina Altamura Taranto Gallipoli
Melfi Venosa Matera
Oppido Tricarico
Atella

Chiaromonte
San Severino Lucano
Morano Cassano
Castrovillari Corigliano Rossano
Altomonte Strongoli
Scalea Acri Rocca
San Marco Bisignano Crotone
Montalto Celico Mesoraca
Paola Rende Cosenza Belcastro
San Lucido Grimaldi Simeri
Amantea Nicastro Catanzaro
Martirano Squillace

Tropea Mileto Stilo
Arena
Nicotera
Seminara Gerace
Sinopoli
Reggio di Calabria
Messina
Santa Lucia
Castroreale
Naso Taormina
San Marco Castiglione
Alcara Randazzo
Cefalù Catania
Geraci Nicosia Paterno
Petralia Augusta
Palermo Termini Polizzi Calascibetta Enna Lentini Syracuse
Caccamo Sclafani Mineo Militello Palazzolo
Piana Ciminna Piazza Armerina Vizzini Caltagirone
Vicari Calanissetta
Alcamo Corleone Castronuovo Cammarata Noto Ragusa
Trapani Salemi Bivona Racalmuto Naro Comiso Modica
Marsala Caltabellota Agrigento Scicli
Castelvetrano Sciacca Licata
Mazara

T y r r h e n i a n   S e a

N

9.
End 1492–beg. 1493—Sicilian
Jews emigrate to southern Italy.

8.
18 June 1492—Edict
of Expulsion of Sicilian
Jews published. After
payment made Jews
granted postponement
until 12 Jan. 1493.

7.
1489—Community
representatives bring donations
to governor for Granada war
expenses. King Ferdinand vows
to protect Jews from mob.

6.
1488—Communities
described by Obadiah
of Bertinoro: Syracuse,
5,000 Jews; Messina, 400
families; Palermo, 850
families; altogether about
50 communities.

Eugenius IV signs contract
Rome's Jewish community
anteeing rights of Italian Jews
turn for annual payment of
gold ounces.

SICILY
(Spain)

RDINIA

73

JEWISH DEMOGRAPHIC CHANGES
From the Thirteenth Century until the Expulsion from Spain

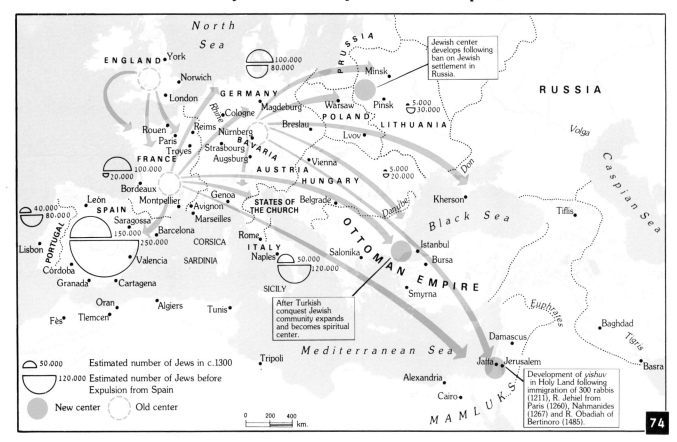

It is difficult to estimate the size of the Jewish population in the Middle Ages. Even were we able to surmise the number of Jews in a particular place, we would still be ignorant of their composition by age and sex or the birth and death rate. We lack not only the absolute numbers but also other factors. It is certain that there were great population fluctuations resulting from expulsions, or from persecutions and massacres, which often destroyed entire communities. Therefore any estimate can be based only upon actual available statistics such as tax records or martyrology lists. These figures are more or less accurate but relate only to a particular time and place. It is clear that we are dealing primarily with an urban Jewish population having diverse occupations which differed from place to place.

Jewish figures from the 15th century.

MAJOR EXPULSIONS

1290	Edward I expels Jews of England
1306	Philip IV expels Jews of France
	(Louis X readmits Jews for a twelve-year period)
1322	Charles IV again expels Jews from France
1367	Expulsion from Hungary
1381	Expulsion from Strasbourg
1394	Charles VI expels Jews of France
1421	Expulsion from Austria
1426	Expulsion from Cologne
1439	Expulsion from Augsburg

1450	Expulsion from Bavaria
1453	Expulsion from Breslau
1467	Expulsion from Tlemcen
1483	Expulsion from Andalusia
1492	Expulsion from Spain
1492	Expulsion from Sardinia
1493	Expulsion from Sicily
1495	Expulsion from Lithuania
1496	Expulsion from Portugal (replaced in 1497 by forced conversion)

England

The statistical information on England relates only to the period of the expulsion. Basing himself on tax records, the historian Georg Caro (1867–1912) estimated the size of the Jewish population in 1280 to 1283, — that is, before the expulsion — at between 2,500 and 3,000. This is a considerably smaller figure than is arrived at by various other calculations, which place the number at between 15,000 and 17,500. The historian S. W. Baron (1895–1989) assumed that the correct figure lies between the two estimates. In London there were apparently no more than 2,000 to 2,500 Jews and the bulk of the Jewish population resided in the rest of England. Therefore it would seem that the total number of Jews in England at the time of expulsion (1290) was about 10,000 — a very small number in relation to the general population, which is estimated at 3,500,000.

France

The statistics for French Jewry are also meager. In the south of what is today France, there was a dense Jewish population. According to Benjamin of Tudela, the town of Arles had two hundred Jewish families when he stopped there in 1160, while in 1194 the Jews were more than 25 percent of the town's population. A similar situation existed in the town of Tarascon. On the other hand, in September 1341, King Robert found that there were 1,205 Jews living in 203 houses in Aix-en-Provence, that is, no more than 10 percent of the general population. Narbonne experienced a decline in Jewish population and in 1305 there were no more than 1,000 Jews in comparison to 15,000 residents (about 7 percent). Toulouse had 15 Jewish families in 1391 and the situation was similar in Béziers, Albi and other towns in southern France. Only in the port town of Marseilles was there a large Jewish community. In 1358 at Avignon, 210 heads of Jewish families swore allegiance to the pope. Its Jewish population grew toward the end of the century and in 1414 the community requested permission to enlarge the area of the cemetery. In the 1490s refugees from Spain arrived at Avignon, but it is still difficult to calculate the size of the Jewish community in a town which was one of the largest in Europe, having 30,000 inhabitants in 1355. Carpentras had 64 Jewish family heads in 1276 and despite the expulsion in 1322, the community grew to 90 family heads in 1343. In 1486 the townspeople exerted pressure to reduce the area of the Jewish quarter, whose members in 1476 numbered 12 percent of the town's population.

In northern France, in the town of Troyes there were no more than 100 Jews during Rashi's time (1040–1105). While the expulsion of 1182 put a halt to Jewish population growth it did not affect the Jews of Champagne, Burgundy, Poitou and Normandy. In 1182 there were equal numbers of Jews and Christians residing in Paris. There was a large concentration of Jews residing in Villejuif near Paris, however, in the thirteenth and fourteenth centuries their numbers in Paris were on the decline. Jews resided in hundreds of small towns and the historian Heinrich Graetz (1817–1891) estimated that in 1306 there were 100,000 Jews who were expelled by Philip IV the Fair.

Germany

Germany's Jewish population increased between the eleventh and thirteenth centuries. During the subsequent two hundred years the population grew only gradually. The Hohenstaufen rulers founded many towns that attracted Jewish settlers. The number of Jews massacred in Mainz during the First Crusade is indicative of the size of this major Jewish community. Jewish sources give a figure of 1,100 to 1,300 killed, while Christian sources cite 1,014. The Nürnberg Jewish community is recorded in a tax list from 1338 as having 212 persons decreasing to 150 by 1449. Another reliable demographic source is the Nürnberg *memorbuch* in which the names of the 628 martyrs of the Rindfleisch massacres in 1298 were recorded. Apparently the community recuperated since the massacres of 1349 claimed 570 victims. To these numbers one must add those Jews who escaped. The community numbered some 1,000 in the thirteenth and fourteenth centuries. Nürnberg recovered after the Black Death and became one of the largest communities in Germany. In 1498, when the Jews were expelled from the town, it had a population of about 20,000.

According to S. W. Baron the total Jewish population of Germany and Austria at the beginning of the fourteenth century was about 10,000. In 1500 there were in all of Germany (the Holy Roman Empire) about 12 million people. Therefore the percentage of Jews was very small. Because the Jewish population was primarily an urban one, it is difficult to calculate the population of every town and village.

Italy

The demography of Jews in Italy differed considerably in the north and the south. In the 1260s Benjamin of Tudela found 500 families (or taxpayers) in Naples, 600 in Salerno, 500 in Otranto, 300 in Capua, 300 in Taranto, 200 in Benevento, 200 in Melfi and 200 in Trani. He found 20 families in the port of Amalfi — at this time the town was in a depression. In this period Sicily was heavily populated with Jews: 200 in Messina, 1,500 families in Palermo — the largest single concentration of Jews in southern Italy. Until the expulsion of 1493 Sicily was the center of Italian Jewish life. Palermo and Syracuse had about 5,000 Jews each at the time of the expulsion. Therefore, Nicolo Ferorelli estimated the number of Jews in Sicily at about 50,000 (1492). This figure seems accurate, since Attilio Milano (1907–1969) arrived at a figure of 37,046 Jews for Sicily — with its 45 communities, and Malta, Gozo and Pantelleria. There was also a community in Sardinia during the period of Aragonese rule. In the sixteenth and seventeenth centuries the community of Rome developed considerably (in 1527 there were 1,738 Jews). Venice in the sixteenth and seventeenth centuries was the largest and most important of the northern communities, numbering several hundred Jews.

During the fifteenth to seventeenth centuries the Jews of Italy migrated from place to place, achieving a degree of communal organization similar to that achieved by the Jews of Ashkenaz and Spain in the thirteenth century.

Frequently the number of Jewish immigrants exceeded those who were native born. Expulsion of the Jews from the southern towns in 1492 to 1511 shifted the Jewish center of gravity to Rome and northward, where the Jewish population was about 25,000 to 30,000, a figure that remained unchanged for several centuries.

Spain

The Jewish population of Castile grew from 60,000 in 1300 to 160,000 by 1492. By contrast the Jewish population in Aragón decreased to 75,000. Navarre had 15,000 Jews. A knowledge of the number of Jews in Spain in 1492 is an essential factor in estimating the size of the Jewish population of Europe, Asia and Africa from the sixteenth century onwards. The number of Jews expelled from Spain has been estimated by both Jewish and Christian sources. The priest-historian Andrés Bernáldez, a contemporary of the expulsion period, estimated that in 1492 there were 35,000 heads of family in Castile and 6,000 in Aragón. One Jewish document calculates 50,000 heads of family, while another estimates that 53,000 were expelled. Isaac Abrabanel (1437–1508) estimated the number that left and crossed the Portuguese border on foot at 300,000 "young and old, children and women," which would mean that in Castile there were between 150,000 to 200,000 Jews at the time of the Expulsion. Another method of calculation is by the size of the communities. For example the Jewish community of Cáceres in Estremadura numbered 130 persons and in the neighboring Talavera de la Reina between the years 1477 and 1487 there were 168 families, these numbers being typical of many other communities. A conservative estimate of the Castilian communities will show that between 1486 and 1491 there were 14,400 to 15,300 families. Estimating six people per family we would reach a figure of under 100,000. If we add to the number of Jews who left Spain some of the conversos, we will arrive at the total Jewish population towards the end of the fifteenth century. A further source of information is the tax paid by the refugees crossing the Portuguese border, each of whom had to pay eight cruzados for permission to cross over and to reside for eight months in the kingdom of Portugal. Here a figure of 120,000 can be reached. We also know that those who went to North Africa in hired ships numbered approximately 50,000. Several thousand refugees crossed the border of the kingdom of Navarre in 1493, having been given certificates of passage and protection so that they might get to Spanish ports whence they could embark. About 50,000 Jews went to Italy and several thousand to Avignon. All these figures bring us close to the estimate of 200,000.

These figures refer only to the Jews of Europe to whom we must add the Jews of Poland-Lithuania estimated at about 50 to 60 communities (30,000 persons) in the fifteenth century. Hungary and the Balkans had very few Jewish communities until the arrival of the Spanish refugees.

By comparison with our knowledge of European Jewish demography we are in the dark concerning the number of Jews in North Africa (including Egypt) and Asia. North Africa had sizable Jewish communities in the tenth and eleventh

centuries but there was a decline in the twelfth and thirteenth centuries. After the persecution of 1391 and the expulsion of 1492, Jews from Spain reached North Africa. In Asia concentrations of Jews could be found in Iran and Iraq and it is reasonable to assume that they numbered several thousands. We have no information about the size of sixteenth-century Jewish communities in Yemen, the Ottoman Empire, Byzantine Asia Minor and Palestine. However, we know that the revival of the Jewish *yishuv* in Palestine in the sixteenth century brought with it a substantial increase in the number of Jews in the Holy Land.

JEWISH POPULATIONS IN EUROPE
(By Percentages)

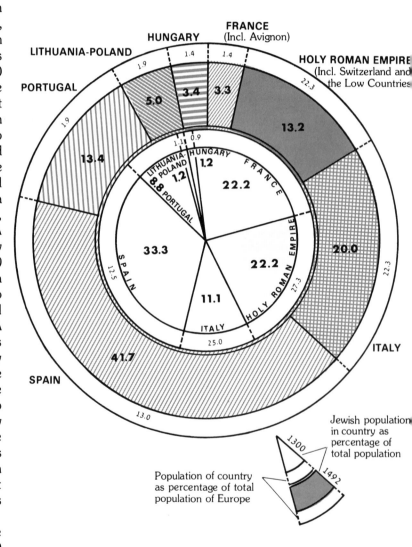

Jewish population in country as percentage of total population

Population of country as percentage of total population of Europe

	1300	1492
Total population	44,000,000	53,800,000
Jewish population	450,000	600,000
Jews as percentage of total population	1.02	1.22

THE EXPULSION ORDER

Don Fernando and Doña Isabela ... by the Grace of God ... etc. ... To the Prince heir don Juan, our very dear and beloved son, to the Infantes, Prelates, Dukes, Marquises, Counts, Masters of Orders, Priors, Ricos omes, Commanders, Alcaldes of Castles and Fortified houses of our Kingdoms and Domains, to all Councils, Alcaldes, Alguasils, Merinos, Calealleros, Escuderos, officials and notables of the very noble and loyal town of Avila, and all the other towns, villages and places of its Bishopry, and to all other Archbishopries and Bishopries and Dioceses of our Kingdoms and Domains, and to the Aljamas of the Jews in the named town of Avila and to all other towns, villages and places of its Bishopry, and to all other towns and villages and Places of our Kingdoms and Domains, and to all other Jews and persons, males and females of any age, and to all other persons of any standing, dignity, preeminence and state they may be, to whom the contents of this Order may concern in any way, grace and greetings.

Know indeed or you must know, that we have been informed that in our kingdoms there were some bad Christians who judaized and apostatized against our holy Catholic Faith, mainly because of the connection between the Jews and the Christians. In the *Cortes* of the past year which we held in Toledo in 1480, we ordered the separation of the above-mentioned Jews in all cities, villages and places in our kingdoms and domains, and to give them Jewish quarters and separate quarters where they should live, hoping that through this separation the matter would be remedied. We further ordered that an inquisition be held in our kingdoms and domains. As you know, this was done and has been the practice for more than twelve years and through it, as is well known, many sinners have been found by the inquisitors, churchmen and many other secular authorities.

Thus the great damage caused to Christians by their participation, connection and conversation they had and are having with the Jews which is proven which they do to subverse and remove from our holy Catholic Faith the devoted Christians and apart them from it and attract and pervert them to their damned faith and opinion instructing them in their ceremonies and observances of their law, organizing meetings in which they read to them and teach them in what they have belief and keep according to their Law, circumcising them and their children, providing them with books in which they recite their prayers, informing them when they have to fast in their fasting days, coming together for readings and teaching them histories of their Law, notifying them the days of their holy days to come, informing them how they are to be observed, giving and bringing from their homes Matzoth and meats slaughtered according to their rituals, advising them from what to abstain in food and in other matters in observance of their Law, convincing them as much as they are able to observe and keep the Law of Moses, making them to understand that there is no other Law nor truth, but theirs, which has been proven through many confessions by the Jews themselves as well by those whom they perverted and deceived, which all caused great damage in detriment of our holy Catholic Faith.

Although we were informed about this beforehand and we know that the real remedy to all the damages and inconveniences is to separate the said Jews and the Christians in all our kingdoms and to expel them from our realm. We had thought it sufficient to order them out of the cities and villages and settlements in Andalusia, where they had already caused great damage, thinking that this would be enough for those living in other cities, villages and places in our kingdoms and domains who would stop acting and sinning as described above.

And because we are aware that this matter, and punishments inflicted on some of these Jews who were found guilty of these great sins and transgressions against our holy Catholic Faith, proved to be insufficient as a complete remedy, in preventing and remedying the great sin and transgression against the holy Catholic Faith and religion; it is not enough for a full remedy in order to cease this great offence to the faith, since we have discovered and seen that Jews pursue their evil and damaging intentions wherever they are found and are in touch; in order that there should be no further damage to our holy Faith, both through those whom God preserved so far and those who failed, but reformed their conduct and were brought back to the fold of the holy Catholic Church — our Holy Mother — and what is bound to happen bearing in mind our human weakness and the deceit and intrigues of the Devil who is continuously fighting us, something that can easily occur, we have decided to remove the main cause for this through the expulsion of the Jews from our kingdoms. Whenever a grave and detestable crime is committed by any member of any society or group, it is proper that that society or group be dissolved or that the low disappear or suffer for the sake of the lofty, the few for the sake of the many. Those who corrupt the good and decent life in towns and villages and contagiously injure others, they should be expelled from these places. If for matters far less consequential which may cause damage to the state we act this way, all the more so for a very serious crime, one of the most dangerous and contagious crimes as this is.

Therefore, in consultation and agreement with the clergy, the higher and lower nobility in our realm, other men of science and conscience from our Council and having deliberated much on the matter, we have agreed to order the expulsion of all Jews and Jewesses in our kingdoms. Never should any one of them return nor come back. We have therefore issued this order. Thus we order all Jews and Jewesses of any age, who live, dwell and are found in our kingdoms and domains, whether born here or elsewhere, and are present here for any reason, must leave our kingdoms and domains until the end of the next month of July this year, together with their sons and daughters, their male and maidservants and their Jewish relatives, old and young, whatever their age. They should not dare to return and live where they previously lived, not for passage or in any other form, under a penalty, that if they fail to do so and to obey the order, and if they are found living in our kingdoms and domains, or come here in any way, they should be put to death, their property being confiscated by our Court and Royal Treasury. These punishments will be inflicted on the basis of the act and law, without trial, verdict and proclamation.

We order and prohibit that no man in our kingdoms, whatever his status, position and level should receive under his protection, should accomodate or defend, openly or secretly, any Jew or Jewess, from the above-mentioned date, the end of next July and onwards, for ever, neither in their lands nor in their houses, or anywhere in our kingdoms and domains, under the penalty of having their property, their vassals, their fortresses and any other thing that passes in inheritance confiscated. They will also lose any acts of mercy they have from us to the advantage of the Court and Royal fisc.

In order that these Jews and Jewesses can sell in a proper way their goods and property during this time until the end of the month of July, we take them and their property, throughout this period, under our protection, auspices and royal defense, so that during this period until the last day of July, could securely move around, sell, exchange or transfer their movables and land, and decide freely and willingly anything connected with them. During this period no harm, evil or injustice should be inflicted on the people and their property against the law, under a penalty against anyone who contravenes the royal safety of the kingdom.

We hereby as well authorize and permit these Jews and Jewesses to take out from our kingdoms and domains their property and goods, by sea or land, as long as they do not take away gold, silver and coins and any other article forbidden by the law of the kingdom, apart from goods which are not prohibited and exchange bills. We also instruct all the Councils and Courts of Justice, the regidores, the *caballeros* and *escuderos*, the officials and notables in the city of Avila, and cities, villages and other places in our kingdoms and domains, all vassals who are under our dominion and natives, that they should keep and fulfil our order and everything written in it, do and give any help and support to anyone who needs it, under the penalty of losing our mercy and having all their property and positions confiscated by the Court and Royal Treasury.

In order that this may reach everyone, and that no one should pretend ignorance, we command that our order be proclaimed in the usual places and squares in this city and major cities, in villages and places in the bishop's domain by the herald and in the presence of the notary public.

No one should act against this under penalty of our mercy and deprivation of all offices and confiscation of his property. And we order any person who would be summoned to appear before us in our Court, wherever we may be, from the day of summons till fifteen days coming, and under the same penalty to appear. And we order any notary public who will be summoned for it, to present the order stamped by his seal so that we shall be informed how our order is carried out.

Given to our city of Granada, the 31st of the month of March in the year 1492. I, the King and I, the Queen. I, Juan de Coloma, the secretary of the King and Queen our Lords, have written as ordered.

(Original text: R. León Tello, Judíos de Avila, Avila 1964, pp. 91–95.)

EXPULSION FROM SPAIN   31 March 1492

The expulsion order came as a surprise to the Jews of Spain. During the month of April unsuccessful efforts were made to rescind the edict, in which Micer Alfonso de la Caballeria among others was involved. On 1 May the edict was promulgated in Castile, and two days earlier in Saragossa. The Jews were allowed three months to wind up their affairs and leave Spain. Spanish Jewry immediately began to prepare to leave. Among those who left for Italy was the family of Don Isaac Abrabanel from the port of Valencia. Compelled to forgo loans he had advanced to the crown, he was permitted to take gold, silver and jewelry out of the country although this was forbidden in the edict. Others attempted to smuggle their valuables out. The authorities were interested in a calm and orderly expulsion. Various personalities, among them descendants of conversos Luis de Santangel and Francisco Pinelo, negotiated with and gave guarantees to ship captains for chartering vessels to carry the evacuees to North Africa and other places. This was a trying period for the communities whose leaders had the additional task of disposing of community property — synagogues, schools, public ritual baths (*Mikvaot*), and cemeteries etc.

The value of property declined drastically; houses, fields and vineyards were sold for the price of a donkey or a mule. By contrast, the price of cloth and silk rose because the refugees were allowed to take such goods with them. The Christians at first hoped for a loss of faith on the part of Spanish Jews and a subsequent readiness to convert and remain in the land where they had resided for close to fifteen hundred years. They were astounded by the Jews' spiritual fortitude as they left for the ports of embarkation with hymns on their lips.

Jews were forbidden ever to return to Spain on pain of death unless they were prepared to convert to Christianity. As a result, Spain was without Jews for hundreds of years. The Spanish expulsion served as a model for expulsions in Lithuania (1495) and Portugal (1496), though the latter was changed by King Emanuel (Manuel) I (1495–1521), for a forced conversion of the Jewish population.

Contemporary descriptions of the hardship and suffering of the banished Jews produced epics unequalled in the annals of human history.

Capital of a column from a synagogue that was to be inaugurated in 1496/7 in Gouveia, Portugal.

"I heard it told by elders, exiles from Spain, that a certain ship was smitten by pestilence and the owner cast the passengers ashore on a desolate site. Whereupon most of them died of starvation, a few attempting to walk until they could find a place of habitation. One Jew among them with his wife and two sons struggled to walk and the woman being barefooted swooned and expired, while the man, carrying his sons, both he and they collapsed from hunger and upon recovering from his swoon, he found the two boys dead. Arising in great distress he cried 'God of the Universe! You do much to cause me to abandon my faith. Know you that despite those who dwell in Heaven, I am a Jew and will remain a Jew, despite all you have brought upon me or will bring upon me.' And so saying he gathered dust and grass, covered the youths, and went to seek an inhabited place."

From Solomon Ibn Verga (late 15th–early 16th centuries), Shevet Yehudah, *Hebrew edition by A. Schochat, Jerusalem 1947, p. 122.*

JEWISH EXODUS FROM SPAIN AND PORTUGAL   1492–1497

The Expulsion from Spain altered the map of Jews in Europe, creating a Diaspora within a Diaspora — Spanish Jewish communities formed within existing Jewish communities. This situation poses two questions. How many Jews left Spain and what were their destinations? It is difficult to calculate the number expelled, but an estimate may be hazarded, on the basis of the number of Jewish residents in various places. The majority of Spanish Jews in the fifteen century resided in Castile. A conservative estimate of this population is 30,000 families, that is, between 120,000 to 150,000 people. In Aragón the estimate is about 50,000 people. This gives us a total of 200,000 expelled — an approximate estimate given in both Jewish and non-Jewish sources.

Most of those banished went to Portugal, where they were offered a temporary eight-month haven for the per capita price of eight cruzados. Twenty-five ships led by Pedro Cabron left Cádiz for Oran but the Jewish passengers fearing to disembark — despite the reassurance of a Genoese pirate named Fragosso — returned to Arsila in North Africa. Storms forced the ships to anchor at Cartagena and Málaga where many of the Jews converted while others died of an epidemic. Those who disembarked at Asilah remained there until 1493. They were joined by a group of Jews who had settled in Portugal and were now on their way to the east (except for 700 heads of family who went to Morocco), paying a considerable sum of money for this privilege.

Other refugees went to North Africa, Italy and further eastward. Some went to the papal state in France. Their

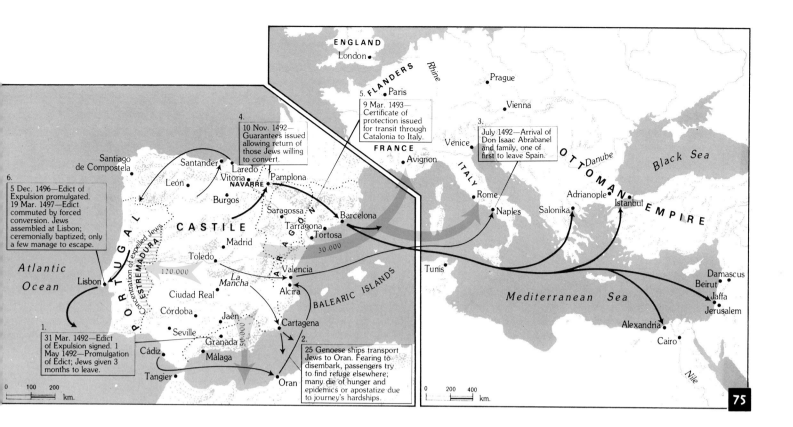

75

journeys were beset with hardship, suffering and affliction, robbery, extortion, and even murder. Many lost their lives on the way.

A cruel fate awaited those Jews who fled to Portugal. John II (1481–1495) accepted 600 wealthy families and skilled craftsmen, granting them permanent residence; others, who were given only temporary residence, were enslaved if they failed to leave on time.

The reign of John II's successor, Manuel I (1495–1521) was a tragic one for the Jews of Portugal. Isabella, daughter of Ferdinand and Isabella, agreed to marry him on condition that he rid Portugal of the Jews. Thus on 5 December 1496 the edict of expulsion was promulgated, the text being an abridged copy of the Spanish edict. In February 1497 Jewish children up to the age of fourteen whose parents intended emigrating, were seized and forcibly baptized. Soon the age limit was extended to twenty, and Jews began to flee the country in every possible way. Many children were detained and transferred to the Portuguese colony on the island of São Tomé in the Gulf of Guinea off the African coast, where they were cruelly ill-treated and most of them died in the jungle.

On 19 March 1497 the expulsion edict was replaced by forced conversion, a change in policy which possibly stemmed from the desire to retain the Jewish population within a sparsely populated nation of about one million people that had recently undertaken large settlement commitments in western Africa. The act of conversion was accomplished through deception, by assembling at Lisbon, the only officially-sanctioned port of embarkation, all those wishing to leave. Those assembled were then ceremonially baptized and declared citizens of the realm. Only a few, among them Abraham b. Samuel Zacuto, were able to resist

and later escaped. On 30 May 1497 the king issued orders that those who converted should be safe from persecution and from the Inquisition for a twenty-year period. From this it would appear that Manuel I was already contemplating the institution of a national inquisition modeled on that of Spain.

Many new communities were established by the Spanish exiles in the Mediterranean basin, the Ottoman Empire proved particularly congenial to Jews and conversos, who developed a comprehensive spiritual network in their communities. The Holy Land also attracted the Spanish exiles and its conquest by the Turks (1517) served as a fulcrum for the expansion and development of the Jewish communities in the country.

"And I Judah, son of my lord the wise and pious R. Jacob may he rest in peace, while residing in Spain savored a smidgen of honey, mine eyes saw the light and my mind was given to seek wisdom and inquire thereof. I went from strength to strength gathering all that was found in the aforementioned book, gleaning a morsel here and a morsel there until I possessed most of what it contained. In true faith I believe it was this knowledge that enabled me to withstand the terrible hardships that befell me upon my expulsion from Spain; and that whosoever heareth of it, both his ears shall tingle; to relate all the hardships, from I know not the numbers thereof but of some I will tell and I shall speak the praises of the Lord.

We traveled, I and my family, with 250 other souls in one vessel, in mid-winter 1493, from Lisbon the great city of the Kingdom of Portugal at the command of the king. The Lord struck us with pestilence to fulfill his word 'I will smite them with pestilence and destroy them...' and this was the reason why no place would receive us — 'Depart ye! unclean! men cried unto them' and we left wandering ceaselessly, four months on the sea with 'meager bread and scant water'. "

R. Judah Hayat, Ma'arekhet ha-Elohut, Mantua, 1558, introduction.

ROUTES TAKEN BY JEWS EXPELLED FROM SPAIN

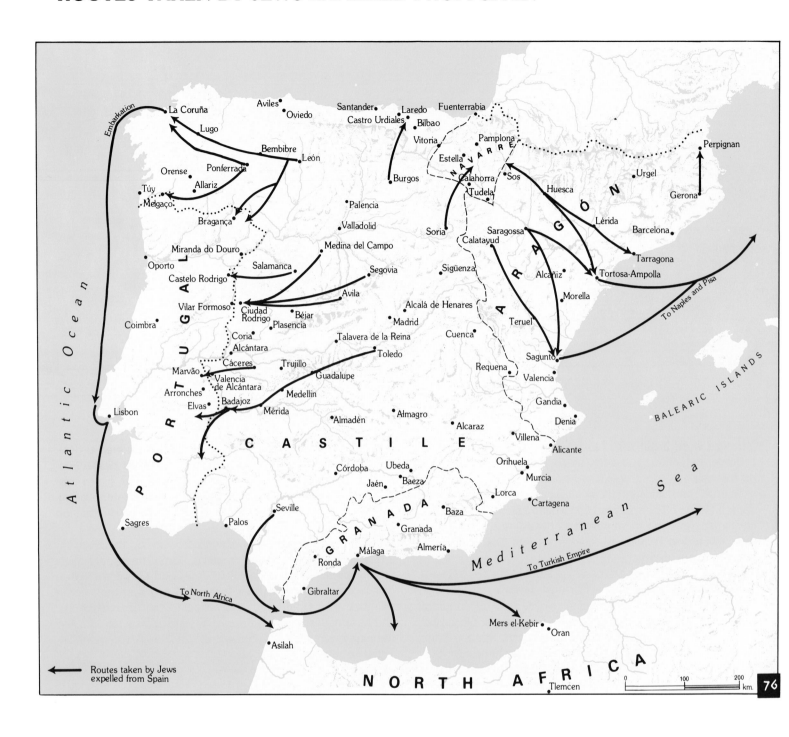

Routes taken by Jews expelled from Spain

THE WANDERINGS OF
R. JUDAH HAYYAT

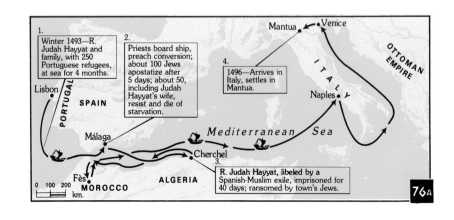

1. Winter 1493—R. Judah Hayyat and family, with 250 Portuguese refugees, at sea for 4 months.

2. Priests board ship, preach conversion; about 100 Jews apostatize after 5 days; about 50, including Judah Hayyat's wife, resist and die of starvation.

3. R. Judah Hayyat, libeled by a Spanish-Muslim exile, imprisoned for 40 days; ransomed by town's Jews.

4. 1496—Arrives in Italy, settles in Mantua.

UNTIL THE CHMIELNICKI MASSACRES
AND SHABBATEAN MOVEMENT

The Turkish fleet besieging a city. Late fifteenth century.

THE OTTOMAN EMPIRE AT THE HEIGHT OF ITS EXPANSION   Until 1683

The expansion of the Ottoman Empire in Europe aroused deep fear in the Christian world, since it seemed that with the fall of Constantinople in 1453 there was no power that could halt this expansion. With great momentum the empire annexed the whole of the southern Mediterranean basin, excluding a few areas under Spanish rule in Morocco. Attempts by various popes to arouse the Christian world to forestall the danger were unsuccessful, particularly since the Christian world was disunited and engaged in wars over the Lutheran Reformation.

The victory of the allied Christian forces in the naval battle of Lepanto (1571) led by Don John of Austria, half brother of King Philip II of Spain (1556–1598), dealt a blow to the Ottoman navy but did not affect the foundation of its empire. Philip had made his plans for war against England and was therefore interested in preserving calm on his Mediterranean flank. Thus in 1578 he succeeded in negotiating an armistice with the Turks. In 1580 Philip ascended the throne of Portugal, intensifying his plans for war with England, which he attacked in 1588, only to be defeated.

For their part, the Turks turned to central Europe, where they already controlled large areas of Hungary, threatening the Holy Roman Empire. On 28 October 1595 the Turks were defeated in the battle of Giurgiu and their expansion was halted.

The existing political climate enabled the Jews to promote immigration to the Holy Land and revitalize the Jewish population there. Within the Ottoman Empire Jews engaged in international trade, particularly with Europe. Philip II of Spain even suspected them of both covertly and overtly supporting Turkish expansion, suspecting the Jewish exiles from Spain who had settled in large numbers in Ottoman-dominated European territories of collusion. Refugee communities were established in many towns in the Balkan Peninsula, the Turks encouraging their residence in important centers. Thus, for example, Jews were ordered to settle in Constantinople after its conquest by the Turks in 1453. In Salonika the Spanish, Portuguese and Italian refugees joined the indigenous Romaniots and the more recently arrived Ashkenazic Jews (1470). The communal organization in Salonika was of a special character, each immigrant group forming its own congregation (*kahal kadosh*) named after its native country or town. At the height of its development the city had thirty such congregations.

A 15th-century woodcut depicting characters from different nations. On the right is a Jew.

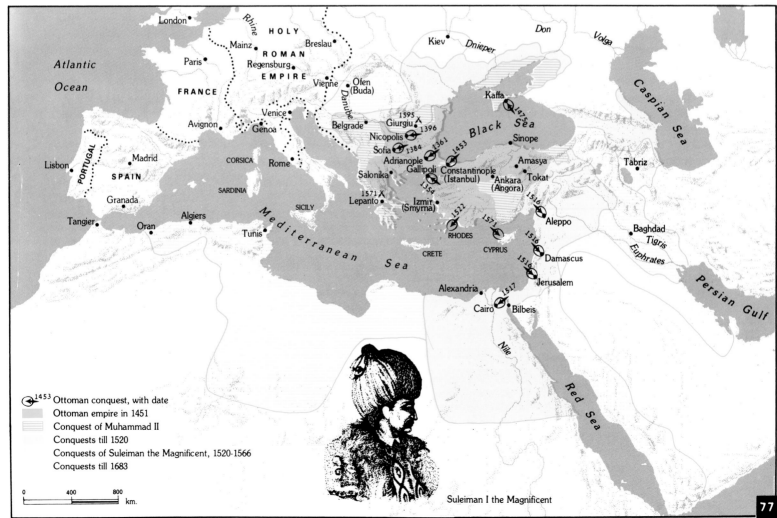

1453 Ottoman conquest, with date

Ottoman empire in 1451

Conquest of Muhammad II

Conquests till 1520

Conquests of Suleiman the Magnificent, 1520-1566

Conquests till 1683

0   400   800
km.

Suleiman I the Magnificent

THE JEWS OF THE BALKAN PENINSULA

Sixteenth Century

"CONGREGATIONS" (SYNAGOGUES)
IN SALONIKA, 16TH CENTURY

4. Arrival of Ashkenazi Jews who immigrated during Reformation and religious wars.

3. 1526—After conquest of Buda many Hungarian Jews arrive; transferred to Balkans.

7. Mid-16th cent.—About 50,000 Jews reside in city; establish 44 synagogues.

9. 1533—Blood libel in Amasya.

6. Stations on Jewish immigration route to Balkans.

5. 1540—Spanish Jews settled in Italy and conversos fleeing from Inquisition leave after conquest of Naples by Charles V.

2. 1522—After conquest of island, 150 Jewish families brought here from Salonika; contribute to developing important commercial center. Island also serves as transit station for immigrants to Holy Land.

1. From late 15th cent.—Refugees arrive from Spain, Portugal and Sicily; important communities established, particularly Salonika.

8. Don Joseph Nasi, minister and adviser to Sultan Suleiman I, increases his influence during reign of Selim II; appointed duke of Naxos, or duke of Aegean Isles.

⊗ Torah center

78

Congregation list
*Aragón
Ashkenazi
Astruc
Baalei Teshuva — 'Community of the Penitent'
Calabria (Old)
Castile
*Castile (Expulsion)
Catalonia
*Catalonia (Expulsion)
Corfu
Etz Hayyim (or *Etz Hada'at*)
Évora
Ishmael
Italy
*Lisbon (Old and New)
Majorca (*Baalei Teshuva*)
Midrash (Castile)
Neot Hen
Otranto
Portugal (New)
Provence
*Pugliese
Shalom (or *Neve Shalom*)
Sicily (Old)
Sicily (New)
Spain (Expulsion)

* Large Congregation

PALESTINE UNDER OTTOMAN RULE

Sixteenth Century

Tombstone of Samuel son of Yoel ibn Shuaib from the Aragonese congregation in Salonika.

3. Safed becomes major Jewish center in country with a population of 15,000 engaged in farming, cloth manufacturing and export of finished goods to Damascus.

5. Late 16th cent.—Beginning of decline; 1576-77—About 1,000 Jews expelled to Cyprus to counterbalance Christian community.

4. Jews in Safed live in their own quarters; in Shechem and Jerusalem in mixed quarters. Four ethnic groups exist: Musta'rabs (native born), Maghrebis (from North Africa), Ashkenazim and Sephardim (refugees from expulsions).

1. 1516—Turkish Sultan Selim I conquers Palestine.

2. 1522—Traveler relates of 1,570 Jews (300 families) living in city.

······· Boundary of Sanjak (province)

79

MAJOR TRADE ROUTES   Sixteenth to Seventeenth Centuries

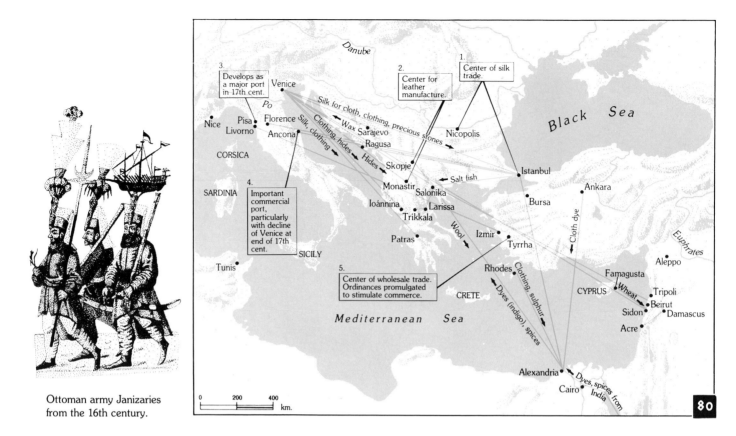

Map labels:

Danube

3. Develops as a major port in 17th cent. — Venice

2. Center for leather manufacture.

1. Center of silk trade.

Black Sea

Po

Nice Pisa Florence Livorno Ancona

Silk for cloth, clothing, precious stones

Silk, clothing Wax Sarajevo

Clothing, hides Ragusa

CORSICA Hides Skopje

Nicopolis

Istanbul

Ankara

SARDINIA

4. Important commercial port, particularly with decline of Venice at end of 17th cent.

Salt fish

Monastir Salonika

Ioánnina Larissa

Tríkkala

SICILY

Patras

Wool Izmir

Tyrrha

Bursa

Cloth dye

Euphrates

Aleppo

5. Center of wholesale trade. Ordinances promulgated to stimulate commerce.

Tunis

Rhodes

Clothing, sulphur

Famagusta Wheat

CYPRUS

Tripoli

CRETE

Dyes (indigo), spices

Sidon Beirut Damascus

Acre

Mediterranean Sea

Alexandria Dyes, spices from India

Cairo

0   200   400
km.

80

Ottoman army Janizaries from the 16th century.

IMMIGRATION TO THE HOLY LAND   Sixteenth and Seventeenth Centuries

The instability stemming from frequent changes of rule in Palestine, the harassment encountered there by Jews, and the heavy taxation imposed upon them all failed to deter Jews immigrating to the country. The immigration wave of the sixteenth century brought new life to the local Jewish population that is described in the accounts left by pilgrims. The Jews resided in a few towns, chiefly Jerusalem, Safed, Tiberias and in some agricultural villages in Galilee. For hundreds of years the Jews of Italy played a special role in strengthening Palestine's Jews by direct support to the communities and by serving as a transit station en route for the immigrants.

Some of the refugees from Spain as well as kabbalists came in the hope of imminent redemption.

Safed of the sixteenth century had an established and growing Jewish community and was the home of many great scholars, among them Jacob (I) Berav, Joseph Caro and Moses Trani. In 1548, nineteen hundred taxpaying families, of whom 716 were Jewish, lived in the town.

In 1560 Doña Gracia Mendes-Nasi obtained concessions in Tiberias from the sultan (confirmed and extended for Joseph Nasi, her nephew, in 1561), intending to rebuild the town and reestablish the Jewish community. Joseph Nasi ordered the

reconstruction of the town's walls (completed in 1565) and the planting of mulberry trees for the silk industry. A call was issued to Jewish communities in the Mediterranean basin inviting them to settle in Tiberias and the entire community of Cori (south of Rome) made preparations to emigrate. After Joseph Nasi's death in 1579 the Tiberias venture was continued by Solomon Abenaes (Ibn Yaish) a Portuguese converso statesman, wealthy merchant and successor of Joseph Nasi at the Turkish court in Constantinople.

The decline in the seventeenth century of the Jewish population in the Holy Land in general and in Galilee in particular reflected the erosion of the Ottoman Empire during this period. The Jewish community of Safed was severely affected by the continuing wars between the Ottoman rulers and the Druzes of Lebanon, as well as by epidemics and a plague of locusts. Despite attempts at reconstituting the Safed community in the 1720s, it never regained its sixteenth-century status and glory. The center of gravity shifted to Jerusalem. Rabbi Isaac ha-Kohen Sholal (Solal), the last *nagid* in Mamluk Egypt from 1502, settled in Jerusalem in 1517. The beginning of the seventeenth century saw a stream of immigrants to Jerusalem, particularly from Italy. The distinguished rabbi, Isaiah b. Abraham ha-Levi Horowitz

IMMIGRATION ROUTES TO THE HOLY LAND

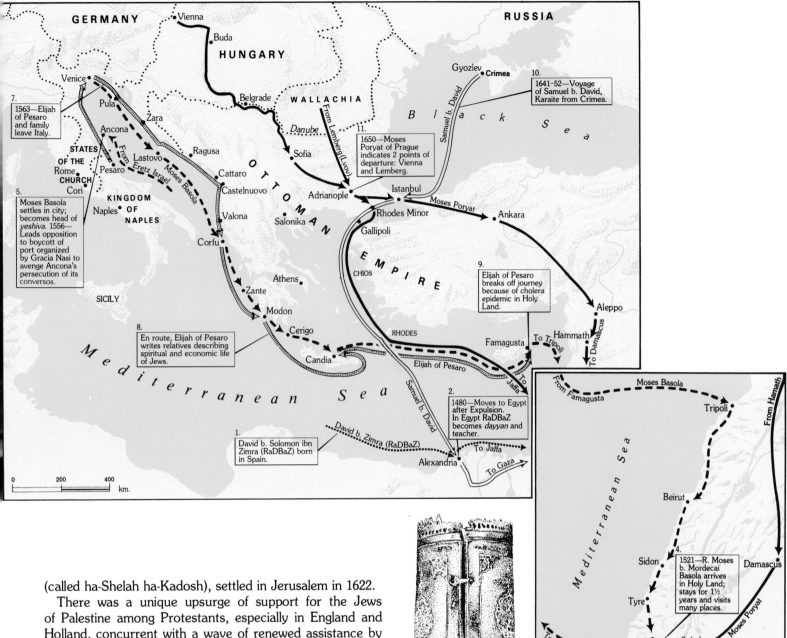

7. 1563—Elijah of Pesaro and family leave Italy.

5. Moses Basola settles in city; becomes head of *yeshiva*. 1556—Leads opposition to boycott of port organized by Gracia Nasi to avenge Ancona's persecution of its conversos.

8. En route, Elijah of Pesaro writes relatives describing spiritual and economic life of Jews.

10. 1641-52—Voyage of Samuel b. David, Karaite from Crimea.

11. 1650—Moses Poryat of Prague indicates 2 points of departure: Vienna and Lemberg.

9. Elijah of Pesaro breaks off journey because of cholera epidemic in Holy Land.

2. 1480—Moves to Egypt after Expulsion. In Egypt RaDBaZ becomes *dayyan* and teacher.

1. David b. Solomon ibn Zimra (RaDBaZ) born in Spain.

4. 1521—R. Moses b. Mordecai Basola arrives in Holy Land; stays for 1½ years and visits many places.

6. Basola returns to Holy Land; dies 1560.

12. Moses Poryat describes 2 routes of travel to Holy Land.

3. 1533—RaDBaZ returns to Jerusalem and later to Safed, where he resides until his death in 1573.

(called ha-Shelah ha-Kadosh), settled in Jerusalem in 1622.

There was a unique upsurge of support for the Jews of Palestine among Protestants, especially in England and Holland, concurrent with a wave of renewed assistance by the Jewish Diaspora, especially for Jerusalem. The Jews of Italy and the Low Countries were particularly generous.

For many generations the Jews in the Holy Land were dependent upon the financial support of the Diaspora, brought by travelers or immigrants via treacherous routes, often at great risk to their lives. However, such support was inadequate, and the local community was forced to send emissaries known as *shadarim* (from *sheluhei de-rabbanan*) out to the entire Diaspora, east and west, to procure contributions. The despatch of these emissaries attested to the close ties between the Jews of the Diaspora and those of the Holy Land.

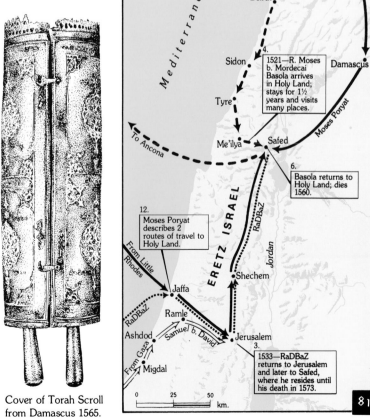

Cover of Torah Scroll from Damascus 1565. Incised copper with silver decoration.

Signature of R. David ben Zimra (the RaDBaZ).

EMISSARIES FROM THE HOLY LAND TO THE DIASPORA
Eighth to Seventeenth Centuries

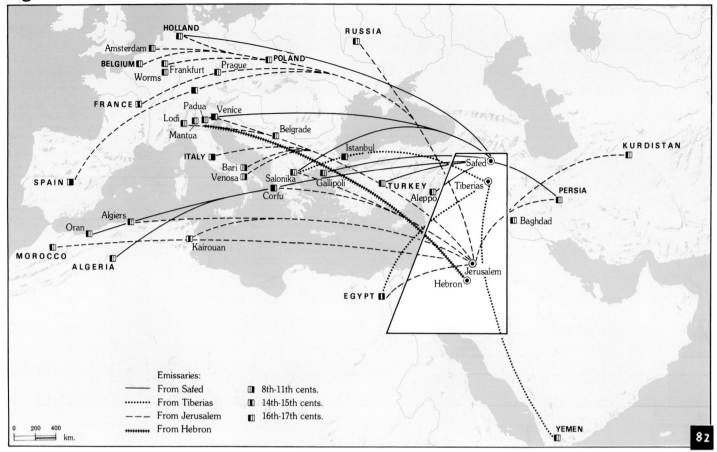

Emissaries:
From Safed — 8th-11th cents.
From Tiberias ⋯⋯ 14th-15th cents.
From Jerusalem – – – 16th-17th cents.
From Hebron ╫╫╫╫

0 200 400 km.

82

IN NORTH AFRICA

JEWISH COMMUNITIES:
Fifteenth to Sixteenth Centuries

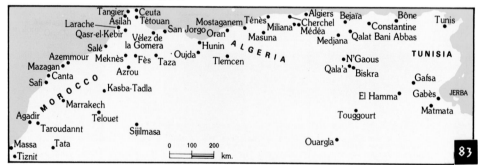

83

IN THE EGYPTIAN DELTA

84

RELATIONS WITH THE RADBAZ

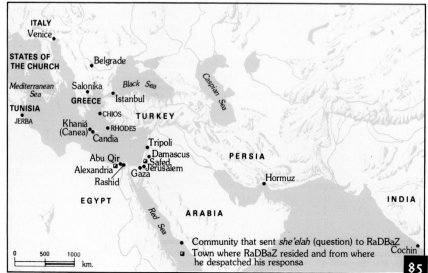

● Community that sent *she'elah* (question) to RaDBaZ
■ Town where RaDBaZ resided and from where he despatched his responsa

0 500 1000 km.

85

92

KABBALISTS AND KABBALISTIC CENTERS
Sixteenth and Seventeenth Centuries

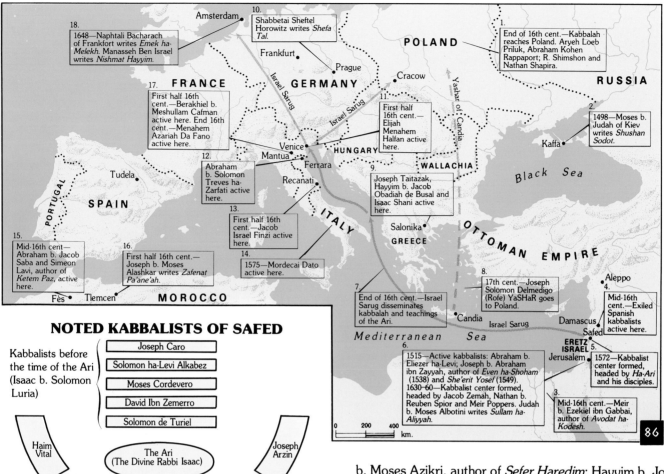

18.
1648—Naphtali Bacharach of Frankfort writes *Emek ha-Melekh*. Manasseh Ben Israel writes *Nishmat Hayyim*.

10.
Shabbetai Sheftel Horowitz writes *Shefa Tal*.

1.
End of 16th cent.—Kabbalah reaches Poland. Aryeh Loeb Priluk, Abraham Kohen Rappaport; R. Shimshon and Nathan Shapira.

17.
First half 16th cent.—Berakhiel b. Meshullam Cafman active here. End 16th cent.—Menahem Azariah Da Fano active here.

11.
First half 16th cent.—Elijah Menahem Halfan active here.

2.
1498—Moses b. Judah of Kiev writes *Shushan Sodot*.

12.
Abraham b. Solomon Treves ha-Zarfati active here.

9.
Joseph Taitazak, Hayyim b. Jacob Obadiah de Busal and Isaac Shani active here.

13.
First half 16th cent.—Jacob Israel Finzi active here.

14.
1575—Mordecai Dato active here.

15.
Mid-16th cent—Abraham b. Jacob Saba and Simeon Lavi, author of *Ketem Paz*, active here.

16.
First half 16th cent.—Joseph b. Moses Alashkar writes *Zafenat Pa'ane'ah*.

8.
17th cent.—Joseph Solomon Delmedigo (Rofe) YaSHaR goes to Poland.

7.
End of 16th cent.—Israel Sarug disseminates kabbalah and teachings of the Ari.

4.
Mid-16th cent.—Exiled Spanish kabbalists active here.

6.
1515—Active kabbalists: Abraham b. Eliezer ha-Levi; Joseph b. Abraham ibn Zayyah, author of *Even ha-Shoham* (1538) and *She'erit Yosef* (1549). 1630–60—Kabbalist center formed, headed by Jacob Zemah, Nathan b. Reuben Spior and Meir Poppers. Judah b. Moses Albotini writes *Sullam ha-Aliyyah*.

5.
1572—Kabbalist center formed, headed by Ha-Ari and his disciples.

3.
Mid-16th cent.—Meir b. Ezekiel ibn Gabbai, author of *Avodat ha-Kodesh*.

86

NOTED KABBALISTS OF SAFED

Kabbalists before the time of the Ari (Isaac b. Solomon Luria)

- Joseph Caro
- Solomon ha-Levi Alkabez
- Moses Cordevero
- David Ibn Zemerro
- Solomon de Turiel

The Ari (The Divine Rabbi Isaac)

Disciples (cubs) of the Ari

Haim Vital

Joseph Ibn Tabul

Samuel de Uzeda

Jonathan Sagiz

Joseph Arzin

The persecutions of 1391 in Spain and the subsequent events, culminating in the Expulsion of 1492, made a deep impression upon the kabbalists of the period and resulted in far-reaching changes in kabbalistic thought. The problem of redemption was heightened, particularly because hopes that the Messiah would come in 1492 (based on the passage in Job 38:7 "When the morning stars sang together" — the numerical value of the Hebrew word, "bron," for "sung" is 1492) proved baseless. The messianic frustration and the catastrophe of expulsion precipitated a soul searching by the kabbalists.

Two books by anonymous authors, published about 1500, were particularly significant: *Sefer ha-Meshiv*, a commentary on the Pentateuch, and *Kaf ha-Ketoret*, a commentary on the book of Psalms. The authors attempted to highlight the apocalyptic meaning of every word in the Bible. There were "seventy modes of expounding the Torah" (Num. R. 13:15) and each generation had its own mode; thus it was expulsion and redemption that occupied their generation, proving to be a particularly dominant theme in *Kaf ha-Ketoret*, which expressed the new weltanschauung of Safed kabbalists and was founded on messianic eschatology.

In the kabbalistic center of Safed, outstanding personalities were: Moses b. Jacob Cordovero, author of *Tomer Devorah*; Elijah b. Moses de Vidas, author of *Reshit Hokhmah*; Eleazar

b. Moses Azikri, author of *Sefer Haredim*; Hayyim b. Joseph Vital, author of *Sha'arei Kedushah*; Joseph b. Ephraim Caro, author of the *Shulhan Arukh*, one of the great halakhists of all time, who apparently met Solomon Molcho, kabbalist and pseudo-messiah, in Salonika and was so deeply impressed by him that when Molcho was martyred at the stake in Mantua in 1532, Caro also expressed a desire to meet a martyr's death. Caro wrote a mystical diary called *Maggid Mesharim* in which he recorded messages revealed to him by a "heavenly mentor" (*maggid*). Another kabbalist living in Safed was Solomon b. Moses ha-Levi Alkabez. Born in 1505 in Salonika, he studied with the greatest of its rabbis, Joseph Taitazak. Around 1535 he settled in Safed, where he died in 1584. Alkabez is the author of the *piyyut Lekhah Dodi*, a hymn welcoming the Sabbath that is woven out of strands of kabbalistic imagery expressing messianic yearning for redemption. Another personality active in the Holy Land was the Hebrew poet, Israel b. Moses Najara (1555?–1625?). Born in Damascus he settled in Gaza around 1587, serving as a rabbi until his death.

The outstanding kabbalist of the sixteenth century was Isaac b. Solomon Luria, known as ha-Ari. He was born in 1534 and was active in Safed from about 1569 until his death in 1572. Luria's originality is in his pioneering conception of the theoretical aspect of *kabbalah* and its permeation with messianic eschatology. In Safed he gathered around him a group of disciples who subsequently expounded, expanded and propogated his teachings. Mid-sixteenth-century Safed was like thirteenth-century Gerona as a center of theoretical *kabbalah*.

THE KARAITES
Sixteenth and Seventeenth Centuries

Sanctuary of the Sovereign, city of peers,
Arise from your ruin,
Too long have you languished in the valley of tears,
The merciful Lord will have pity on you.
No longer shall you be shamed or humiliated.
Why are you downcast and disquieted?
The needy of My people shall find shelter in Zion,
And the city shall be rebuilt on its mound.

From Lekhah Dodi *("Come My Beloved") by Solomon Alkabez.*

NOVGOROD

2.
16th cent.—Young Karaites sent to Istanbul to study; return as community leaders.

5.
End of 17th cent.—Solomon of Troki writes *Appiryon Asa Li.*

3.
Karaites sporadically reside in city.

4.
End of 16th cent.— Development of literary activity. Isaac b. Abraham of Troki writes anti-Christian polemic, *Hizzuk Emunah.*

SWEDEN

Baltic Sea

Birzai
Panevèžys
Vilna
Naumiestis
Troki

LITHUANIA

MOSCOW

POLAND

HOLY ROMAN EMPIRE

Krasnystaw
Lutsk
Derazhnya
Lvov
Galich

1.
From 14th cent.—Karaites from Crimea reach Poland.

0   100   200
km.

HUNGARY

87

Area of Karaite settlement

JEWISH PRINTERS AND ADMISSION OF JEWS TO UNIVERSITIES
Fifteenth to Seventeenth Centuries

About twenty years after Johann Gutenberg developed a new method of printing and printed his forty-two-line Bible in 1455, there are verified accounts of Jewish printers printing books in Hebrew. Books printed before 1501 are known as incunabula and at present there are 175 extant editions of books printed with Hebrew letters. These deal with the whole Bible or various parts of it, biblical commentaries, tractates of the Babylonian Talmud, prayer books, Passover *haggadot,* and books on the *halakhah.* Italy was the cradle of Jewish printing in the fifteenth century with presses operating in at least eleven towns including Piove di Sacco and Reggio di Calabria, 1475; Mantua, 1476; Soncino, 1483; and Brescia, 1491. Jewish printing continued in the sixteenth and seventeenth centuries with presses operating in Venice, Cremona and Sabbioneta. Both Jewish and non-Jewish craftsmen contributed to the development of Hebrew printing.

Spain was the next largest center for Jewish printers and their presses. In 1476 Solomon b. Moses Alkabez (grandfather of the Kabbalist Solomon Alkabez) established a press in Guadalajara and Eliezer Alantansi in Híjar in Aragón in 1485; one was set up in Zamora in 1487. For Portugal there are extant incunabula attesting to printing presses in Lisbon in 1473; in Faro in 1487 operated by Eliezer Toledano the printer; and in Leiria in 1492 operated by the printers Samuel D'Ortas and sons.

Constantinople had one incunabulum, *Arba'a Turim* by Jacob b. Asher, completed in December 1493 by the printers David and Samuel ibn Nahmias.

In the sixteenth century presses were established in other Jewish centers such as Prague (1512), Salonika (1513), Fès (1516) and Augsburg (1533). Amsterdam became an important center for Hebrew printing in the seventeenth century, after Manasseh ben Israel established the first press in 1626.

Christian printers were also active in printing Hebrew texts both for Jewish and non-Jewish clients; such presses operated in Basle (1516) and Lyons (1520).

UNIVERSITIES

The medieval universities founded in the twelfth and thirteenth centuries were naturally closed to Jews, since their curriculum was largely theologically oriented. The few "Jews" who were able to attend these universities were apostates. The universities of Oxford, Paris and Salamanca established faculties for the study of Hebrew and Judaica, particularly for men studying to be priests. Medicine was one of the few subjects that interested Jews, but few places were open to them. Eventually a number of Jews were able to study medicine at the University of Padua. At the beginning of the seventeenth century a larger number succeeded in gaining admission to Dutch universities, particularly Leiden.

In Spain the conversos were able to study at many of the universities until the end of the fifteenth century, when a number of universities limited the intake of conversos, thus compelling some of them to obtain forged documents attesting to their Christian ancestry. The University of Salamanca established a faculty of Hebrew in 1314 and when the University of Alcalá de Henares was founded in 1509 some conversos were admitted. However, the major converso admittance into universities was in the sixteenth and seventeenth centuries, some of them even attained high status. The Inquisition kept a close watch on university students, fearing the spread of heretical ideas.

Printers in the 16th century.

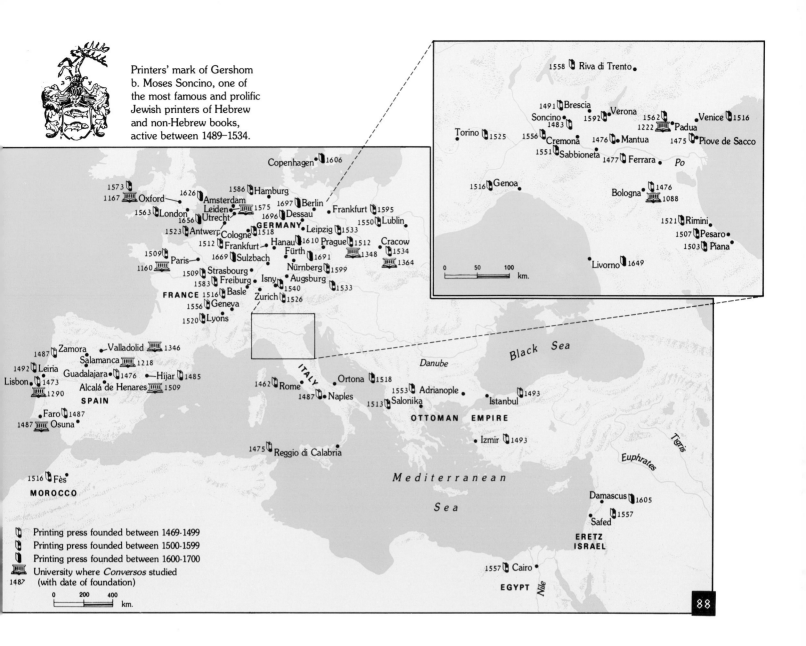

Printers' mark of Gershom
b. Moses Soncino, one of
the most famous and prolific
Jewish printers of Hebrew
and non-Hebrew books,
active between 1489–1534.

Printing press founded between 1469-1499
Printing press founded between 1500-1599
Printing press founded between 1600-1700
University where *Conversos* studied
(with date of foundation)

THE JEWS OF ITALY   Sixteenth and Seventeenth Centuries

The history of the Jews in Italy in the sixteenth and seventeenth centuries is as complex as that of the two preceding centuries. The Italian Peninsula was fragmented into many states, between which constant rivalry played an important part in both the establishment of new Jewish communities and in the expulsion of Jews and and their constant emigration. Jewish emigrants from Germany, most of whom settled in northern Italy, as well as refugees from Spain and Portugal, among them conversos who reverted to Judaism, were assimilated by the Italian Jewish communities. Each group of immigrants brought with it customs and traditions of communal organization which they reestablished and continued to practice for many generations in their new communities, quite distinct from one another.

The Jewish fate in sixteenth-century Italy was one of expulsions from various towns and areas. Persecutions, as in Spain, were uniformly applied in the Spanish-ruled territories of southern Italy. After Spain took control of Milan and northern Italy, it was extended to these areas as well. In the 1570s Spain exerted its influence upon Savoy and its environs. With regard to the Jews, Spain was concerned about the rise of Islam and the expansion of the Ottoman Turks and saw the Jews as collaborators with the Turks. Philip II of Spain, who succeeded in uniting the kingdoms of Spain and Portugal in 1580, was particularly troubled by this matter, seeing himself as the protector of Christianity against its external enemies and guardian of the faith against internal heresy.

Internal power struggles in sixteenth-century Italy and external pressures also affected the popes, some of whom (particularly popes Julius II, 1503–1513, and Leo X, 1513–1521) were patrons of the arts. They encouraged and supported artists, philosophers and architects, and transformed their domains into centers of culture. Others, assisted by the Inquisition, supported the persecution and expulsion of Jews.

During the papacy of Leo X (Giovanni de' Medici) Rome blossomed, its population increased from forty to ninety thousand, the Jewish community also grew. Elijah (Bahur) Levita, Hebrew philologist, grammarian and lexicographer, lived and worked in Rome from 1514 to 1527.

The papacies of Julius III (1550–1555) and Paul IV (1555–1559) were years of grief and suffering for the Jews

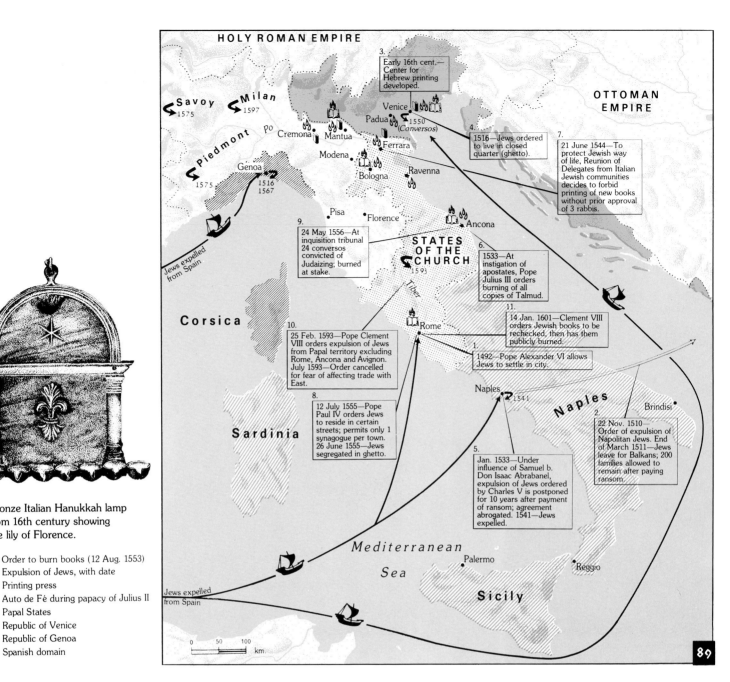

OTTOMAN EMPIRE

3. Early 16th cent.—Center for Hebrew printing developed.

Savoy 1575

Milan 1597

Piedmont

Po

Cremona

Mantua

Modena

Ferrara

Venice

Padua 1550 (Conversos)

4. 1516—Jews ordered to live in closed quarter (ghetto).

7. 21 June 1544—To protect Jewish way of life, Reunion of Delegates from Italian Jewish communities decides to forbid printing of new books without prior approval of 3 rabbis.

Genoa 1516 1567 1575

Bologna

Ravenna

Jews expelled from Spain

Pisa

Florence

Ancona

9. 24 May 1556—At inquisition tribunal 24 conversos convicted of Judaizing; burned at stake.

STATES OF THE CHURCH 1593

6. 1533—At instigation of apostates, Pope Julius III orders burning of all copies of Talmud.

Corsica

Tiber

11. 14 Jan. 1601—Clement VIII orders Jewish books to be rechecked, then has them publicly burned.

10. 25 Feb. 1593—Pope Clement VIII orders expulsion of Jews from Papal territory excluding Rome, Ancona and Avignon. July 1593—Order cancelled for fear of affecting trade with East.

Rome

1. 1492—Pope Alexander VI allows Jews to settle in city.

8. 12 July 1555—Pope Paul IV orders Jews to reside in certain streets; permits only 1 synagogue per town. 26 June 1555—Jews segregated in ghetto.

Naples 1541

Naples

Brindisi

2. 22 Nov. 1510—Order of expulsion of Napolitan Jews. End of March 1511—Jews leave for Balkans; 200 families allowed to remain after paying ransom.

Sardinia

5. Jan. 1533—Under influence of Samuel b. Don Isaac Abrabanel, expulsion of Jews ordered by Charles V is postponed for 10 years after payment of ransom; agreement abrogated. 1541—Jews expelled.

Mediterranean Sea

Palermo

Reggio

Sicily

Jews expelled from Spain

0 50 100
km.

89

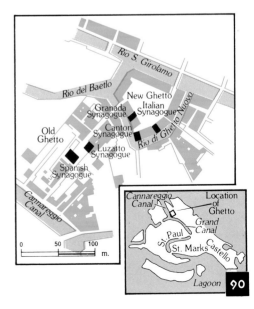

Bronze Italian Hanukkah lamp from 16th century showing the lily of Florence.

- Order to burn books (12 Aug. 1553)
- 1575 Expulsion of Jews, with date
- Printing press
- Auto de Fé during papacy of Julius II
- Papal States
- Republic of Venice
- Republic of Genoa
- Spanish domain

of Italy. Paul IV revived the Inquisition and was the author of the bull *Cum nimis absurdum* ("because it is absurd") of 14 July 1555, which determined the official attitude of the church toward the Jews. The bull decreed the segregation of Jews into separate streets or quarters (ghettos) and the wearing of a yellow badge and hat. On 30 April 1556 he ordered the arrest of the Conversos who had come from Portugal and settled in Ancona. An inquisition tribunal sentenced fifty of them; twenty-four were burned at the stake. Doña Gracia Nasi and her nephew Joseph Nasi, former conversos, attempted to intervene on behalf of those condemned to the stake by organizing a boycott of the port of Ancona and transferring commerce to nearby Pesaro. The boycott was unsuccessful but the attempt was significant as an instance of exertion of Jewish power through the use of economic sanctions against Christian authorities. The policies of Pope Gregory XIII (1572–1585) toward the Jews were less severe.

Despite their hardships, the Jews of Italy continued to maintain an active community life and even increased their support of the Jews of the Holy Land.

THE JEWISH GHETTO IN VENICE

Rio S. Girolamo

Rio del Baetlo

New Ghetto

Granada Synagogue

Italian Synagogue

Old Ghetto

Canton Synagogue

Luzatto Synagogue

Rio di Ghetto Nuova

Spanish Synagogue

Cannareggio Canal

0 50 100
m.

Cannareggio Canal

Location of Ghetto

Grand Canal

St. Paul

St. Marks

Castello

Lagoon

90

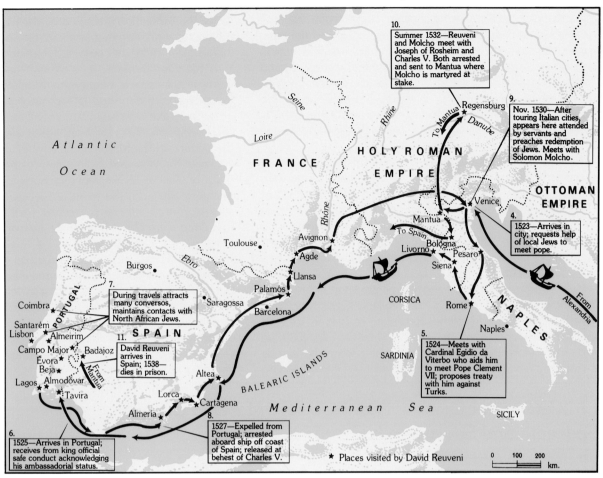

10.
Summer 1532—Reuveni and Molcho meet with Joseph of Rosheim and Charles V. Both arrested and sent to Mantua where Molcho is martyred at stake.

9.
Nov. 1530—After touring Italian cities, appears here attended by servants and preaches redemption of Jews. Meets with Solomon Molcho.

4.
1523—Arrives in city; requests help of local Jews to meet pope.

7.
During travels attracts many conversos, maintains contacts with North African Jews.

11.
David Reuveni arrives in Spain; 1538—dies in prison.

5.
1524—Meets with Cardinal Egidio da Viterbo who aids him to meet Pope Clement VII; proposes treaty with him against Turks.

6.
1525—Arrives in Portugal; receives from king official safe conduct acknowledging his ambassadorial status.

8.
1527—Expelled from Portugal; arrested aboard ship off coast of Spain; released at behest of Charles V.

★ Places visited by David Reuveni

0   100   200
km.

In 1524–1525, shortly after Palestine was conquered by Sultan Selim, David Reuveni appeared from the east and proposed the grandiose scheme of organizing a Jewish-Christian military campaign against the Ottoman Empire, which was threatening Christianity. His plan called for Pope Clement VII to make peace between the Emperor Charles V and King Francis I of France, and then to give him a letter of recommendation to the emperor of Ethiopia. The combined forces would execute a flanking military campaign against the Ottoman Empire while the Jews of Habor, led by Reuveni's brother, would join the forces and conquer Palestine. The plan was based upon the belief that the soldiers of Habor were brave warriors who lacked only weapons for their assured victory.

It is important to note that this plan was proposed by a Jew to the Christian world for a war against the Ottomans who, after conquering Palestine, opened their gates to Jewish and converso refugees from Spain. Reuveni relates in his diary that the pope found the plan plausible but said he was unable to make peace between Charles V and Francis I, who was at that time negotiating for a treaty with the Turks. The pope referred Reuveni to John III, king of Portugal,

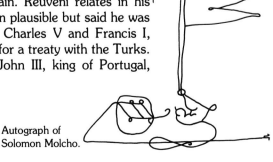

Autograph of
Solomon Molcho.

1.
1480s—Presumed birth date.

3.
Meets Abraham Castro.

2.
Journey along Nile.

0 100 200
km.

91

giving him a letter of recommendation. In referring Reuveni to Portugal, the pope no doubt wished to rely on Portuguese experience of voyages and discovery. In particular, he may have borne in mind their reputation for voyages to the east, perhaps thinking that they might operate from their overseas colonies or from places discovered in their voyages around Africa. However, doubt has been cast on this supposition by a non-Jewish source. A letter by Marco Foscari, the Venetian representative in Rome, written on 13 March 1524 (while Reuveni was still in Rome) states that it was Reuveni who suggested the visit to Portugal.

Reuveni requested and also received a second letter to the emperor of Ethiopia, from which we learn that he promised the pope his loyalty to the Holy See and the Christian world if his plan succeeded. His appearance before the king of Portugal had a resounding effect upon the conversos, one of whom, Diogo Pires, inspired by Reuveni, returned to Judaism, circumcised himself and took the Hebrew name of Solomon Molcho.

Solomon probably spent some time studying *kabbalah* in Salonika, where he possibly met Joseph Caro, who was greatly impressed by Molcho. Returning to Italy in 1529 he was by then convinced he was the Messiah. In 1530 he appeared before Pope Clement VII, who recognized him as a visionary, after he correctly predicted the Tiber's flooding

of Rome in 1530. The strange appearance of David Reuveni and Solomon Molcho jointly and severally before pope and kings, the protection proffered by the pope — particularly to Molcho (considering that he was a converso who returned to Judaism) — and their combined mission to Emperor Charles V is food for thought. It is difficult to determine whether this was a messianic phenomenon linked to a political plan, for this was the period of eschatological fervor. Even a personality like Don Isaac Abrabanel had calculated the year of redemption, first 1503 and then 1531, as the year for the coming of the Messiah.

David Reuveni and Solomon Molcho were arrested by order of Charles V. Reuveni imprisoned, died in an inquistion prison in Spain (in the town of Llerena) while Molcho died as a martyr at the stake. Despite their tragic end, the fact that Jews were able to negotiate openly with heads of state is most significant. If we examine this fact in conjunction with the activities of former conversos during the sixteenth century, we may perhaps gain some insight into the origin of the new ideas and weltanschauung in Jewish thinking. There is no doubt that they were fully acquainted with the political climate and balance of power within Christianity and the rest of the world and were therefore able to present a plausible case to the heads of state. The appearance of David Reuveni caused a great stir amongst Jews and conversos.

EMIGRATION OF CONVERSOS FROM PORTUGAL
Sixteenth and Seventeenth Centuries

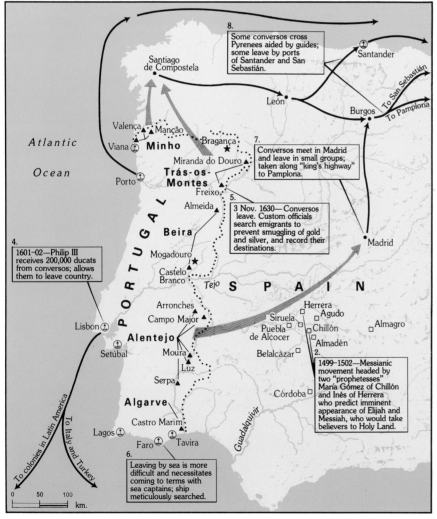

□   Center of Messianic movement

★   Major converso community

▲   Customs post

⊕   Port of embarkation

THE READMISSION OF JEWS TO ENGLAND; CONVERSO DISPERSION
Seventeenth Century

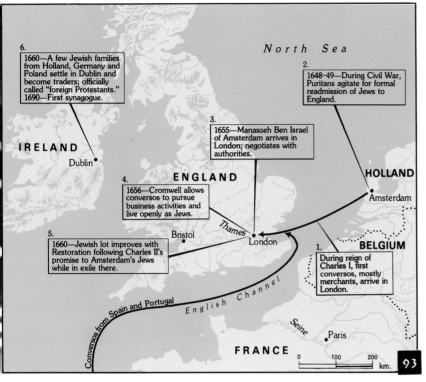

Map annotations:

6. 1660—A few Jewish families from Holland, Germany and Poland settle in Dublin and become traders; officially called "foreign Protestants." 1690—First synagogue.

2. 1648-49—During Civil War, Puritans agitate for formal readmission of Jews to England.

3. 1655—Manasseh Ben Israel of Amsterdam arrives in London; negotiates with authorities.

4. 1656—Cromwell allows conversos to pursue business activities and live openly as Jews.

5. 1660—Jewish lot improves with Restoration following Charles II's promise to Amsterdam's Jews while in exile there.

1. During reign of Charles I, first conversos, mostly merchants, arrive in London.

North Sea — IRELAND — Dublin — ENGLAND — HOLLAND — Amsterdam — Bristol — *Thames* — London — BELGIUM — *English Channel* — *Conversos from Spain and Portugal* — *Seine* — Paris — FRANCE

0 100 200 km. **93**

Petition from Manasseh Ben Israel (first signator) and six Jews living in London to Oliver Cromwell, requesting permission to conduct services in their homes. 24 March 1655/6.

One of the outcomes of the Expulsion of Jews from Spain was a Sephardic diaspora within the existing Diaspora — a new reality in the history of the Jews. Those expelled settled and established communities in many places in the countries of the Mediterranean basin, particularly in the domains of the Ottoman Empire. In due course, these communities absorbed the indigenous Jewish communities, transplanting their communal organization from Spain. However, the refugees from Spain were not alone in establishing the new Sephardic communities. At the beginning of the sixteenth century the first refugees from the forced conversions in Portugal in 1497 joined the newly established Sephardic communities, after first forming communities of their own.

From the sixteenth century these new Jewish communties were joined by conversos who had succeeded by various means and routes in escaping from the Iberian peninsula. By the mid-sixteenth century many conversos settled in Jewish centers in France and in the Low Countries. They were the first Jews to settle in Amsterdam toward the end of the sixteenth century, as well as in Hamburg and Glückstadt at the beginning of the seventeenth century.

Manasseh ben Israel (1604–1657) was a man of considerable achievements who undertook to work for the readmission of Jews to England, believing in its messianic significance (to scatter the Jews to "the end of the earth" [Deut 28:64], the medieval Hebrew for *Angle-Terre*). He was also interested in the reported discovery in South America of the Ten Lost Tribes. In 1655 Manasseh negotiated unsuccessfully with Oliver Cromwell for the formal readmission of Jews to England. However, in 1656 the small converso community was allowed to live openly as Jews, thus de facto renewing the community that had been expelled in 1290.

The conversos of Spain and Portugal who continued in secret to observe the precepts of the Torah had powerful spiritual resources. During the years 1499 to 1502 a turbulent messianic movement developed, based on the anticipation of — and expressing the yearning for — the coming of Elijah and the Messiah, both of whom would both lead the Jews to the Promised Land. Among the leaders of the movement were two "prophetesses": María Gómez of Chillón and Inés, the twelve-year old daughter of the shoemaker Juan Estéban from the town of Herrera. The remembrance of their Judaism sustained the conversos for hundreds of years until they were able to cast off their disguise and openly join Jewish communities and profess and practice their religion.

In the 1630s, Jacob Cansino (d. 1666), the Jewish interpreter of the governor of Algeria, negotiated with the count-duke of Olivares (1587–1645), prime minister of Philip IV of Spain, for the return of Jews to Spain and the founding of a community in Madrid. Although the plan was foiled by the Inquisition, it is significant that the prime minister was prepared to give serious consideration to Cansino's private proposal.

During the sixteenth and seventeenth centuries Sephardi Jews developed a wide range of economic activities which included distant voyages of trade to the Far East and the New World. The Jews and conversos expelled from Spain developed a particular spiritual tradition that reached its peak in Holland with the works of Juan Prado, Baruch Spinoza, Isaac Orobio De Castro and Daniel Levi De Barrios.

AREA OF JEWISH SETTLEMENT IN THE CITY OF LONDON

Printer's mark of Manasseh Ben Israel.

JEWISH COMMUNITIES IN ALSACE
Seventeenth Century

3. Jews allowed to reside without citizenship; forced to pay many taxes: poll tax for right of residence, tax for king's protection, and municipal tax.

2. 1681—Town seized by French; closed to Jews to protect Christian merchants; Jewish merchants allowed to spend 24 hours in town upon payment of double toll.

1. Ashkenazi Jewish population increases with French control of Alsace from 1648 (Peace of Westphalia).

4. 1689—Some 525 families (391 in lower Alsace, 134 in upper Alsace) totaling about 4,000 people.

5. Rabbis headed communities; a number of communities banded together to form regional associations headed by rabbis and *parnassim* (elected lay leaders).

FRANCE · Lower Alsace · Upper Alsace · GERMANY · SWITZERLAND

Wissembourg, Bouxwiller, Neuwiller, Etterdorf, Haguenau, Saverne, Bischheim, Strasbourg, Westhoffen, Mutzig, Rozenwiller, Benfeld, Sélestat, Ribeauvillé, Marckolsheim, Wintzenheim, Colmar, Freiburg, Soultz, Mulhouse, Rixheim, Sierentz, Hegenheim, Basle

🕎 Synagogue
🏛 *Bet Midrash* (Seminary)
⌂ Jewish cemetery

JEWISH COMMUNITIES IN HOLLAND
Seventeenth Century

Tombstone of David Israel Mendez in the Ouderkerk cemetery near Amsterdam.

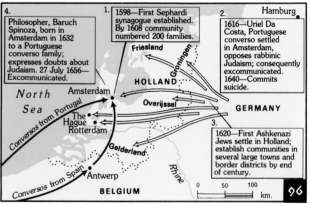

4. Philosopher, Baruch Spinoza, born in Amsterdam in 1632 to a Portuguese converso family; expresses doubts about Judaism. 27 July 1656—Excommunicated.

1. 1598—First Sephardi synagogue established. By 1608 community numbered 200 families.

2. 1616—Uriel Da Costa, Portuguese converso settled in Amsterdam, opposes rabbinic Judaism; consequently excommunicated. 1640—Commits suicide.

3. 1620—First Ashkenazi Jews settle in Holland; establish communities in several large towns and border districts by end of century.

North Sea · Friesland · Groningen · HOLLAND · Amsterdam · Overijssel · GERMANY · The Hague · Rotterdam · Gelderland · Hamburg · Antwerp · BELGIUM · Rhine · Conversos from Portugal · Conversos from Spain

Document of excommunication pronounced upon Baruch Spinoza.

MAJOR VOYAGES OF DISCOVERY AND SPHERES OF DOMINION IN THE NEW WORLD

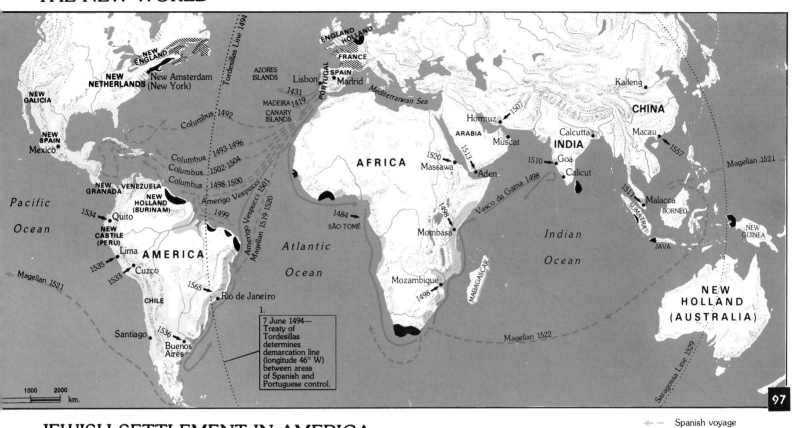

NEW ENGLAND
NEW NETHERLANDS
New Amsterdam (New York)
NEW GALICIA
NEW SPAIN
Mexico
NEW GRANADA
VENEZUELA
NEW HOLLAND (SURINAM)
Quito
NEW CASTILE (PERU)
Lima
Cuzco
CHILE
Santiago
Buenos Aires
Rio de Janeiro

Columbus 1492
Columbus 1493-1496
Columbus 1502-1504
Columbus 1498-1500
Amerigo Vespucci 1501
1499
Amerigo Vespucci 1499-1520
Magellan 1519-1520
1534
1535
1533
1565
1536

Pacific Ocean
Atlantic Ocean
Magellan 1521

AMERICA

Tordesillas Line 1494
AZORES ISLANDS
MADEIRA 1419
CANARY ISLANDS
Lisbon 1431
PORTUGAL **SPAIN** Madrid
ENGLAND **HOLLAND**
FRANCE

Mediterranean Sea

AFRICA
Massawa
1484
SÃO TOMÉ
Mombasa 1498
Mozambique 1498
MADAGASCAR

Hormuz 1507
ARABIA Muscat 1513
1520 Aden
1510 Goa Calcutta
INDIA Calicut
Vasco da Gama 1498
Indian Ocean

Kaifeng
CHINA
Macau 1557
1511 Malacca
SUMATRA BORNEO
JAVA
NEW GUINEA

Magellan 1521
Saragossa Line 1529

NEW HOLLAND (AUSTRALIA)

Magellan 1522

1. 7 June 1494—Treaty of Tordesillas determines demarcation line (longitude 46° W) between areas of Spanish and Portuguese control.

1000 2000
km.

97

Legend:
← — Spanish voyage
← — Portuguese voyage
Under Portuguese control
Under Spanish control
Under Dutch control
Under English control
Under French control

JEWISH SETTLEMENT IN AMERICA
Seventeenth Century

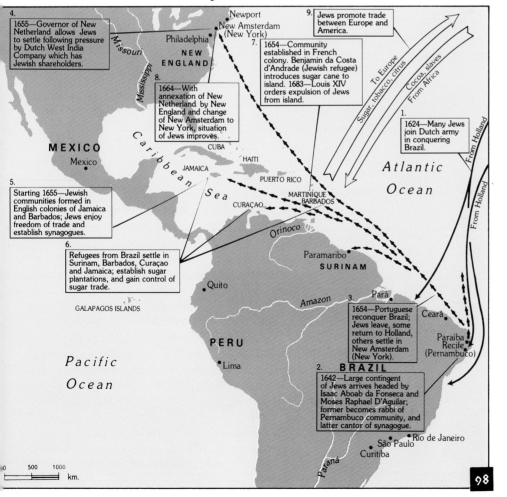

4. 1655—Governor of New Netherland allows Jews to settle following pressure by Dutch West India Company which has Jewish shareholders.

5. Starting 1655—Jewish communities formed in English colonies of Jamaica and Barbados; Jews enjoy freedom of trade and establish synagogues.

6. Refugees from Brazil settle in Surinam, Barbados, Curaçao and Jamaica; establish sugar plantations, and gain control of sugar trade.

8. 1664—With annexation of New Netherland by New England and change of New Amsterdam to New York, situation of Jews improves.

7. 1654—Community established in French colony. Benjamin da Costa d'Andrade (Jewish refugee) introduces sugar cane to island. 1683—Louis XIV orders expulsion of Jews from island.

9. Jews promote trade between Europe and America.

1. 1624—Many Jews join Dutch army in conquering Brazil.

3. 1654—Portuguese reconquer Brazil; Jews leave, some return to Holland, others settle in New Amsterdam (New York).

2. 1642—Large contingent of Jews arrives headed by Isaac Aboab da Fonseca and Moses Raphael D'Aguilar; former becomes rabbi of Pernambuco community, and latter cantor of synagogue.

Newport
New Amsterdam (New York)
Philadelphia
NEW ENGLAND
Missouri
Mississippi
MEXICO
Mexico
CUBA
JAMAICA
HAITI
PUERTO RICO
MARTINIQUE
BARBADOS
CURAÇAO
Caribbean Sea
Atlantic Ocean
To Europe
Sugar, tobacco, citrus
Cocoa, slaves From Africa
From Holland
Orinoco
Paramaribo
SURINAM
Quito
Amazon
Pará
Ceará
Paraiba Recife (Pernambuco)
PERU
Lima
BRAZIL
São Paulo
Curitiba
Rio de Janeiro
Paraná
GALAPAGOS ISLANDS
Pacific Ocean

0 500 1000
km.

98

The Santa Maria, Columbus' flagship on his voyage to the New World.

JEWISH SETTLEMENT IN INDIA Sixteenth and Seventeenth Centuries

The Inquisition standard at Goa.

Vasco da Gama

8.
1689—Abraham Navarro, a Jew from London, appointed by East India Company as ambassador to Mogul Emperor Aurangzeb.

7.
Jewish communities originating from Persia and Khurasan.

1.
1510—Conquest by Portugal brings Portuguese conversos. 1560—Inquisition established. Aug. 1575—public Auto de fés held; in each one 17 conversos burned.

6.
Community of Portuguese Jews promote English trade in India, primarily in diamonds and pearls.

2.
1524—Portuguese destroy town; Jews move to Cochin.

3.
Wave of conversos arrive from Spain and Portugal.

5.
1662—Dutch fail to conquer town; assisted in their retreat by Cochin Jews. In revenge, Portuguese burn Jewish quarter. Jews flee to highlands; return with Dutch conquest in 1663.

4.
Rajah of Cochin appoints chief (*mudaliar*) of Jewish community, grants religious and cultural autonomy. 1568—Paradesi synagogue built. End of cent.—About 900 families reside in town.

Map labels: Srinagar, Kashmir, Lahore, Himalaya Mts., Indus, Fatehpur, Delhi, Agra, Ganges, Brahmaputra, Bengal, Calcutta, Surat, INDIA, Bombay, Bay of Bengal, Deccan, Goa, Fort St. George (Madras), Cranganur, Cochin, Mattancheri, CEYLON, Indian Ocean

0 100 200 km.

99

JEWISH PLANTATIONS IN SURINAM

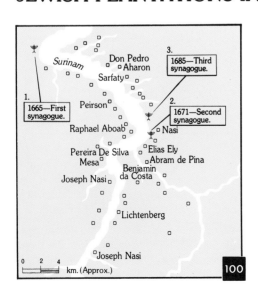

Map labels: Surinam, Don Pedro, Aharon, Sarfaty, Peirson, Raphael Aboab, Pereira De Silva, Mesa, Joseph Nasi, Benjamin da Costa, Nasi, Elias Ely, Abram de Pina, Lichtenberg, Joseph Nasi

1.
1665—First synagogue.

3.
1685—Third synagogue.

2.
1671—Second synagogue.

0 2 4 km. (Approx.)

100

Although Jewish and converso settlement in South American colonies was forbidden, in the sixteenth century conversos succeeded in gradually settling in the Spanish colonies of Mexico and Peru. Occasionally the crown would permit entry for commercial reasons and the conversos fully exploited these opportunities to infiltrate and settle in Spanish and Portuguese colonies. During the seventeenth century there was an increase of immigrants to the New World; but significant Jewish settlement began in 1624 with the conquest of the northern region of Brazil by the Dutch — a campaign in which Jews participated — later settling in Pernambuco and leading full Jewish lives. Following Dutch colonial expansion, Jews also settled in Carribean islands. The Jewish community in Brazil was short-lived, dispersing after the reconquest of the northern territories by the Portuguese in 1654. Some of the refugees arrived in the same year at New Amsterdam, settling there despite the governor's opposition. They were the first Jewish settlers in North America.

Conversos also reached India, settling chiefly in the Portuguese colony of Goa, which also had an active inquisition tribunal. The converso commercial ties in the Far East brought spices and precious gems to Europe.

Cochin in India had a Jewish community whose origin and foundation date are uncertain. There are accounts of Jews from Egypt and Aden trading with India and of Jewish merchants who stayed on in the country for several years on business. We also know that the Rambam's brother drowned in the Indian Ocean (1169) while on a business trip.

The first news of a Jewish community in Kaifeng, China, reached Europe in 1605 in a report from the Italian Jesuit missionary, Matteo Ricci, who resided in Peking. Jewish merchants probably arrived in Kaifeng via Persia and Afghanistan in the first quarter of the twelfth century.

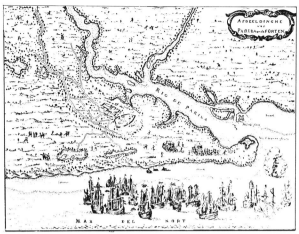

The Dutch fleet anchored in Paraíba (1640).

INQUISITION TRIBUNALS IN SPAIN AND PORTUGAL

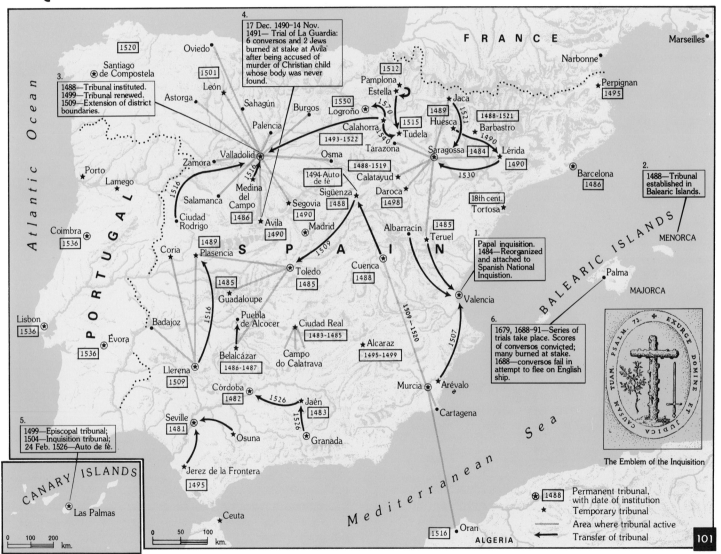

The Inquisition organized its activities most methodically, slowly spreading its network in Spain. A tribunal was founded in Seville in 1481 and in Córdoba in 1482; the tribunal whose jurisdiction was over all Castile was at first located at Ciudad Real (1483); later it moved to Toledo in 1485. Thus the inquisition organized tribunals throughout the country, eventually extending its authority to the New World, first in Mexico (1532), later founding tribunals in Cartagena (Colombia) and in Lima (Peru). In Portugal the inquisition had three centers

— Lisbon, Évora and Coimbra — and when it began its activities against the conversos in Brazil, the Inquisition sent visiting commissaries. In 1621 the first tribunal was founded in Brazil in the Bahia district, but most of the suspects were sent to Portugal for trial.

Both the Spanish and Portuguese inquisition tribunals persisted in persecuting the conversos who returned to Judaism, even though they managed to leave the Peninsula and settle in regions where the Inquisition did not function.

Tomás de Torquemada, first head of the Spanish Inquisition.

HEADS OF THE INQUISITION

Tomás de Torquemada	1481–1489	Prior of Santa Cruz in Segovia
Diego Deza	1498–1506	Bishop of Palencia
Francisco Jiménez de Cisneros	1505–1517	Archbishop of Toledo
Adrian of Utrecht	1517–1522	Cardinal; later Pope Adrian VI
Alfonso Manrique	1523–1538	Archbishop of Seville
Juan Pardo de Távira	1538	Archbishop of Toledo
García de Loaysa	1538–1546	Cardinal; Father Confessor to Charles V
Fernando Valdés	1546–1566	
Diego Espinosa	1566–1571	Cardinal and Bishop of Sigüenza
Pedro Ponce de León	1571–1573	Bishop of Plasencia
Gaspar de Quiroga	1573–1594	Archbishop of Toledo
Jerónimo Manrique de Lara	1594–1595	
Pedro de Portocarrero	1595–1599	Bishop of Córdoba
Fernando Nuño de Guevara	1599–1602	Cardinal; Archbishop of Seville
Juan de Zúñiga	1602–1603	Bishop of Cartagena
Juan Bautista de Azevedo	1603–1607	Head of the Church in South America
Bernardo Sandoval y Rojas	1607–1618	Cardinal; Archbishop of Toledo; Adviser to the Crown
Luis de Aliaga	1618–1625	Dominican; Father-Confessor to Philip III
Andrés Pacheco	1621–1625	
Antonio de Zapata	1626–1643	Cardinal; Archbishop of Burgos; Head of the Church in South America
Antonio de Sotomayor	1632–1643	Dominican; Father-Confessor to King
Diego de Arce y Reinoso	1643–1665	
Pascual de Aragón	1665–1666	Cardinal; Archbishop of Toledo
Juan Eduardo Nithard	1666–1669	German; Father-Confessor to the Queen
Diego Sarmiento de Valderas	1669–1694	Archbishop; Head of the Council of Castile
Juan Tomás de Rocaberti	1694–1699	Archbishop of Valencia
Alfonso Fernández de Córdoba y Aguilar	1699	
Balthasar de Mendoza y Sandoval	1699–1705	Bishop of Segovia
Vidal Marín	1705–1709	Bishop of Ceuta
Antonio Ibáñez de la Riva Herrera	1709–1710	Archbishop of Saragossa
Francisco Giudici	1710–1716	Italian priest
José de Molinas	1717–1720	
Juan de Arcemendi	1720	Counselor of the Suprema
Diego de Astorga y Cespedes	1720	Bishop of Barcelona
Juan de Camargo	1720–1733	Bishop of Pamplona
Andrés de Urban y Lariategui	1733–1740	Archbishop of Valencia; Chairman of Council of Castile
Manuel Isidoro Manrique de Lara	1742–1758	Archbishop of Santiago
Franciso Pérez de Pardo y Cuesta	1745–1758	Bishop of Teruel
Manuel Quintana Bonifas	1758–1761	
Felipe Beltrán	1761–1783	Bishop of Salamanca
Agustin Rubib de Celoallos	1783–1792	Bishop of Jaén
Manuel Abad y la Sierra	1792–1794	
Francisco Antonio de Lorenzano	1794–1797	Cardinal; Archbishop of Toledo
Ramón José de Arce	1797–1808	Head of the Church in South America
Francisco de Mier y Campillo	1814–1820	

THE AMRAPHEL SCROLL

Sermon held by R. Abraham b. Eliezer ha-Levi exhorting Jews and Conversos not to lose heart because of the persecutions. He advises those tried to declare openly that they are Jews and not to be frightened when put on trial. He alludes to the Auto-de-fés of the Inquisition. The sermon is based on the Midrash Shir ha-Shirim Raba. The power of the person's love of the Almighty is stronger than earthly fire.

INQUISITION TRIBUNALS IN ITALY

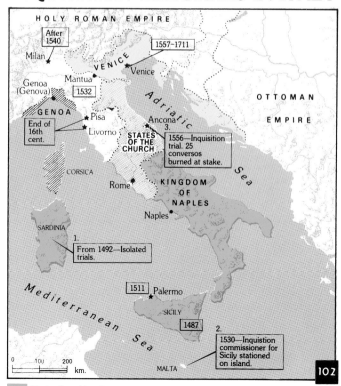

HOLY ROMAN EMPIRE

After 1540 — Milan
1557–1711
VENICE — Venice
Mantua
Genoa (Genova) — 1532
GENOA
End of 16th cent. — Pisa
Livorno — STATES OF THE CHURCH
Ancona 3.
1556—Inquisition trial. 25 conversos burned at stake.
CORSICA
Rome — KINGDOM OF NAPLES
Naples
Adriatic Sea
OTTOMAN EMPIRE
SARDINIA
1. From 1492—Isolated trials.
Mediterranean Sea
1511 Palermo
SICILY
1487
2. 1530—Inquisition commissioner for Sicily stationed on island.
MALTA

0   100   200 km.

Under Spanish rule
★ Inquisition tribunal

102

INQUISITION TRIBUNALS

Fifteenth to Seventeenth Centuries

Seal of the Catholic Monarchs Ferdinand (1474–1506) and Isabella (1474–1504) after Unification of Kingdom of Castile and Aragón.

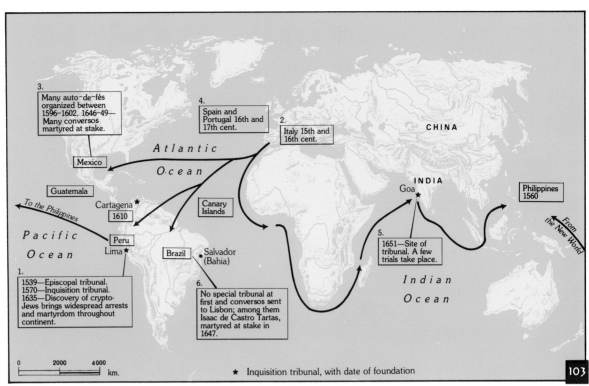

3. Many auto-de-fés organized between 1596–1602. 1646–49—Many conversos martyred at stake.

Mexico

Guatemala

Cartagena 1610

To the Philippines

Peru
Lima

1. 1539—Episcopal tribunal. 1570—Inquisition tribunal. 1635—Discovery of crypto-Jews brings widespread arrests and martyrdom throughout continent.

4. Spain and Portugal 16th and 17th cent.

2. Italy 15th and 16th cent.

Canary Islands

Brazil

Salvador (Bahia)

6. No special tribunal at first and conversos sent to Lisbon; among them Isaac de Castro Tartas, martyred at stake in 1647.

CHINA

INDIA

Goa

Philippines 1560

5. 1651—Site of tribunal. A few trials take place.

From the New World

Atlantic Ocean

Pacific Ocean

Indian Ocean

| 0 | 2000 | 4000 |

km.

★ Inquisition tribunal, with date of foundation

103

RELIGIOUS DIVISIONS IN EUROPE 1560

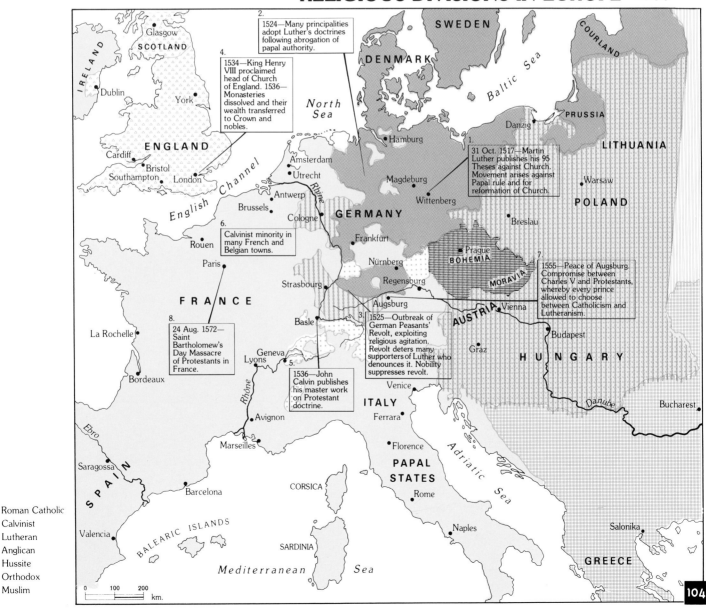

2. 1524—Many principalities adopt Luther's doctrines following abrogation of papal authority.

4. 1534—King Henry VIII proclaimed head of Church of England. 1536—Monasteries dissolved and their wealth transferred to Crown and nobles.

1. 31 Oct. 1517—Martin Luther publishes his 95 Theses against Church. Movement arises against Papal rule and for reformation of Church.

6. Calvinist minority in many French and Belgian towns.

7. 1555—Peace of Augsburg. Compromise between Charles V and Protestants, whereby every prince allowed to choose between Catholicism and Lutheranism.

8. 24 Aug. 1572—Saint Bartholomew's Day Massacre of Protestants in France.

3. 1525—Outbreak of German Peasants' Revolt, exploiting religious agitation. Revolt deters many supporters of Luther who denounces it. Nobility suppresses revolt.

5. 1536—John Calvin publishes his master work on Protestant doctrine.

SWEDEN · DENMARK · COURLAND · IRELAND · SCOTLAND · Glasgow · Dublin · York · ENGLAND · Cardiff · Bristol · Southampton · London · Amsterdam · Utrecht · Antwerp · Brussels · Cologne · Rouen · Paris · La Rochelle · Bordeaux · Saragossa · SPAIN · Barcelona · Valencia · Marseilles · Avignon · Lyons · Geneva · Basle · Strasbourg · FRANCE · Hamburg · Magdeburg · Wittenberg · GERMANY · Frankfurt · Nürnberg · Regensburg · Augsburg · Prague · BOHEMIA · MORAVIA · AUSTRIA · Vienna · Graz · Budapest · HUNGARY · Danzig · PRUSSIA · LITHUANIA · Warsaw · POLAND · Breslau · Venice · Ferrara · Florence · ITALY · PAPAL STATES · Rome · Naples · CORSICA · SARDINIA · BALEARIC ISLANDS · Salonika · GREECE · Bucharest

North Sea · *Baltic Sea* · *English Channel* · Rhine · Rhône · Ebro · *Adriatic Sea* · Danube · *Mediterranean Sea*

	Roman Catholic
	Calvinist
	Lutheran
	Anglican
	Hussite
	Orthodox
	Muslim

| 0 | 100 | 200 |

km.

104

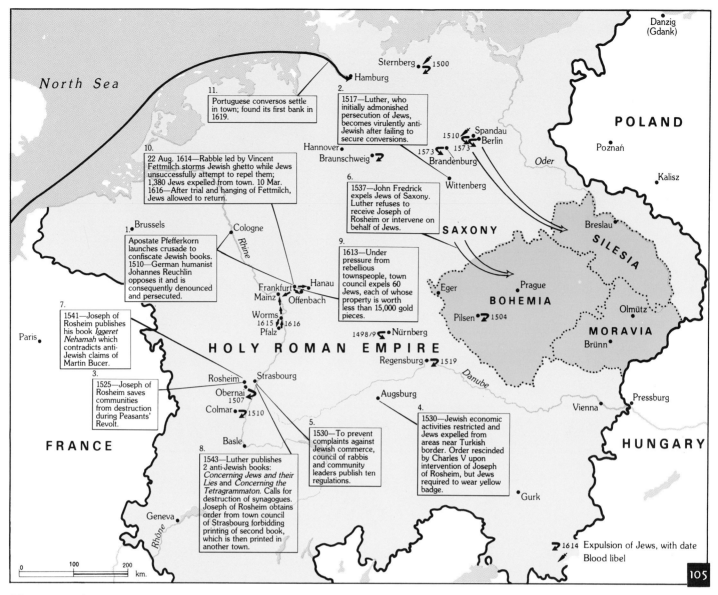

The map contains the following labeled text boxes and annotations:

North Sea

Danzig (Gdank)

POLAND

Poznań

Kalisz

Breslau

SILESIA

MORAVIA

Olmütz

Brünn

BOHEMIA

Prague

Eger

Pilsen 1504

Pressburg

Vienna

HUNGARY

Gurk

Hamburg

Sternberg 1500

Spandau Berlin
1510
1573 1573
Brandenburg

Hannover
Braunschweig

Wittenberg

SAXONY

Oder

11. Portuguese conversos settle in town; found its first bank in 1619.

2. 1517—Luther, who initially admonished persecution of Jews, becomes virulently anti-Jewish after failing to secure conversions.

10. 22 Aug. 1614—Rabble led by Vincent Fettmilch storms Jewish ghetto while Jews unsuccessfully attempt to repel them; 1,380 Jews expelled from town. 10 Mar. 1616—After trial and hanging of Fettmilch, Jews allowed to return.

6. 1537—John Fredrick expels Jews of Saxony. Luther refuses to receive Joseph of Rosheim or intervene on behalf of Jews.

9. 1613—Under pressure from rebellious townspeople, town council expels 60 Jews, each of whose property is worth less than 15,000 gold pieces.

Brussels

Cologne

Rhine

1. Apostate Pfefferkorn launches crusade to confiscate Jewish books. 1510—German humanist Johannes Reuchlin opposes it and is consequently denounced and persecuted.

Frankfurt   Hanau
Mainz   Offenbach
Worms
1615   1616
Pfalz

1498/9   Nürnberg

HOLY ROMAN EMPIRE

Regensburg 1519

Danube

7. 1541—Joseph of Rosheim publishes his book *Iggeret Nehamah* which contradicts anti-Jewish claims of Martin Bucer.

Paris

Rosheim   Strasbourg
Obernai
1507
Colmar 1510

Augsburg

3. 1525—Joseph of Rosheim saves communities from destruction during Peasants' Revolt.

5. 1530—To prevent complaints against Jewish commerce, council of rabbis and community leaders publish ten regulations.

4. 1530—Jewish economic activities restricted and Jews expelled from areas near Turkish border. Order rescinded by Charles V upon intervention of Joseph of Rosheim, but Jews required to wear yellow badge.

FRANCE

Basle

Geneva

Rhône

8. 1543—Luther publishes 2 anti-Jewish books: *Concerning Jews and their Lies* and *Concerning the Tetragrammaton*. Calls for destruction of synagogues. Joseph of Rosheim obtains order from town council of Strasbourg forbidding printing of second book, which is then printed in another town.

0   100   200 km.

1614 Expulsion of Jews, with date
Blood libel

The sixteenth century was not auspicious for the Jews of Germany-Austria. Though they resided in many villages and towns, pressures exerted by the German emperors and the many expulsions greatly depleted the Jewish communities. The rise of Protestantism did not encourage the renewal of Jewish settlement. Charles V, the Holy Roman Emperor, fought the spread of Protestantism but was not antagonistic toward the Jews, who were represented at court by the *shtadlan* (intercessor) Joseph b. Gershon of Rosheim. Martin Luther was at first tolerant toward the Jews, hoping to attract and convert them to Protestantism, but later, disappointed at their rejection, he became violently hostile to them. The Jews of Germany were subjected to the anti-Jewish polemic of the apostate Antonius Margarita (1530), who followed in the footsteps of another apostate and anti-Jewish agitator, Johannes Pfefferkorn. The activities of these agitators were opposed by a number of humanists led by Johannes Reuchlin, who engaged Pfefferkorn in written and verbal attacks and counterattacks from 1511 to 1521. Anti-Jewish propaganda also found its expression in a number of plays depicting the Jews as the killers of Christ.

The Jewish center of gravity moved eastward. Despite the adverse effect on the Jewish community of the expulsions from the crown cities in Bohemia and Moravia to the countryside and villages, Jews somehow managed to withstand the trials and tribulations of this period.

The expulsion of Jews from Frankfort on the Main in 1614. Engraving by Georg Keller.

The Thirty Years' War destroyed these communities and increased the numbers who fled to eastern Europe, Poland and Lithuania, joining the already established and growing Jewish communities of these countries within the superbly organized structure known as the Council of Four Lands.

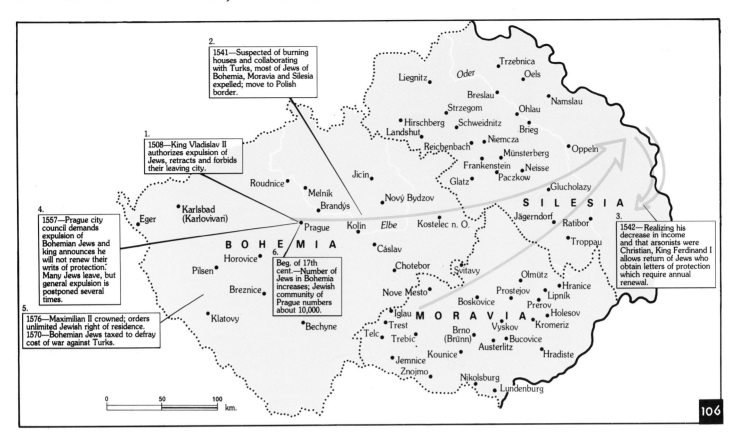

2.
1541—Suspected of burning houses and collaborating with Turks, most of Jews of Bohemia, Moravia and Silesia expelled; move to Polish border.

1.
1508—King Vladislav II authorizes expulsion of Jews, retracts and forbids their leaving city.

4.
1557—Prague city council demands expulsion of Bohemian Jews and king announces he will not renew their writs of protection. Many Jews leave, but general expulsion is postponed several times.

5.
1576—Maximilian II crowned; orders unlimited Jewish right of residence.
1570—Bohemian Jews taxed to defray cost of war against Turks.

6.
Beg. of 17th cent.—Number of Jews in Bohemia increases; Jewish community of Prague numbers about 10,000.

3.
1542—Realizing his decrease in income and that arsonists were Christian, King Ferdinand I allows return of Jews who obtain letters of protection which require annual renewal.

Place names on map: Trzebnica, Oels, Oder, Liegnitz, Breslau, Namslau, Strzegom, Ohlau, Hirschberg, Schweidnitz, Brieg, Landshut, Niemcza, Reichenbach, Münsterberg, Oppeln, Roudnice, Frankenstein, Neisse, Melník, Glatz, Paczkow, Glucholazy, Brandýs, Nový Bydzov, SILESIA, Jicín, Karlsbad (Karlovivari), Eger, Prague, Kolín, Elbe, Kostelec n. O., Jägerndorf, Ratibor, Cáslav, Troppau, Horovice, Chotebor, Olmütz, Pilsen, Svitavy, Hranice, Breznice, Nove Mesto, Prostejov, Lipník, Prerov, Holesov, Boskovice, Klatovy, Iglau, MORAVIA, Vyskov, Kromeriz, Trest, Brno (Brünn), Bucovice, Hradiste, Telc, Trebic, Austerlitz, Bechyne, Kounice, Jemnice, Znojmo, Nikolsburg, Lundenburg, BOHEMIA

0 50 100 km.

106

JEWISH FOUNDATIONS IN THE CITY OF PRAGUE

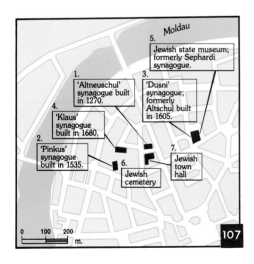

Moldau

5.
Jewish state museum; formerly Sephardi synagogue.

1.
'Altneuschul' synagogue built in 1270.

3.
'Dusni' synagogue; formerly Altschul built in 1605.

4.
'Klaus' synagogue built in 1680.

2.
'Pinkus' synagogue built in 1535.

6.
Jewish cemetery

7.
Jewish town hall

0 100 200 m.

107

Figure of a Jew from a woodcut illustration to the Prague Haggadah, 1526.

Entrance to the Pinkus synagogue in Prague.

THE JEWS OF HUNGARY UNDER TURKISH AND AUSTRIAN RULE

Though there is very little information about early Jewish presence in Hungary, it seems there was a well-integrated settlement in the eleventh century, Esztergom (Gran) being the most important community. The church council of Szabolcs in 1092 prohibited Jews from marrying Christian women, working on Christian festivals and purchasing slaves. During the First Crusade King Kálman (1095–1116) protected the Jews of his domain against attacks by remnants of the crusader army passing through Hungary. From the twelfth century Jews played a role in the economic life of the country, but in 1222 an order was issued forbidding them to hold any office that would give them authority to judge Christians or to receive titles of nobility.

We do not know what befell the Jews during the Mongol invasion of Hungary in 1241 when King Bela IV (1235–1270) was severely defeated and the country overrun and devastated. But in 1251 the king granted a privilege to the Jews that was similar to those granted in Germany. It would appear that Bela wished to encourage Jewish settlement. Despite this privilege, the church council of Buda in 1279 ordered Jews to wear a distinguishing badge.

The Black Death led to the first expulsion of Jews in 1349 and to a further general expulsion decree in 1360. In 1364 Jews were allowed to return, subject to restrictions. In 1365 the king instituted the office of "judge of the Jews," appointing one of the nobles to represent the Jews before the crown in matters relating to collection of taxes and protection of their rights. Only in the second half of the fifteenth century, during the reign of Matthias Corvinus (1458–1490), did the status of the Jews improve, despite the animosity of the townspeople, who were mostly of German origin. The Jewish population increased and Buda emerged as the largest community in the kingdom.

A blood libel case in Tyrnau (Trnava; 1494) led to both the arrest of sixteen Jews who were then burned at the stake and to anti-Jewish riots in the town. At the beginning of the sixteenth century there were anti-Jewish riots in Pressburg and Buda, but none during the reign of Louis II (1516–1526).

The Turks first invaded Hungary in 1526, the year in which

Boundary of Holy Roman Empire, 1550
Territory under Austrian control
Territory under Turkish control

the Jews were expelled from Esztergom (Gran) in northern Hungary — an expulsion that is thought to have been the result of an accusation of Jewish collusion with the invading Turks. From this point there was a distinct difference between the status of the Jews living in Turkish-held territories and those living in the domains of the Holy Roman Empire. In the former, they enjoyed satisfactory treatment while in the latter they were persecuted. Jews even emigrated to other parts of the Ottoman Empire.

THE THIRTY YEARS' WAR
1618–1648

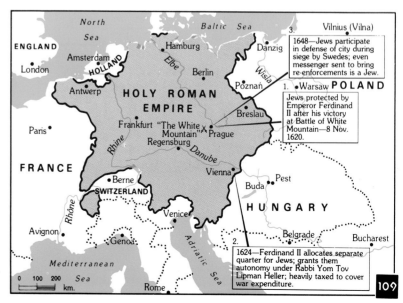

——— Boundary of Holy Roman Empire at end of Thirty Years' War —
Peace of Westphalia (1648)

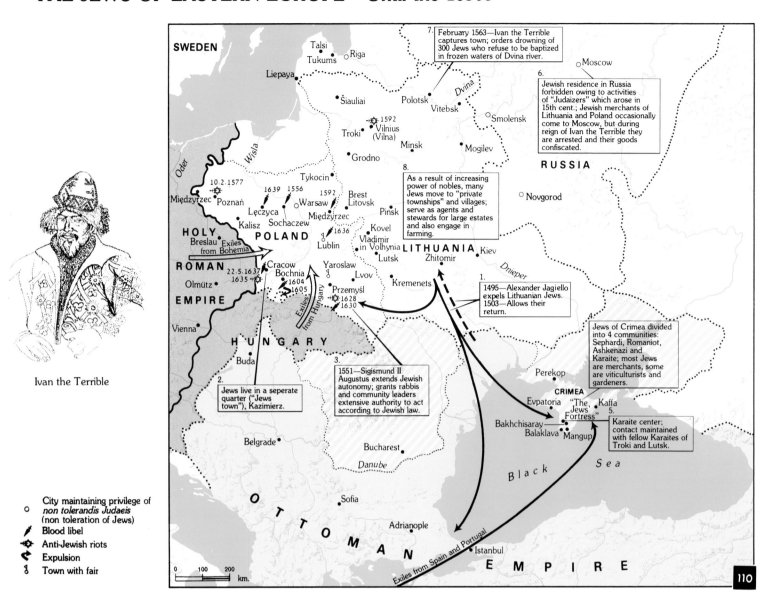

Ivan the Terrible

7. February 1563—Ivan the Terrible captures town; orders drowning of 300 Jews who refuse to be baptized in frozen waters of Dvina river.

6. Jewish residence in Russia forbidden owing to activities of "Judaizers" which arose in 15th cent.; Jewish merchants of Lithuania and Poland occasionally come to Moscow, but during reign of Ivan the Terrible they are arrested and their goods confiscated.

8. As a result of increasing power of nobles, many Jews move to "private townships" and villages; serve as agents and stewards for large estates and also engage in farming.

1. 1495—Alexander Jagiello expels Lithuanian Jews. 1503—Allows their return.

Jews of Crimea divided into 4 communities: Sephardi, Romaniot, Ashkenazi and Karaite; most Jews are merchants, some are viticulturists and gardeners.

3. 1551—Sigismund II Augustus extends Jewish autonomy; grants rabbis and community leaders extensive authority to act according to Jewish law.

2. Jews live in a seperate quarter ("Jews town"), Kazimierz.

5. Karaite center; contact maintained with fellow Karaites of Troki and Lutsk.

o   City maintaining privilege of *non tolerandis Judaeis* (non toleration of Jews)
⚡ Blood libel
✡ Anti-Jewish riots
↻ Expulsion
⚱ Town with fair

0   100   200
km.

110

In 1495 Alexander Jagiellon, grand prince of Lithuania and later (1501) king of Poland and Lithuania, expelled the Jews of Lithuania. Though some of the leading wealthy Jews apostatized, the majority immigrated to Kaffa (Feodosiya in Crimea), to Constantinople or to Poland (where they were allowed to remain an additional year). The folly of the expulsion was soon recognized and in 1503 the Jews were allowed to return, their communal property being restored. Conditions for those who returned were difficult, since they had to redeem their property from the German inhabitants, pay a special tax, and pay for the annual upkeep of one thousand cavalry.

The major Jewish communities in Poland were Cracow, Poznań and Lvov, the latter being a commercial center for the trade routes to Kiev and Istanbul.

Two outstanding rabbinic personalities in Poland were Rabbi Jacob b. Joseph Pollack who opened the first yeshiva in Poland, and his pupil Rabbi Shalom Shakhna b. Joseph (died in Lublin in 1559), founder of Talmudic scholarship in Poland. R. Pollack (1460/1470–after 1522) was born and studied in Bavaria and was later rabbi in Prague, from which he moved to Cracow.

There was a considerable growth of Jewish communities during the reign of Sigismund II Augustus (1548–1572), partly due to immigration from Moravia and Bohemia; in some places the Jewish population doubled toward the end of the sixteenth century. A conspicuous example was the community of Lublin, a town that, in the mid-sixteenth century, was famous for its trade fair.

In the middle of the sixteenth century the major Jewish communities in Lithuania were Brest Litovsk (which had 160 Jewish homes in 1566; though they were all burned in 1568, the community succeeded in rehabilitating itself); and Grodno, out of which developed the community of Tykocin and Pinsk. The Vilna community developed slowly; being a town with the privilege of *non tolerandis Judaeis* (1527) very few Jews could reside there, but by 1568 there are records of an organized community. Toward the end of the sixteenth century communities also developed in Lutsk, Kovel and Kremenets.

The death of Sigismund II (1572), the last of the Jagiellon dynasty, and the election of Henry III of Valois in 1574 resulted in a deterioration of Jewish status in Poland-Lithuania that was ameliorated beyond recognition with the election in 1576 of Stephen Báthory, who reigned until 1586. Jews were active in his court, successfully representing the interests of the Jewish community at large. During the reign of Sigismund III Vasa (1587–1632) the situation deteriorated for Poland in general and for the Jews in particular.

Polish-Lithuanian Jewry was fortunate in having great rabbinic leaders and a central institution of self-government called the Council of the Lands (also known as the Council of Four Lands). The council led the communities from the middle of the sixteenth century until 1764 and among its many achievements was support of the development of a study of Torah that was a synthesis of Ashkenazic erudition, Kabbalah and Talmudic sophistry (*pilpul*).

THE JEWS OF POLAND WITHIN THE COUNCIL OF FOUR LANDS
Seventeenth Century

The Jewish quarter in Kazimierz.

Boundary of the Lands
Boundary of province
⊙ Provincial (Land) capital
■ Principal community
◄ Town with fair

* The place names are based upon contemporary Jewish sources (*see appendix to "Pinkas" of Council of the Four Lands" by Israel Halpern*).

The Jews of Poland created a national institution for self-government known as the Council of Four Lands, consisting of representatives of the four lands or provinces: Great Poland, Little Poland, Red Russia and Volhynia. Lithuania was a separate entity; its council probably functioned as early as the 1560s.

Basically there was cooperation and coordination between the two councils in matters relating to Jewry at large, though relations were sometimes strained over divergent approaches to local problems.

The two councils, initially established to deal with matters of taxation and protection of the Jewish community, soon became institutions dealing with internal community affairs. In the first half of the sixteenth century we have evidence of a central rabbinical court for the Jews of Poland; a similar court already existed in Lithuania.

Representatives of the four provinces (*roshei ha-glilot*) formed a council of elders who governed Polish Jewry. They would usually assemble at the annual fairs of Lublin in February and Jaroslaw in September and deal with such subjects as the election of rabbis, taxation and personal matters. In 1549 the Polish government, realizing its administrative inability to collect Jewish poll taxes, imposed this task upon the council. The Council of Four Lands probably started functioning from the middle of the sixteenth century (the earliest extant record from its official minute book [*pinkas*] is dated 1580) and was dissolved by the Polish Sejm in 1764.

The nonrabbinical delegates (*roshei ha-medinot*) of the provinces elected one of their number as the *parnas* (community leader) of the House of Israel of the Four Lands; he headed the council, presided at the assemblies, and negotiated on its behalf with the king. They also elected a *ne'eman* (trustee) of the House of Israel of the Four Lands to serve as a treasurer and secretary. This appointment was for one year, with salary and expenses, and was also open to rabbinical candidates (rabbis qualified to be elected to the assembly of judges). In later years a number of trustees were elected, dividing the tasks among them.

In Lithuania the council's executive consisted of an elected *parnas* and a number of *shelihim* (emissaries) whose duties were to visit the Jewish communities, check the population rolls and assess their ability to pay taxes. These emissaries were eventually replaced by appointed clerks who dealt with tax collection in the province. The trustees were responsible for tax collection and the secretaries of the council recorded the regulations.

Representatives of the two councils would meet to discuss and settle matters relating to the obligations of Polish-Lithuanian Jewry as well as determining their relations with one another.

The institution declined following the destruction of the Polish-Lithuanian community in the Chmielnicki massacres of 1648–1649 and in the Russian and Swedish wars against Poland.

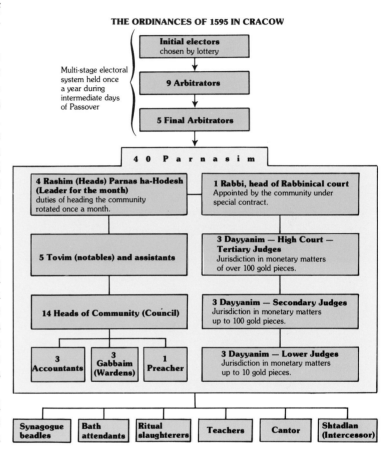

THE ORDINANCES OF 1595 IN CRACOW

Multi-stage electoral system held once a year during intermediate days of Passover

- **Initial electors** chosen by lottery
- **9 Arbitrators**
- **5 Final Arbitrators**

40 Parnasim

4 Rashim (Heads) Parnas ha-Hodesh (Leader for the month) duties of heading the community rotated once a month.

1 Rabbi, head of Rabbinical court Appointed by the community under special contract.

5 Tovim (notables) and assistants

3 Dayyanim — High Court — Tertiary Judges Jurisdiction in monetary matters of over 100 gold pieces.

14 Heads of Community (Council)

3 Dayyanim — Secondary Judges Jurisdiction in monetary matters up to 100 gold pieces.

3 Accountants — **3 Gabbaim (Wardens)** — **1 Preacher**

3 Dayyanim — Lower Judges Jurisdiction in monetary matters up to 10 gold pieces.

Synagogue beadles — **Bath attendants** — **Ritual slaughterers** — **Teachers** — **Cantor** — **Shtadlan (Intercessor)**

THE CHMIELNICKI MASSACRES   1648–1649

Toward the latter half of the seventeenth century two calamitous events shattered Polish Jewry: externally, the Cossack rebellion led by Bogdan Chmielnicki (Bohdan Khmelnytsky; 1599–1657) and the major wars on Polish territory which followed; and internally, the Shabbetai Zevi crisis, which shook the very foundations of the community. Repercussions were still felt in the second half of the eighteenth century.

The massacres of 1648–1649 decimated Polish Jewry, scattering the survivors throughout many countries. The anti-Jewish propoganda presented the Jewish lessee as an exploiter of the peasants and agent of the nobility. Many Jews died in the rebellion of Pavoloch and other uprisings. In 1637 three hundred Jews were killed east of the Dnieper and many communities were destroyed. The anti-Jewish ag-itation in the 1640s found a leader in Chmielnicki, whose rebellion dealt a crushing blow to the Polish army near Korsun (1648). In the course of his campaigns against the Poles, Chmielnicki, at the head of a Cossack army and the peasant-serf paramilitary bands of Haidamacks, destroyed Polish Jewry and their communities. The Jews were betrayed by the Poles despite their mutual defense pacts, the latter suggesting apostasy as a mode of rescue. Entire communities resisted this temptation, preferring martyrdom. Following the never-to-be-forgotten slaughter of the Tulchin and Nemirov communities, the shocked Polish nobility went to battle against the Cossacks and Haidamacks but were defeated. Chmielnicki's forces lashed out on all fronts, wreaking havoc and death while those taken captive were sold by the Tatars as slaves. The Jewish communities of Istanbul, Salonika, Venice, Rome, Hamburg and Amsterdam did everything in their power to ransom the captives. The Russian and Swedish invasions of Poland completed the destruction of the Jewish communities.

Jews did not reside in the principality of Moscow. In the area that was the Soviet Union and was then Polish, Jews resided in Vitebsk, Smolensk and Polotsk and the adjacent villages. By 1667, following the wars involving Russia, Poland and Sweden, the grand duchy of Lithuania was destroyed and the Jews who were taken captive were ransomed under the terms of the Truce of Andrusovo (1667). Jewish refugees fleeing westward were also caught by the invading Swedes and Brandenburgers and very few succeeded in reaching Amsterdam or Hamburg. In other towns, such as Lublin, the Jews were handed over to the Russians, many being sold into slavery. In Lvov they were spared after paying a huge ransom. The deteriorating situation brought complete ruin upon the Jews of Lithuania, Reisen, Podolia and Volhynia.

The Truce of Andrusovo stabilized Poland's eastern border, the entire area east of the Dnieper remaining in Russian hands. Attempting to rationalize their defeats, the Poles laid the blame on those who had forsaken Catholicism — the Eastern Orthodox, Protestants and Jews. In Lvov and Cracow there were anti-Jewish pogroms. John III Sobieski (1674–1696) — exemplary for the privileges he granted the Jews of Zolkiew, his town of residence — did much to revive the Jewish communities during his reign and with his death in 1696 the Jews lost a patron. In 1699 a blood libel in Sandomir (Sandomierz) had grave consequences for the community.

Renewed invasions by the Russians, Swedes and Saxons dealt crushing blows to the Jewish communities. On the eve of the eighteenth century the Jews of Poland faced a crisis of actual existence.

Jews had been predominant in the Polish economy for several centuries — in national and international trade and commerce, in leasing large estates and salt mines, banking and crafts and participation at the trade fairs of Lublin and Jaroslaw; but this predominance was gravely affected by anti-Jewish propaganda and the consequent molestation was one of the major factors that contributed to the destruction of the Polish economy.

Of some they removed their skins and the flesh they threw to the dogs; some they cut off their arms and legs and cast them on the wayside to be driven over by carriages and horses; on some they inflicted many wounds but not enough for them to die, and threw them out so that they would not die soon and would convulse in their blood until their spirit would depart from them; and many they buried alive, and slaughtered children in the presence of their mothers; they cut up many children like fish; and they cut the stomachs of pregnant women and wrenched the foetus from them and beat their faces; some, they cut their stomachs and put a live cat in them and sewed up the stomach, and cut off their hands so that they could not tear out the live cat; and they hung children on the breasts of their mothers; and they speared children on sticks and burned them on the fire and brought them to their mothers to be eaten by them: and sometimes they took the children of Jews and made bridges of them to pass over. There was no form of gory death which they spared them — the four forms of death, by trial, stoning, burning and strangulation.

From Yeven Metzula *by Nathan Nata Hanover, Venice 1653, (ed. Ein Harod 1945, p. 32).*

THE CHMIELNICKI MASSACRES

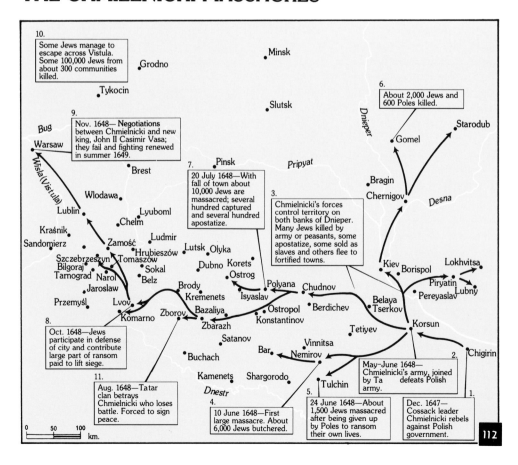

SHABBETAI ZEVI: ACTIVITIES AND TRAVELS

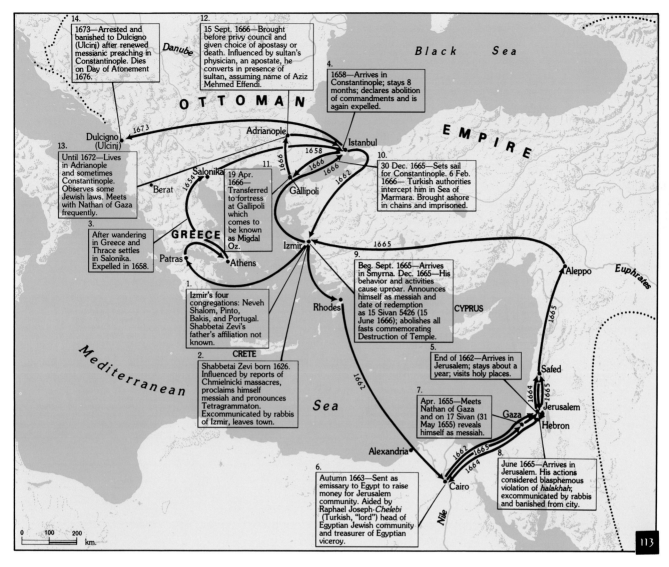

14. 1673—Arrested and banished to Dulcigno (Ulcinj) after renewed messianic preaching in Constantinople. Dies on Day of Atonement 1676.

12. 15 Sept. 1666—Brought before privy council and given choice of apostasy or death. Influenced by sultan's physician, an apostate, he converts in presence of sultan, assuming name of Aziz Mehmed Effendi.

4. 1658—Arrives in Constantinople; stays 8 months; declares abolition of commandments and is again expelled.

13. Until 1672—Lives in Adrianople and sometimes Constantinople. Observes some Jewish laws. Meets with Nathan of Gaza frequently.

11. 19 Apr. 1666—Transferred to fortress at Gallipoli which comes to be known as Migdal Oz.

10. 30 Dec. 1665—Sets sail for Constantinople. 6 Feb. 1666— Turkish authorities intercept him in Sea of Marmara. Brought ashore in chains and imprisoned.

3. After wandering in Greece and Thrace settles in Salonika. Expelled in 1658.

9. Beg. Sept. 1665—Arrives in Smyrna. Dec. 1665—His behavior and activities cause uproar. Announces himself as messiah and date of redemption as 15 Sivan 5426 (15 June 1666); abolishes all fasts commemorating Destruction of Temple.

1. Izmir's four congregations: Neveh Shalom, Pinto, Bakis, and Portugal. Shabbetai Zevi's father's affiliation not known.

5. End of 1662—Arrives in Jerusalem; stays about a year; visits holy places.

2. Shabbetai Zevi born 1626. Influenced by reports of Chmielnicki massacres, proclaims himself messiah and pronounces Tetragrammaton. Excommunicated by rabbis of Izmir, leaves town.

7. Apr. 1655—Meets Nathan of Gaza and on 17 Sivan (31 May 1655) reveals himself as messiah.

8. June 1665—Arrives in Jerusalem. His actions considered blasphemous violation of *halakhah*; excommunicated by rabbis and banished from city.

6. Autumn 1663—Sent as emissary to Egypt to raise money for Jerusalem community. Aided by Raphael Joseph *Chelebi* (Turkish, "lord") head of Egyptian Jewish community and treasurer of Egyptian viceroy.

Mordecai Zevi orginated from Greece (probably Patras), and settled in Smyrna (Izmir) where his son Shabbetai was born on the Sabbath, Ninth of Av (August) 1626. As a youth Shabbetai Zevi studied with Rabbi Joseph Escapa and seems to have been ordained a *hakham* (scholar) when he was eighteen. Shabbetai Zevi early began showing signs of mental instability — extreme manic-depressive psychosis — which plagued him for his entire life. During his manic spasms he committed acts that ran counter to religious law, including pronouncing the Ineffable Name of God and proclaiming himself the Messiah. These repeated violations led the rabbis to banish him from Smyrna at some time between 1651 and 1654. Wandering through Greece and Thrace, visiting Athens, Patras and Salonika, he arrived in Constantinople in 1658, staying there for eight months, before being expelled because of his blasphemous pronouncements and behavior. Returning to Smyrna, he remained there until 1662, when he decided to settle in Jerusalem.

Traveling via Rhodes and Cairo, where he established contacts with leaders of the Jewish community, he arrived in Jerusalem at the end of 1662. In the autumn of 1663 he was sent by the community as an emissary to Egypt to raise money. On 31 March 1664 in Cairo he married Sarah, his third wife, who was rumored to be a woman of easy virtue. Returning from Egypt, he stopped at Gaza in April 1665, where he met Abraham Nathan b. Elisha Hayyim Ashkenazi. Nathan convinced Shabbetai Zevi of his messianic destiny and on 17 Sivan (31 May 1665) Shabbetai Zevi proclaimed himself the Messiah.

Shabbetai Zevi

Letters despatched from Palestine, Egypt and Smyrna to the many communities of the Jewish Diaspora proclaiming the need for repentance to facilitate the coming redemption, created a fervent revivalist atmosphere which developed into a mass movement of people who believed in Shabbetai Zevi as the revealed Messiah of the Jewish people. In eastern Europe the Chmielnicki massacres and the Russian-Swedish war provided fertile soil for the growth of such a movement.

The messianic revelation had special significance in Poland-Lithuania, and in several places it resulted in massacres (Pinsk — 20 March 1666; Vilna — 28 March; Lublin — 27 April). A number of delegations were despatched from Poland to Shabbetai Zevi, both while in Smyrna and when he was imprisoned in Migdal Oz in Gallipoli. His meeting with one of the emissaries, Nehemiah ha-Kohen, was destined to play a crucial role in Shabbetai's life. Other prominent Jewish communities, such as Salonika, Amsterdam and Livorno (Leghorn) were caught up in the fervor, and many became his followers.

The movement's vital energy sprang from the Holy Land and the belief in redemption which would originate from it, as well as from the renewal of prophecy that was confirmed by the rabbi of Gaza, Jacob Najara, and some other scholars. The overwhelming enthusiasm that swept over and united Jews all over the world brought people from all walks of life to the movement: from the punctiliously observant kabbalists to the simple folk, all were united in repentance and in anticipation of the coming redemption. Ashkenazim, Sephardim, conversos returning to Judaism, Jews from Yemen and Persia, and in fact the entire Diaspora, were engulfed by these expectations.

The Shabbatean movement included many rabbis and scholars among its adherents: David Yitshaki of Salonika, Samuel Primo of Bursa, Judah Sharaf, and Mattathias Bloch Ashkenazi. It also had many opponents, the greatest of whom was Jacob Sasportas, rabbi and erudite scholar, who narrated the story of his polemic with the Shabbateans in a book called *Zizat Novel Zevi*. Shabbetai Zevi also had many opponents in Egypt, Jerusalem and Safed.

The tumult and messianic fever caused by Shabbetai Zevi and his followers prompted the authorities to arrest and imprison him in Constantinople (30 December 1665). He was later transferred to the fortress at Gallipoli (19 April). On 3 or 4 September he was visited by the Polish kabbalist Nehemiah ha-Kohen. After an angry debate with Shabbetai, he declared his willingness to convert to Islam and was taken to Adrianople where he denounced Shabbetai Zevi. On 15 September Shabbetai was brought to Adrianople and given the choice of death or apostasy. He converted, assuming the name of Aziz Mehmed Effendi. His apostasy was emulated by many of his adherents.

News of Shabbetai Zevi's apostasy spread quickly, causing shock and consternation amongst the Jews. For some, it was proof of their errors while others tried to rationalize

THE TRAVELS OF NATHAN OF GAZA

Nathan of Gaza

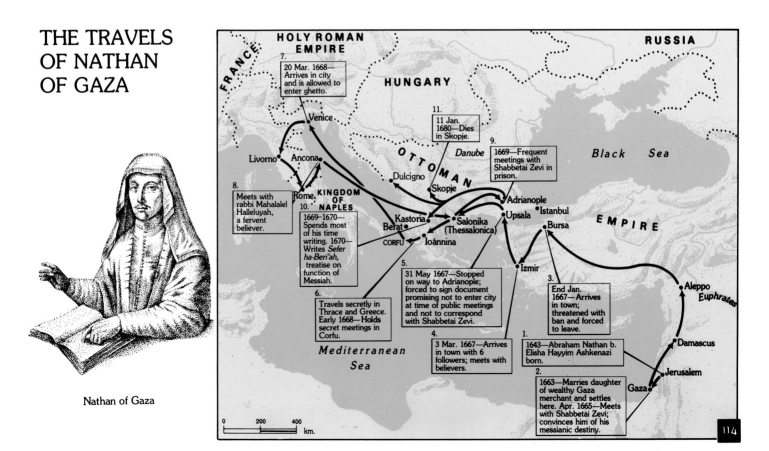

the apostasy, continuing to believe in Shabbetai Zevi and his mission. Shabbetai Zevi continued his activities even after his apostasy trying to persuade adherents to follow him into Islam. Denounced and arrested in Constantinople on 16 August 1672, he was exiled to Dulcigno in January 1673, dying there on the Day of Atonement (17 September) 1676.

Following the apostasy, secret sects of believers sprang up in various places. In Turkey a sect of believers arose called the Doenmeh, who followed in Shabbetai Zevi's footsteps by converting to Islam without renouncing their Judaism.

Nathan of Gaza persisted in his activities even after the apostasy and on his travels secretly visited Shabbetai Zevi in Adrianople (mid-1667). Nathan continued writing, preaching and explaining Shabbetai Zevi's actions, defending his apostasy and his messianic mission. For the next ten years (from 1670) he remained in Macedonia and Bulgaria staying mainly in Sofia, Adrianople and Kastoria. He died in Skopje on 11 January 1680.

The crisis caused by the Shabbatean messianic movement was felt in the Jewish world for many years.

LEADERS OF THE SHABBATEAN MOVEMENT AFTER THE DEATH OF SHABBETAI ZEVI

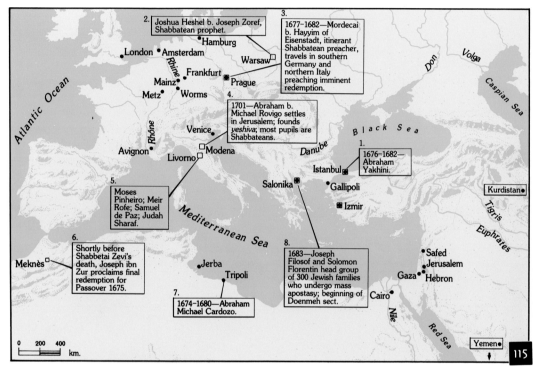

2. Joshua Heshel b. Joseph Zoref, Shabbatean prophet.

3. 1677–1682—Mordecai b. Hayyim of Eisenstadt, itinerant Shabbatean preacher, travels in southern Germany and northern Italy preaching imminent redemption.

4. 1701—Abraham b. Michael Rovigo settles in Jerusalem; founds *yeshiva*; most pupils are Shabbateans.

1. 1676–1682—Abraham Yakhini.

5. Moses Pinheiro; Meir Rofe; Samuel de Paz; Judah Sharaf.

6. Shortly before Shabbetai Zevi's death, Joseph ibn Zur proclaims final redemption for Passover 1675.

8. 1683—Joseph Filosof and Solomon Florentin head group of 300 Jewish families who undergo mass apostasy; beginning of Doenmeh sect.

7. 1674–1680—Abraham Michael Cardozo.

0 200 400 km.

- • Shabbatean center during lifetime of Shabbetai Zevi
- ▢ Shabbatean center after death of Shabbetai Zevi

THE JEWISH DIASPORA AND THEIR LANGUAGES
End of the Seventeenth Century

This general map reveals the entire Jewish world as it was on the eve of the year 1700. The dispersion of the Jews reveals the increased numbers that occurred after the Jews emerged from a past of upheavals, crises, crusades, Black Death, local and national expulsions and a messianic movement that was unprecedented in scope. Substantial Jewish communities can be found in central and eastern Europe, Asia and North Africa. In its formative years the New World opened its gates to Jewish pioneers of the Spanish and Portuguese settlements.

The beginning of the eighteenth century is marked by a display of Jewish attachment to the Holy Land. Judah Hasid (Segal) ha-Levi arrived in Jerusalem in October 1700 with several hundred immigrants, the harbingers of a renewed Zion.

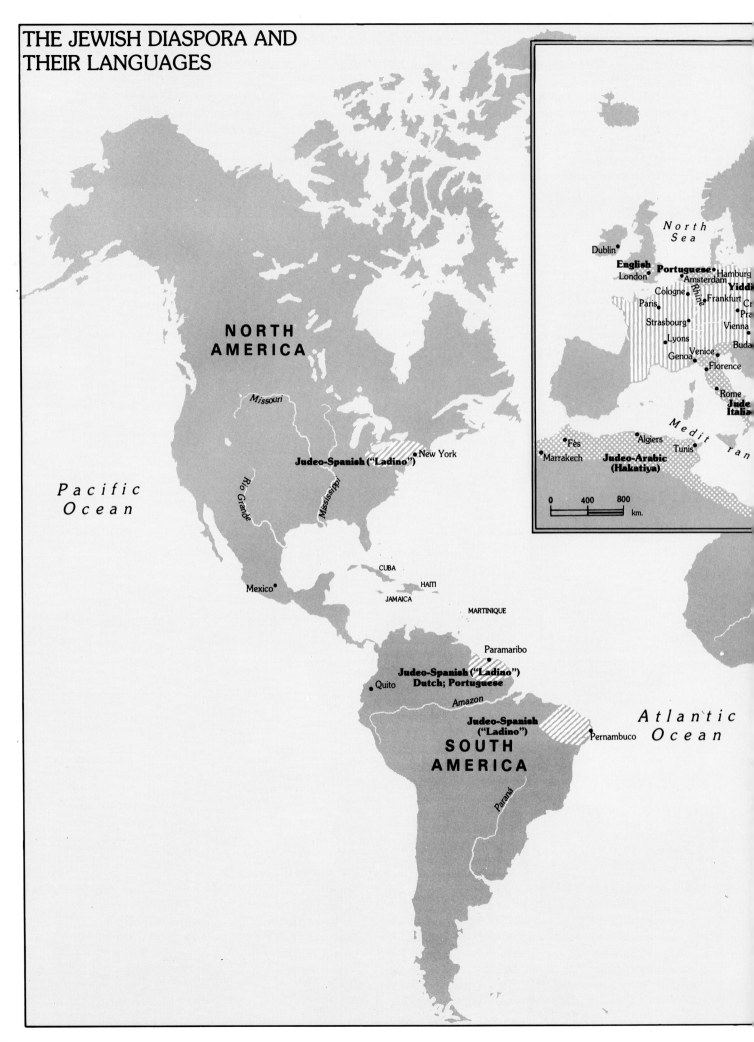

THE JEWISH DIASPORA AND THEIR LANGUAGES

NORTH AMERICA

Pacific Ocean

Missouri

Rio Grande

Mississippi

Judeo-Spanish ("Ladino") • New York

CUBA

HAITI

JAMAICA

• Mexico

MARTINIQUE

Paramaribo

Judeo-Spanish ("Ladino")
Dutch; Portuguese

• Quito

Amazon

Judeo-Spanish ("Ladino")

SOUTH AMERICA

Atlantic Ocean

• Pernambuco

Paraná

North Sea

• Dublin

English   **Portuguese** • Hamburg
London   • Amsterdam   **Yiddi**
Cologne   Frankfurt   Cr
• Paris   *Rhine*   Pra
Strasbourg   Vienna
Lyons   Buda
Genoa   Venice
Florence
• Rome
Jude
Italia

Medit

• Algiers
• Fès   Tunis
Marrakech   **Judeo-Arabic**
(Hakatiya)   *ran*

0   400   800
km.

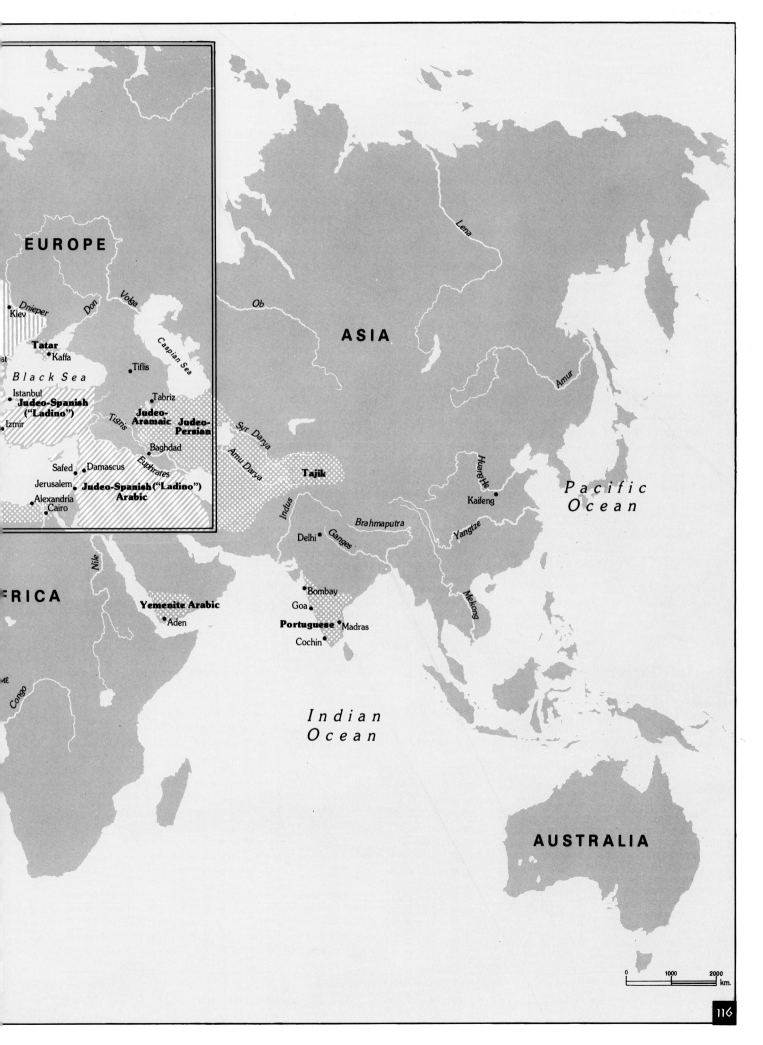

EUROPE

Dnieper
Kiev

Tatar
Kaffa

Tiflis

Black Sea

Istanbul
**Judeo-Spanish
("Ladino")**

Izmir

Tabriz

**Judeo-
Aramaic**

Tigris

Baghdad

**Judeo-
Persian**

Safed
Damascus

Jerusalem
**Judeo-Spanish("Ladino")
Arabic**
Alexandria
Cairo

Nile

Yemenite Arabic
Aden

Congo

AFRICA

Don
Volga

Caspian Sea

Euphrates

Ob

ASIA

Syr Darya

Amu Darya

Tajik

Indus

Delhi
Ganges

Brahmaputra

Lena

Amur

Huang He
Kaifeng

Yangtze

Mekong

*Pacific
Ocean*

Bombay
Goa
Portuguese Madras
Cochin

*Indian
Ocean*

AUSTRALIA

0   1000   2000
km.

116

SELECT BIBLIOGRAPHY

The following books and articles have been selected for suggested reading. This list does not purport to be a full description of proposed reading. Research in Jewish history is ever-expanding and new vistas are constantly being opened. This bibliography contains only those sources which have served in the preparation of the maps themselves and does not include many others which throw light on the subjects dealt with in this atlas. Hebrew sources of which there are many have not been listed here, nor have articles from academic periodicals in Jewish history in any language.

The bibliography is arranged alphabetically according to subjects.

GENERAL READING

I. Abrahams, *Jewish Life in the Middle Ages*, London 1932.
S. W. Baron, *A Social and Religious History of the Jews*, 2nd rev. ed., 18 vols. New York 1952–1980.
S. W. Baron, *The Jewish Community: Its History and Structure to the American Revolution*, 3 vols. Philadelphia 1942.
G. Caro, *Sozial- und Wirtschaftsgeschichte der Juden im Mittelalter und der Neuzeit*. 2 vols. Leipzig 1908–1920.
A. Lukyn Williams, *Adversus judaeus*, Cambridge 1935.
L.I. Newman, *Jewish Influence on Christian Reform Movements*, New York 1925.
J. Parkes, *The Conflict of the Church and the Synagogue: A Study in the Origins of Antisemitism*, London 1934.
J. Parkes, *The Jew in the Medieval Community: A Study of his Political and Economic Situation*, London 1938.
O.S. Rankin, *Jewish Religious Polemic*, Edinburgh 1956.
J. Trachtenberg, *The Devil and the Jews: the Medieval Conception of the Jew and its Relation to Modern Antisemitism*, New Haven 1934.
J. Trachtenberg, *Jewish Magic and Superstition: A Study in Folk Religion*, New York 1939.

SOURCE MATERIAL (COLLECTIONS; TRAVELOGUES)

I. Abrahams, *Hebrew Ethical Wills*, 2 vols. Philadelphia 1948.
R. Chazan, (ed.), *Church, State and Jew in the Middle Ages*, New York 1980.
S. Grayzel, *The Church and the Jews in the XIIIth Century: A Study of their Relations during the Years 1198–1254 based on the Papal Letters and the Conciliar Decrees of the Period*, Philadelphia 1933.
J. Marcus, (ed.), *The Jew in the Medieval World: A Source Book 315–1791*, Cincinnati 1938.

MESSIANIC MOVEMENTS, KABBALAH, JEWISH THOUGHT

J. Greenstone, *The Messianic Idea in Jewish History*, Philadelphia 1906.
A.H. Silver, *A History of Messianic Speculation in Israel from the First to the Seventeenth Centuries*, New York 1927.
D.J. Silver, *Maimonidean Criticism and the Maimonidean Controversy, 1180–1240*, Leiden 1965.

KABBALAH

J. Husik, *A History of Medieval Jewish Philosophy*, Philadelphia 1946.
G. Scholem, *Major Trends in Jewish Mysticism*, New York 1954.
G. Scholem, *The Messianic Idea in Judaism and Other Essays on Jewish Spirituality*, New York 1971.

KARAITES

Z. Ankori, *Karaites in Byzantium: The Formative Years, 970–1100*, New York—Jerusalem 1959.
J. Mann, *Texts and Studies in Jewish History and Literature*, Vol. 2., *Karaitica*, Cincinnati 1935.
L. Nemoy, *Karaite Anthology: Excerpts from the Early Literature*, New Haven, Conn.—London 1952.

ITALY

A. Milano, *Storia degli ebrei in Italia*, Torino 1963.

L. Poliakov, *Jewish Bankers and the Holy See: From the Thirteenth to the Seventeenth Century*, London 1977.

ASHKENAZ (INCLUDING GERMANY AND FRANCE; THE CRUSADES)

I. Agus, *The Heroic Age of Franco-German Jewry*, New York 1969.
I. Agus, *Urban Civilization in Pre-Crusade Europe: A Study of Organized Town-Life in North western Europe during the Tenth and Eleventh Centuries based on Responsa Literature*, New York 1965.
J. Aronius, (ed.), *Regesten zur Geschichte der Juden im Fränkischen und Deutschen Reiche bis zum Jahre 1273*, Berlin 1902.
B. Blumenkranz, (ed.), *Histoire des Juifs en France*, Toulouse 1972.
R. Chazan, *Medieval Jewry in Northern France: A Political and Social History*, Baltimore 1973.
S. Eidelberg, *Jewish Life in Austria in the XVth Century*, Philadelphia 1962.
L. Finkelstein, *Jewish Self-Government in the Middle Ages*, New York 1924.
Germania Judaica, 3 vols. Tübigen 1963–1968.
H. Gross, *Gallia Judaica: Dictionnaire geographique de la France*, Paris 1897.
G. Kisch, *The Jews in Medieval Germany: A Study of their Legal and Social Status*, Chicago 1949.
A. Neubauer, (ed.), *Medieval Jewish Chronicles and Chronological Notes*, 2 vols. Oxford 1887–1895.
A. Neubauer—M. Stern, (eds.), *Hebräische Berichte über die Judenverfolgungen während der Kreuzzüge*, Berlin 1892.
L. Rabinowitz, *The Social Life of the Jews of Northern France in the XII–XIV Centuries*, London 1938.
S. Salfeld, (ed.), *Das Martyrologium des Nürnberger Memorbuches*, Berlin 1898.

THE KHAZARS

D.M. Dunlop, *The History of the Jewish Khazary*, Princeton 1954.

ENGLAND

Stars and Jewish Charters 1–3 (ed. H. Loewe), London 1932.
A. Hyamson, *The Sephardim in England: A History of the Spanish and Portuguese Jewish Community 1492–1951*, London 1951.
J. Jacobs, *The Jews of Angevin England: documents and records*, London 1893.
V.D. Lipman, *The Jews of Medieval Norwich*, London 1967.
H. Richardson, *The English Jewry under Angevin Kings*, London 1960.
C. Roth, *History of the Great Synagogue*, London 1950.
C. Roth, *A History of the Jews in England*, Oxford 1964.

SPAIN, PORTUGAL, THE INQUISITION

Y.F. Baer, *Die Juden im christlichen Spanien*, 2nd, ed. 2 vols., Farnborough 1970.
Y. Baer, *A History of the Jews in Christian Spain*, 2 vols., Philadelphia 1961–1966 (expanded and revised edition: 1981 — translated into Spanish by J.L. Lacave).
R.D. Barnett, (ed.), *The Sephardi Heritage: Essays on the History and Cultural Contribution of the Jews of Spain and Portugal*, London 1971.
H. Beinart, *Conversos on Trial: The Inquisition in Ciudad Real*, Jerusalem 1981 (expanded and revised edition).
H. Beinart, (ed.), *Records of the Trials of the Spanish Inquisition in Ciudad Real*, 4 vols., Jerusalem 1974–1985.

H. Beinart, *Trujillo: A Jewish Community in Extramadura on the Eve of the Expulsion from Spain*, Jerusalem 1980.

F. Cantera Burgos, *Sinagogas Españolas*, Madrid 1955.

F. Cantera Burgos—J. Ma. Millàs Vallicrosa, *Las Inscripciones Hebraicas de España*, Madrid 1956.

S. Katz, *The Jews in Visigothic and Frankish Kingdoms of Spain and Gaul*, Cambridge, Mass. 1937.

M. Kayserling, *Geschichte der Juden in Portugal*, Leipzig 1867.

H.C. Lea, *A History of the Inquisition of Spain*, 1-4, New York—London 1906-1908.

B. Netanyahu, *Don Isaac Abravanel*, Philadelphia 1972.

J. Régné, (ed.), *History of the Jews in Aragon: Regesta and Documents 1213-1327*, Compiled, edited and annotated by Yom Tov Assis, Jerusalem 1978.

L. Suárez Fernández, *Documento acerca de la Expulsión de los Judíos*, Valladolid 1964.

EASTERN EUROPE

S. Dubnov, *History of the Jews in Russia and Poland from the Earliest Times to the Present Day*, 3 vols., Philadelphia 1916-1920.

EGYPT, NORTH AFRICA AND ARAB COUNTRIES

A. Chouraqui, *Between East and West: A History of the Jews of North Africa*, Philadelphia 1968.

M.R. Cohen, *Jewish Self Government in Medieval Egypt*, Princeton 1980.

W. Fischel, *Jews in the Economic and Political Life of Medieval Islam*, London 1937.

S.D. Goitein, (ed.), *Letters of Medieval Jewish Traders*, Princeton 1973.

S.D. Goitein, *A Mediterranean Society: The Jewish Communities of the Arab World as Portrayed in the Documents of the Cairo Geniza*, 5 vols., Berkeley—Los Angeles—London 1967-1989.

J. Mann, *The Jews of Egypt and Palestine under the Fatimid Caliphs*, 2 vols., London—Oxford 1920-1922.

J. Mann, *Texts and Studies*, 1, Cincinnati 1931.

J. Mann, *The Collected Articles*, Gedera 1971.

N. Stillman, *The Jews of Arab Lands: A History and Source Book*, Philadelphia 1979.

ASIA MINOR AND BYZANTIUM

A. Sharf, *Byzantine Jewry from Justinian to the Fourth Crusade*, London 1971.

J. Starr, *Jews in the Byzantine Empire 641-1204*, Athens 1939.

J. Starr, *Romania: The Jewries of the Levant after the Fourth Crusade*, Paris 1949.

ERETZ ISRAEL AND THE OTTOMAN EMPIRE

I.M. Goldman, *The Life and Times of Rabbi David Ibn Abi Zimra*, New York 1970.

M.S. Goodblatt, *Jewish Life in Turkey in the XVth Century*, New York 1952.

INDEX TO MAPS
(Numbers represent map numbers)

B

SUBJECT INDEX

INDEX TO PERSONS